Metropolitan Governance

Metropolitan Governance offers a cross-national analysis of contemporary issues and challenges for the governing of urban regions throughout Europe and North America.

The authors develop an analytical framework built on the premise that issues of metropolitan governance are best understood by focusing not only on the characteristics of the local government systems and of state–society relations, but also on the dynamics of place. They argue that area-wide governance in urban regions can draw on flexible networks and involve public–private partnerships as well as requiring institutional reform. This book includes chapters focusing on Germany, Spain, France, Greece, the Netherlands, Finland, the UK, Switzerland and North America and lays particular emphasis on democratic legitimacy and the tensions that arise when strengthening the capacity of metropolitan governance.

An original contribution to the debates on the nature of metropolitan governance, this book puts forward the argument that 'place matters'. It will be of interest to all students and researchers of public administration, governance and urban research.

Hubert Heinelt is Professor of Public Administration, Public Policy and Urban Research at the Institute for Political Science, Darmstadt University of Technology, Germany.

Daniel Kübler is Assistant Professor at the University of Zurich, Switzerland and currently visiting researcher at the University of New South Wales, Australia.

Routledge/ECPR Studies in European Political Science
Edited by Thomas Poguntke,
Keele University, UK

and

Jan W. van Deth, *University of Mannheim, Germany on behalf of the European Consortium for Political Research*

The Routledge/ECPR Studies in European Political Science series is published in association with the European Consortium for Political Research – the leading organisation concerned with the growth and development of political science in Europe. The series presents high-quality edited volumes on topics at the leading edge of current interest in political science and related fields, with contributions from European scholars and others who have presented work at ECPR workshops or research groups.

1 **Regionalist Parties in Western Europe**
Edited by Lieven de Winter and Huri Türsan

2 **Comparing Party System Change**
Edited by Jan-Erik Lane and Paul Pennings

3 **Political Theory and European Union**
Edited by Albert Weale and Michael Nentwich

4 **Politics of Sexuality**
Edited by Terrell Carver and Véronique Mottier

5 **Autonomous Policy Making by International Organizations**
Edited by Bob Reinalda and Bertjan Verbeek

6 **Social Capital and European Democracy**
Edited by Jan van Deth, Marco Maraffi, Ken Newton and Paul Whiteley

7 **Party Elites in Divided Societies**
Edited by Kurt Richard Luther and Kris Deschouwer

8 **Citizenship and Welfare State Reform in Europe**
Edited by Jet Bussemaker

9 **Democratic Governance and New Technology**
Technologically mediated innovations in political practice in Western Europe
Edited by Ivan Horrocks, Jens Hoff and Pieter Tops

10 **Democracy without Borders**
Transnationalisation and conditionality in new democracies
Edited by Jean Grugel

11 **Cultural Theory as Political Science**
Edited by Michael Thompson, Gunnar Grendstad and Per Selle

12 **The Transformation of Governance in the European Union**
Edited by Beate Kohler-Koch and Rainer Eising

13 **Parliamentary Party Groups in European Democracies**
Political parties behind closed doors
Edited by Knut Heidar and Ruud Koole

14 **Survival of the European Welfare State**
Edited by Stein Kuhnle

15 **Private Organisations in Global Politics**
Edited by Karsten Ronit and Volker Schneider

16 **Federalism and Political Performance**
Edited by Ute Wachendorfer-Schmidt

17 **Democratic Innovation**
Deliberation, representation and association
Edited by Michael Saward

18 **Public Opinion and the International Use of Force**
Edited by Philip Everts and Pierangelo Isernia

19 **Religion and Mass Electoral Behaviour in Europe**
Edited by David Broughton and Hans-Martien ten Napel

20 **Estimating the Policy Position of Political Actors**
Edited by Michael Laver

21 **Democracy and Political Change in the 'Third World'**
Edited by Jeff Haynes

22 **Politicians, Bureaucrats and Administrative Reform**
Edited by B. Guy Peters and Jon Pierre

23 **Social Capital and Participation in Everyday Life**
Edited by Paul Dekker and Eric M. Uslaner

24 **Development and Democracy**
What do we know and how?
Edited by Ole Elgström and Goran Hyden

25 **Do Political Campaigns Matter?**
Campaign effects in elections and referendums
Edited by David M. Farrell and Rüdiger Schmitt-Beck

26 **Political Journalism**
New challenges, new practices
Edited by Raymond Kuhn and Erik Neveu

27 **Economic Voting**
Edited by Han Dorussen and Michaell Taylor

28 **Organized Crime and the Challenge to Democracy**
Edited by Felia Allum and Renate Siebert

29 **Understanding the European Union's External Relations**
Edited by Michèle Knodt and Sebastiaan Princen

30 **Social Democratic Party Policies in Contemporary Europe**
Edited by Giuliano Bonoli and Martin Powell

31 **Decision Making Within International Organisations**
Edited by Bob Reinalda and Bertjan Verbeek

32 **Comparative Biomedical Policy**
Governing assisted reproductive technologies
Edited by Ivar Bleiklie, Malcolm L. Goggin and Christine Rothmayr

33 **Electronic Democracy**
Mobilisation, organisation and
participation via new ICTs
Edited by Rachel K. Gibson,
Andrea Römmele and
Stephen J. Ward

34 **Liberal Democracy and**
Environmentalism
The end of environmentalism?
Edited by Marcel Wissenburg and
Yoram Levy

35 **Political Theory and the European**
Constitution
Edited by Lynn Dobson and
Andreas Follesdal

36 **Politics and the European**
Commission
Actors, interdependence,
legitimacy
Edited by Andy Smith

37 **Metropolitan Governance**
Capacity, democracy and
the dynamics of place
Edited by Hubert Heinelt and
Daniel Kübler

38 **Democracy and the Role of**
Associations
Political, organizational and social
contexts
Edited by Sigrid Roßteutscher

39 **The Territorial Politics of Welfare**
Edited by Nicola McEwen and
Luis Moreno

40 **Health Governance in Europe**
Issues, challenges and theories
Edited by Monika Steffen

41 **Republicanism in Theory and**
Practice
Edited by Iseult Honohan and
Jeremy Jennings

Also available from Routledge in association with the ECPR:

Sex Equality Policy in Western Europe
Edited by Frances Gardiner

Democracy and Green Political Thought
Edited by Brian Doherty and
Marius de Geus

The New Politics of Unemployment
Edited by Hugh Compston

Citizenship, Democracy and Justice in
the New Europe
Edited by Percy B. Lehning and Albert Weale

Private Groups and Public Life
Edited by Jan W. van Deth

The Political Context of Collective
Action
Edited by Ricca Edmondson

Theories of Secession
Edited by Percy Lehning

Regionalism Across the North/South
Divide
Edited by Jean Grugel and Wil Hout

Metropolitan Governance

Capacity, democracy and
the dynamics of place

**Edited by
Hubert Heinelt and
Daniel Kübler**

Routledge
Taylor & Francis Group

LONDON AND NEW YORK

First published 2005
by Routledge
2 Park Square, Milton Park, Abingdon, Oxon OX14 4RN

Simultaneously published in the USA and Canada
by Routledge
270 Madison Ave., New York, NY 10016

Routledge is an imprint of the Taylor & Francis Group

Typeset in Times New Roman by
Newgen Imaging Systems (P) Ltd, Chennai, India
Printed and bound in Great Britain by
Antony Rowe Ltd, Chippenham, Wiltshire

British Library Cataloguing in Publication Data
A catalogue record for this book is available from the British Library

Library of Congress Cataloging in Publication Data
Metropolitan governance: capacity, democracy and the dynamics of
place/edited by Hubert Heinelt and Daniel Kübler.
        p. cm.
Includes bibliographical references and index.
1. Metropolitan government – Europe – Case studies. 2. Metropolitan
government – North America – Case studies. 3. Comparative
government. 4. Political planning. I. Heinelt, Hubert.
II. Kübler, Daniel.

   JS3000.3.A8M48 2005
   320.8'5–dc22   2004010762

ISBN 0–415–33778–X (hardback)

Contents

List of illustrations   ix
Notes on contributors   x
Acknowledgements   xii

1 **Introduction**   1
  DANIEL KÜBLER AND HUBERT HEINELT

2 **Metropolitan governance, democracy**
  and the dynamics of place   8
  DANIEL KÜBLER AND HUBERT HEINELT

3 **The new French dice: metropolitan institution**
  building and democratic issues   29
  EMMANUEL NÉGRIER

4 **Building metropolitan governance in Spain:**
  Madrid and Barcelona   47
  MARIONA TOMÀS

5 **The emergence of metropolitan governance**
  in Athens   63
  PANAGIOTIS GETIMIS AND NIKOLAOS HLEPAS

6 **The experience of metropolitan government**
  in England   81
  MICHAEL GOLDSMITH

7 **Arrested metropolitanism: limits and contradictions**
  of municipal governance reform in Los Angeles,
  Montreal and Toronto   100
  ROGER KEIL AND JULIE-ANNE BOUDREAU

viii *Contents*

8 **The coming of age of metropolitan governance in Helsinki?** 117

ANNE HAILA AND PATRICK LE GALÈS

9 **Reform and democracy in the Rotterdam region: an evaluation of the attempt to create a regional government** 133

LINZE SCHAAP

10 **Metropolitan governance in Germany** 151

DIETRICH FÜRST

11 **Governing without government: metropolitan governance in Switzerland** 169

DANIEL KÜBLER, FRITZ SAGER AND BRIGITTE SCHWAB

12 **Conclusion** 188

HUBERT HEINELT AND DANIEL KÜBLER

Index 203

Illustrations

Figures

2.1   Segments of metropolitan governance   17
2.2   Cube of democratic metropolitan governance   23

Tables

2.1   Segments of interest intermediation, decision modes, types of actors and characteristics of citizenship   18
4.1   Basic data for Madrid and the Autonomous Community of Madrid (2001)   50
4.2   Basic data for Barcelona, its metropolitan area, the province of Barcelona and the Autonomous Community of Catalonia (2001)   51
5.1   Basic data for Greece and the metropolitan area of Athens   64
9.1   Democracy evaluation criteria   143
9.2   Evaluation of present democracy in the Rotterdam City-Region   146
11.1   The ten largest metropolitan areas in Switzerland   171

Notes on contributors

Julie-Anne Boudreau, Assistant Professor in the Department of Political Science at York University, Toronto, specialising in comparative and urban politics.

Dietrich Fürst, Professor of Spatial Planning and Public Administration, University of Hanover.

Panagiotis Getimis, Professor at the Department for Regional Economy and Development and Head of the Research Institute of Urban Environment and Human Resources at the Panteion University in Athens.

Michael Goldsmith, Professor of Government and Politics at the University of Salford and Visiting Professor at the Fondation Nationale des Sciences Politiques, Paris.

Anne Haila, Professor of Urban Studies, University of Helsinki.

Hubert Heinelt, Professor for Public Administration/Public Policy and Urban Studies at the Institute for Political Science.

Nikolaos Hlepas, Assistant Professor of Local Government and Regional Administration at the National University of Athens, Department of Political Science and Public Administration.

Roger Keil, Professor at the Faculty of Environmental Studies, York University.

Daniel Kübler, Assistant Professor at the Institute of Political Science, University of Zurich and currently visiting researcher at the Faculty of the Built Environment, University of New South Wales, Sydney.

Patrick Le Galès, Directeur de recherché CNRS and Associate Professor of Politics and Sociology, Sciences po Paris.

Emmanuel Négrier, CNRS researcher at the CEPEL (Centre d'Etudes Politiques de l'Europe Latine), University of Montpellier and visiting researcher at the University of Barcelona.

Fritz Sager, Assistant Professor for Policy Analysis and Evaluation at the Institute of Political Science, University of Bern.

Linze Schaap, Assistant Professor for Public Administration and Coordinator of the Centre for Local Democracy at the Department of Social Sciences at the Erasmus University Rotterdam.

Brigitte Schwab, Researcher at the Deutsches Institut für Urbanistik, Berlin, and Teaching Assistant at the University of Lausanne.

Mariona Tomàs, Research Fellow the National Institute of Scientific Research (INRS), Université du Québec, Montréal.

Acknowledgements

The editors are indebted to a large number of people who made this book possible. They include, of course, the authors of the individual chapters. Furthermore, we should point out that this book originates from a workshop on 'The Politics of Metropolitan Governance' held in Turin during the ECPR Joint Sessions in April 2002. The participants of this workshop contributed a lot to the argumentation presented in this book through a lively and supportive discussion of earlier drafts of most of the chapters. We also acknowledge the funding of a workshop held in Darmstadt in December 2003 by Peter Benz, the Mayor of Darmstadt, which gave us the opportunity to discuss some of the chapters with the authors. We thank the Centre for Interdisciplinary Research in Technology of Darmstadt University of Technology for financial support which allowed us to employ Oliver Wolf (Darmstadt University of Technology), who transformed the text delivered by the authors into a form acceptable to our publisher. In addition Randall Smith and Claudia Steffens worked hard on editing the language in some of the chapters. Finally, Daniel Kübler acknowledges support for his work on metropolitan governance from a post-doctoral scholarship by the Swiss National Science Foundation.

Hubert Heinelt
Daniel Kübler
Darmstadt and Zürich, March 2004

1 Introduction

Daniel Kübler and Hubert Heinelt

The twenty-first century will be metropolitan. In the ongoing globalisation of economic, social and cultural processes, metropolitan areas play the role of nodal points where human activities concentrate. They have entered a global competition and hierarchisation, and thereby participate in the making and the shaping of a global order of centrality. This has also led to internal change within metropolitan areas, notably to the transformation of the relationships between traditional core-cities and their surrounding territory. Assessing these dual exterior and interior dynamics, four elements have been put forward to characterise contemporary metropolitan areas across the world: (1) *urban sprawl* has broken up the historic boundaries of the city, extending on the surrounding rural space by waves of suburbanisation; (2) *functional specialisation of space* has intensified social segregation, that is, homogeneity of luxury residential areas, distressed neighbourhoods, single purpose zones etc. has grown simultaneously; (3) *spatial mobility of persons and goods* has become the lifeblood of the metropolitan system of economic production and social reproduction; (4) *cosmopolitan localism* has become the organising principle of metropolitan politics and culture, where global endowments are considered necessary to international competitiveness, but must be rooted in local culture in order to be socially and politically acceptable.[1]

Although it is clearly the forces of free-market capitalism that drive the emergence and development of metropolitan areas, public policies still play an important role. On the one hand, a high-performance public infrastructure is crucial to the competitiveness of a metropolitan area (e.g. transportation and communication networks, education and research, etc.). On the other hand, as spatially concentrated expressions of modern capitalism and its contradictions, metropolitan areas also entail the drawbacks of growth, and most of these (e.g. pollution, social distress, etc.) can only be addressed by state action. There is thus reason to argue that the future of metropolitan areas strongly depends on public governance capacity, able to channel economic development and, particularly, to equilibrate competitiveness with social cohesion and liveability at the metropolitan level (OECD 2001).

Aims of this book

This book, then, is about building metropolitan governance capacity at the dawn of the twenty-first century. The authors of this volume are interested in the latest developments and (new) paths towards achieving area-wide governance in metropolitan areas, favouring and impeding factors in this process, successes and failures, as well as consequences especially with respect to political and democratic issues. Unlike much of the earlier literature on this topic, none of the authors has espoused the assumption that there would be 'one best way' towards building governance capacity in metropolitan areas. Drawing on case studies in eleven OECD countries, they show indeed that a multiplicity of solutions has emerged, varying not only across but also within countries. Although we have deliberately refrained from referring to some sort of common ideal-type for metropolitan governance, the empirical analysis in this book is informed by an analytical framework that is intended to provide guidance through a wide variety of empirical constellations.

More precisely, this analytical framework, presented in Chapter 2, builds on the premise that issues of metropolitan governance may be understood by contextual conditions such as nationally specific local government traditions and state–society relations. But at the same time, emphasis should be given to the dynamics of place, that is, the fact that problems of metropolitan governance, as well as the responses to these problems, are structured by a set of factors whose combination and interaction are locally specific. In this sense, a first central argument put forward by this book is that 'place matters' in building metropolitan governance capacity. Whereas Chapter 2 provides the theoretical underpinning for this argument, each of the empirical chapters highlights the specific set of factors found in the different countries and metropolitan regions under scrutiny – so as to show *how* place matters in empirical situations. In addition, a second argument provides guidance throughout the texts in this book, namely that the tensions between the building of metropolitan governance capacity and democratic legitimacy merit particular attention. It is the case that the implications of metropolitan governance for democratic legitimation have been raised as an issue by many contemporary analyses of metropolitan governance, but have rarely been systematically assessed. Therefore, addressing the democratic question within metropolitan governance is the second main objective of this book, not only by suggesting a coherent analytical framework (developed in Chapter 2), but also by assessing empirical evidence from different countries in the light of this framework in the subsequent empirical chapters.

Presentation

As briefly mentioned above, and as is further developed in Chapter 2, the underlying analytical framework of this volume makes a strong case for the local government typology developed by Hesse and Sharpe (1991). This typology distinguishes three major types of local government traditions in the Western world: the Franco group, the Anglo group and the North and Middle European variant. Considering that this typology provides a useful conceptual lens for approaching issues of metropolitan governance in an internationally comparative perspective (see Chapter 2), it also provides the logic behind the structuring and presentation of the empirical chapters in this book.

The Franco group countries

More precisely, the first three chapters present cases drawn from countries belonging to the Franco group, namely France, Spain and Greece.

In Chapter 3, Emmanuel Négrier assesses the impact of a 1999 law aiming at the enhancement of governance capacity in French metropolitan areas through the creation of structures of cooperation between communes (the *Communautés d'agglomération*). He argues that the effect of financial incentives to communes should not be exaggerated in explaining the success of this law. On the one hand, institutional routines formed through pre-existing networks of intercommunal cooperation appeared as more important. On the other hand, political leadership has proven crucial in order to make an area-wide policy scope emerge and to overcome parochial resistance. In this respect, metropolitan areas in France must be seen as new political territories. However, the rules of the political game, and especially the role of democratic citizen participation remain to be invented. Given the very different combinations of factors that explain the coming about of *Communautés d'agglomération* in the various metropolitan areas, Négrier concludes that it is unlikely that a single model will be found for the political regulation of French metropolitan areas.

In Chapter 4, Mariona Tomàs draws on the cases of Madrid and Barcelona in order to outline conditions and prospects for metropolitan governance in Spain. In spite of evolving in the same national context, metropolitan governance patterns differ greatly between the two places. In Madrid, area-wide governance is mainly the matter of the Autonomous Community (the Spanish regional level), whose boundaries happen to coincide more or less with the extension of the metropolitan area. As a consequence, governance here is mainly state-centred, involving selected corporate actors but is generally rather closed to other civil society actors. This strongly contrasts with Barcelona, where, due to institutional fragmentation and political conflicts between different tiers of government (basically between the core city and the Autonomous Community of Catalonia), area-wide governance has come about mainly through pluralised networks of cooperation between the public and the private sector, mostly framed by visionary projects such as the 1992 Olympic Games. In both places however, and similarly to the French cases, the Spanish local government tradition implies that political leaders are at the centre of the governance building process.

Drawing on the case of Athens, Chapter 5, written by Panagiotis Getimis and Nikolaos Hlepas, presents issues and prospects of metropolitan governance in Greece. Long considered a 'hopeless case' due to extreme institutional fragmentation and persisting political conflict, area-wide governance in metropolitan Athens has gained new momentum through the challenge of organising the Olympic Games in 2004. Issue- and project-based mechanisms of coordination have come about, most of them involving private and societal organisations.

Getimis and Hlepas argue that metropolitan governance will continue to be an issue even after the Olympics: indeed, three concrete scenarios for strengthening area-wide governance have been intensely discussed in Athens. Reviewing each of these scenarios, Getimis and Hlepas identify two critical conditions for success: moving away the focus of local government from the primacy of politics and towards service production, as well as increasing civil society involvement.

The Anglo group countries

Still following Hesse and Sharpe's typology of local government, the next part of the book reunites case studies from the Anglo group of countries: the United Kingdom, Canada and the United States.

In Chapter 6, Michael Goldsmith reviews the English experience in which initiatives have been taken to increase governance capacity in metropolitan areas. It shows the absolutely crucial influence of central government, which has extensively used opportunities to make radical changes to institutional conditions for the emergence of certain forms of metropolitan governance. Depending on whether central government has been dominated by the Conservative or the Labour parties, English metropolitan areas have seen institutionalised area-wide governments (the metropolitan councils), their abolition parallel to the weakening of local government and the establishment of a multitude of quasi-governmental agencies/organisations in the Thatcher era, and, under 'New Labour', the re-establishment of a politically strong Greater London Authority with a directly elected mayor and assembly, as well as the foundation of strong Regional Development Agencies outside London. Goldsmith concludes that, while there have been some attempts at democratic renewal of local government, governance of metropolitan areas still remains concerned primarily with efficient service provision, and that although civil society actors such as voluntary associations have real opportunities to become engaged at the metropolitan level they find it far more difficult than big business to be involved in decision making in governing metropolitan regions.

Chapter 7, by Roger Keil and Julie-Anne Boudreau, reports on metropolitan governance restructuring in North America. Drawing on the cases of Toronto, Montreal and Los Angeles, it shows that recent reforms have introduced a scalar change of urban governance processes and institutions. Keil and Boudreau argue that, in spite of the different results of these reforms – consolidation in Toronto and Montreal, secession in Los Angeles – they must all be understood as a neo-liberal answer to urban globalisation. In all three cases, the political debate on amalgamation and secession was tied in with discourses on efficiency and democracy. However, little attention was paid to the internal democracy of metropolitan areas, and the democratic deficits of metropolitan politics were not significantly addressed by any of the three reforms. In addition, social movements pursuing the agenda of internal democratisation were significantly weakened by government rescaling in all three cases. Therefore, Keil and Boudreau conclude, this means that those three metropolitan areas may prove to be insufficiently prepared for stabilising an acceptable mode of political regulation over central policy issues that they will have to arbitrate in the near future.

The North and Middle European group

Finally, the remaining part of the book analyses issues of metropolitan governance capacity and democracy in countries belonging to the North and Middle European group: Finland, the Netherlands, Germany and Switzerland.

Chapter 8, by Anne Haila and Patrick Le Galès, presents the contradictions of metropolitan governance in Finland, drawing on the example of the Helsinki area. More precisely, it is focused on the tensions generated by the attempt to develop an international strategy for competing in the globalised economy while maintaining local welfare services against the national government's initiative for a restructuring of the extensive Finnish welfare state. Hence, the coming about of area-wide governance has been driven by communal interests reuniting against the central state, a coalition of actors interested in economic development, as well as through professional networks in the field of social service provision. Interestingly, the issue of democracy has not been at the forefront of the debate on metropolitan governance in Helsinki. Local democracy is seen as embedded in single municipalities, thereby serving as an argument against institutionalised area-wide governance. Haila and Le Galès conclude that, given its origins, metropolitan governance in Helsinki will continue to rely on a mix of robust government and dynamic issue-based networks involving private actors, and therefore presents oligarchic tendencies.

Chapter 9, by Linze Schaap, discusses attempts at metropolitan governance building in the Netherlands. More particularly, it reviews the reform aiming at the creation of a new governmental institution for the Rotterdam metropolitan area. Paying particular attention to the democratic content of the reform, Schaap shows that not only the process but also its intended end result (the City Province) did not meet the requirements of either representative or participatory democracy – a fact not unrelated to the spectacular failure of the reform project. Today it appears that the failure of the City Province reform has also impacted upon existing area-wide cooperation. In particular, the regional scope of these bodies seems to have retreated behind interest representation by single municipalities. Schaap concludes that the current system places most emphasis on representative democracy, whereas the potential to build legitimacy of metropolitan governance by direct citizen involvement is too often overlooked.

Chapter 10, by Dietrich Fürst, scrutinises current developments in metropolitan governance building in Germany. He observes that the prospects for developing area-wide schemes of governance in German metropolitan areas are now better than in the past. They are not only favoured by state incentives granted for area-wide cooperation in metropolitan areas, but most notably by a 'paradigm change' at the level of local authorities, who have become increasingly aware of their mutual interdependence as well as of the benefits of the regional scale. However, German municipalities are still anxiously trying to preserve their relatively high autonomy against each other, upper-level government and societal actors in governing local affairs. Reviewing two current models of metropolitan governance (Stuttgart and Hanover), Fürst shows that an area-wide political body expanded governance capacity by providing an institutionalised arena in which a strong definition of the common regional interest could emerge. However, the drawback of such strong forms of democratic area-wide governance seems to be that they tend to further state impingements on the private sector and may therefore hamper metropolitan dynamism in the mid-term.

In Chapter 11, Daniel Kübler, Fritz Sager and Brigitte Schwab discuss the problems and prospects of area-wide governance in metropolitan areas in Switzerland. In the absence of significant reform of urban territorial institutions since the early twentieth century, institutional fragmentation of Swiss metropolitan areas is very high and area-wide governance has relied exclusively on intergovernmental cooperation. So far, conflict-avoiding behaviour appears to have been the major factor of success for achieving area-wide governance, but new initiatives taken by the federal government will probably see financial incentives become more important in building metropolitan governance capacity. With respect to the democratic issue of metropolitan governance, the authors argue that democratic legitimacy of metropolitan policies is high, not least because of direct democratic instruments, allowing the creation of issue-based legitimacy in order to regulate political conflicts. Citizen participation is extensive, sometimes to the point of making area-wide governance difficult.

In their concluding chapter, Hubert Heinelt and Daniel Kübler try to summarise the empirical findings (1) by assessing the democratic quality of presented cases according to the model developed at the end of Chapter 2, that is, according to input and output legitimacy, the openness and closure of policy networks built into metropolitan governance arrangements and the involvement of civil society and (2) by answering the question what supports the evolvement and strengthening of metropolitan governance. Here, the above-mentioned hypothesis that 'place matters' is addressed against the background of the empirical findings. Related to this, emphasis is given to 'critical junctures' and how local actors have made use of them to break up frozen landscapes (or path dependency) determined by organisational settings as well as by established 'meaning systems' and interests.

Note

1 This list is drawn from Bassand and Kübler (2001: 122) and inspired by reflections made by authors such as Sassen (1991), Choay (1994), Ascher (1995), Castells (2000).

Bibliography

Ascher, F. (1995) *Métapolis ou l'avenir des villes*, Paris: Odile Jacob.
Bassand, M. and Kübler, D. (2001) 'Introduction: Metropolization and Metropolitan Governance', *Swiss Political Science Review*, 7: 121–123.
Castells, M.E. (2000) *The Rise of the Network Society*, Oxford: Blackwell Publishers.

Choay, F. (1994) 'Le règne de l'urbain et la mort de la ville', in Centre G. Pompidou (ed.), *La ville, art et architecture en Europe 1870–1933*, Paris: Centre Pompidou.

Hesse, J.J. (ed.) (1991) *Local Government and Urban Affairs in International Perspective*, Baden-Baden: Nomos Verlag.

Hesse, J.J. and Sharpe, L.J. (1991) 'Conclusions', in J.J. Hesse (ed.), *Local Government and Urban Affairs in an International Perspective*, Baden-Baden: Nomos Verlag, pp. 603–621.

Organisation for Economic Cooperation and Development (OECD) (2001) *Cities for Citizens. Improving Metropolitan Governance*, Paris: OECD.

Sassen, S. (1991) *The Global City*, Princeton: Princeton University Press.

2 Metropolitan governance, democracy and the dynamics of place

Daniel Kübler and Hubert Heinelt

Introduction

Continuing urban sprawl combined with faltering or failed attempts of local government reform have resulted in a growing divergence between functional and institutional urban spaces in most industrialised countries. Today, cities in the (Weberian) sense of territorially integrated socio-economic entities no longer exist. The urban phenomenon is better described by the notion of *metropolitan areas*, that is multi-centred urban regions which have developed mainly along functional networks, cutting across institutionally defined territorial boundaries. This situation of *governmental fragmentation* leads to difficulties for the solution of public problems in these areas.

Drawing on the long-running debate over the appropriate institutional structure for governing fragmented metropolitan areas, this chapter reflects upon the relationship between the architecture of metropolitan governance on the one hand, and metropolitan democracy on the other. The chapter comprises three sections. It begins with a presentation of the debate on metropolitan governance as a succession of three waves: the metropolitan reform tradition, the public choice approach and the so-called new regionalism. The main arguments of the latter approach are developed, as related to the ongoing discussion on 'modern governance' (i.e. new forms and modes of political steering through bargaining systems). In the next section, we retrace the ways in which each wave of the debate on metropolitan governance has conceptualised the relationship between governance and democracy. We argue that although new regionalist thinking has pointed to some important elements for the study of this relationship, it yet lacks a framework suitable for cross-national comparison. The final section suggests a framework through which 'the democratic question' within metropolitan governance can be comparatively addressed. More precisely, we argue that an assessment of metropolitan democracy should work out the 'place'-specific combinations of three conditioning factors.

Debating metropolitan governance: three waves

The nature of metropolitan governance has continued to be a central issue in regional economics, public administration research and (urban) political science.

Generations of scholars have debated the 'right way' to overcome the growing disparities between functional urban territories and the institutional structure of local government. This long-running debate on metropolitan governance used to be one between two different intellectual traditions: the metropolitan reform tradition and the public choice approach (Ostrom 1972). During the 1990s, however, several scholars and policy advocates have made the case for a 'new regionalism' (Frisken and Norris 2001) or 'new metropolitan governance' (Brenner 2003).

The *metropolitan reform tradition* views the existence of a large number of independent public jurisdictions within a metropolitan area as the main obstacle to efficient and equitable urban service delivery.[1] Based on this perspective and with a somewhat Weberian trust in the rationality and planning capacity of large public bureaucracies, metropolitan reformers have advocated governmental consolidation, whereby institutional boundaries would be brought to match the territorial scale of the economic and social development of metropolitan areas. Consolidation, they argue, should be achieved either through annexation of suburbs by centre-cities, or by the creation of metropolitan governments, that is, two-tier institutions with extensive competencies and autonomy, whose territorial scope covers the functional metropolitan area as a whole.

The *public choice perspective* on metropolitan governance rejects the idea of institutional consolidation as a way to resolve metropolitan problems.[2] It argues that, far from being pathological, the institutional fragmentation of metropolitan areas into a multitude of autonomous local jurisdictions is beneficial for effective and efficient metropolitan service delivery. Drawing on Tiebout's (1956) classic idea of 'voting with one's feet', public choice scholars think that the existence of a range of autonomous local constituencies allows citizens to choose the jurisdiction with the tax/service package that corresponds best to their personal preferences. At the aggregate level, they argue, the competition between local governments to attract new residents leads not only to effective matching of urban service demands, but also to efficiency in the allocation of public resources used to produce these services.

Over the second half of the twentieth century, the debate on metropolitan governance was largely dominated by the dispute between these two classic schools of thought. It has not only resulted in an impressive amount of empirical research, but has also informed political discussion over metropolitan government reforms in many OECD countries.[3] However, both schools of thought proved to provide only limited guidance for debating contemporary issues of metropolitan governance. On the one hand, institutional consolidation is not really a success story: most reforms have failed and many experiences with two-tier metropolitan authorities have proved disappointing (Lefèvre 1998). On the other hand, the public tenet of unbiased competition between autonomous local authorities also appears as a theoretical position that lacks empirical underpinning (Frey and Eichenberger 2001). In reality, most metropolitan problems are addressed through purpose-oriented networks of coordination and cooperation, involving municipalities, governmental agencies at various levels, as well as private service providers. Such networks usually fall short of institutional consolidation advocated by metropolitan reformers. At the same time, coopera-tion within these networks is not always entirely voluntary and sometimes significantly hampers local autonomy which is considered essential by public choice theorists.

This observation is taken as a starting point by a new perspective which draws on research conducted during the 1990s on metropolitan policy coordination in North America (see Downs 1994; Rusk 1995) and Western Europe (see van den Berg *et al.* 1997; Benz 2001). Labelled '*new regionalism*' by some North-American authors (see Savitch and Vogel 2000; Frisken and Norris 2001), this new perspective conveys the notion that effective metropolitan governance does not necessarily require institutional consolidation. Instead, it argues that area-wide governance is achieved through cooperative arrangements that stabilise networks of policy-relevant actors. These networks usually are heterogeneous conglomerates of actors and agencies with various backgrounds and competen-cies who define and deliver urban services in a way that is independent from the territorial boundaries of the traditional local government structure. New region-alism is not focused on institutional structures or on the behaviour of autonomous localities, but rather on re-harnessing relations between various public agencies and private actors at different territorial levels for the purpose of area-wide governance.

As Savitch and Vogel (2000) argue, the 'new regionalist' perspective on metropolitan governance mirrors the debate on the transformation of the state, 'from government to governance' as some have put it (see Kooiman 1993; Le Galès 1995; Rhodes 1996; Stoker 1998). Informed by neo-corporatist analyses (see Schmitter and Lehmbruch 1979) as well as by the policy-network approach (see Marin and Mayntz 1991), this debate emphasises the growing importance of *functional interest intermediation* between market and hierarchy, in comparison to *territorial interest intermediation* based on territorially defined systems of representation and parliamentary decision making. It also emphasises that a weak state on the one hand and the growing importance of policy networks and strong societal actors on the other are expressions of societal modernisation addressing the challenges resulting from the increased complexity of modern societies (Mayntz 1993: 41).

New regionalism thus focuses on the emergence of metropolitan governance through the interaction between a variety of actors rather than through state hier-archy. Following Fritz Scharpf, it can be argued that the steering capacity of new regionalist modes of metropolitan governance depends on the ability to avoid the 'joint decision trap' (Scharpf 1988), that is, when defenders of the status quo block all changes due to a *de facto* unanimity rule resulting from high interdependence between actors. Accordingly, research in the wake of new regionalism has pointed to three factors crucial to area-wide steering capacity. The first factor relates to actor behaviour. Indeed, the risk of a joint decision trap is reduced when actors adopt conflict-avoiding strategies (see Benz 2001): formulating 'soft' norms rather than obligations; consulting all relevant interests; allocating financial resources in an equitable way; finding compromises through solutions which only marginally alter the status quo ('pragmatism'); and relying not only on 'positive coordination' (through negotiation) but also on 'negative coordination' (by anticipating interests and possible reactions of peers without necessarily negotiating with them). A second factor is incentive structures set by higher level institutions. Although generally not directly involved in metropolitan problem solving, supra-local bodies such as states or provinces, but also national states and – in the case of the European Union – even international institutions' can set (financial) incentives and thereby significantly influence metropolitan actors' willingness to cooperate (see Baraize and Négrier 2001; Gainsborough 2001; Kübler *et al.* 2003). Finally, political leadership also plays an important role. Mobilisation around strong visions put forward by political leaders can provide motivation to act towards a common goal and thereby facilitate cooperation among relevant actors (see Jouve and Lefèvre 1999, and more generally Stone 1995; Elcock 2001).

With adequate actor behaviour, incentive structures and political leadership as the critical ingredients for metropolitan governance, new regionalism acknowledges that paths towards such governance may include very different combinations of these three factors and therefore vary greatly across metropolitan areas. Unlike the two classic schools of thought new regionalism does not assume that there is one only true way. Instead, routes towards new regionalism are likely to be strongly shaped by existing prerequisites on the three critical dimensions. As Le Galès (1998) has argued, a single model of governance is not likely to emerge, since the construction of steering capacity is strongly determined by the social, political and economic dynamics of place, that is, the locally specific combinability between actor behavior, incentive structures and political leadership for the construction of an area-wide steering capacity.

Metropolitan governance and democracy

To date, the debate on metropolitan governance has mainly focused on questions of equity, effectiveness and efficiency in public service provision within metropolitan areas, as well as of competitiveness of metropolitan areas on a global scale. So far, the debate has essentially revolved around economic arguments (Swanstrom 2001). By way of contrast, questions about the democratic quality of policy-making in metropolitan areas appear far less prominent in this debate. Nevertheless, some scholars did focus on these questions, especially in the wake of the two traditional schools of thought.

Institutional consolidation and community building

For a long time, scholars pertaining to the metropolitan reform tradition implicitly or explicitly 'celebrated professional management over democratic politics, at best reserving the public a right of final judgement via a short ballot' (Lowery 2001: 131–132). Only recently have there been endeavours to examine the institutional architecture of metropolitan areas in the light of various conceptions of citizenship. Among the more significant figures the inquiry by Lyons *et al.* (1992), who analyse the relationship between metropolitan institutions, community attachment and individual political behaviour. Based on surveys in two metropolitan areas – one consolidated and one fragmented – they compare levels of community attachment as well as citizen responses to dissatisfaction. The latter are classified according to the so-called EVLN (*Exit, Voice, Loyalty* and *Neglect*) model, placing responses to dissatisfaction on two dimensions: active–passive and constructive–destructive. With respect to rival conceptions of citizenship, the authors argue that *liberal* conceptions of citizenship stress Exit and Loyalty, whereas *communitarian* conceptions of citizenship put most stress on Voice (Lowery *et al.* 1992: 71). Neglect – for example, alienation, cynicism and distrust – is seen as inappropriate to both liberal and communitarian notions of citizenship.

Based on this survey, Lowery *et al.* (1992) report that local government structures have a strong effect on how citizens react to dissatisfaction. More precisely, they found that community attachment was much higher in consolidated than in fragmented settings. They also found that a high level of community attachment makes the constructive responses of Voice and Loyalty more likely, and the destructive responses of Exit and Neglect less likely. The conclusion is that consolidated metropolitan institutions promote use of the constructive problem-solving behaviours better than fragmented metropolitan settings. Unlike consolidated institutions, the localities in fragmented metropolitan settings do not provide the appropriate scale in relation to many issues of concern to residents and therefore are not seen as a meaningful arena for getting constructively involved in public affairs.

The results of this study provide a new – that is, non-economic – argument in favour of the metropolitan reform agenda, namely that consolidated metropolitan institutions tend to foster and enhance democratic citizenship (Lowery 1999; 2001). In this sense, the metropolitan reform tradition has approached integrative theories of democracy whose focus lies on the 'ability of democratic institutions to produce democratic citizens' (Sørensen 1997: 555).

Fragmentation, civic virtues and happiness

Public choice theorists of metropolitan governance have from the outset emphasised the role of citizen participation and democratic institutions. In one of the earliest texts explaining the public choice perspective on metropolitan governance, Ostrom *et al.* (1961) emphasise the importance of political representation. Through participation in democratic government structures, citizens can express their preferences for certain tax/service packages and sanction those who are responsible for the supply of these services (elected members of government) when the demand is not appropriately met. This argument is a central tenet of public choice theory which goes beyond the issue of metropolitan governance; in several empirical studies, public choice scholars have found support for the hypothesis that there is a positive relationship between the extensiveness of democratic procedures and efficient allocation of public resources (see Frey and Stutzer 1999; Freitag and Vatter 2000).

Some public choice scholars have recently reversed the question and started to investigate the effect of participation rights on individual citizen behaviour, combining institutional rational choice theory and social psychology in order to study the effect of institutions on what is called *intrinsic motivation* of individuals, such as moral incentives or civic virtues (see Frey 1997). More precisely, it is argued that external interventions crowd-out (i.e. destroy) intrinsic motivation if they are perceived to be controlling and they crowd-in (i.e. increase) intrinsic motivation if they are perceived to be supportive. In particular, the possibilities for institutional participation by individuals are seen as critical. Extensive participation rights foster civic virtues, whereas restricted participation tends to destroy them. Some scholars showed, for instance, that in local settings with extensive institutional participation rights, tax evasion is significantly lower than in settings with restricted participation (Pommerehne and Weck-Heckmann 1996; Frey 1997). They argue that when people have a greater chance to participate in and to influence government, they identify more with the policy choices of the government, making them less likely to cheat. Others have found that extensive participation rights increase individual happiness (Stutzer 2000). This seems to be particularly the case for direct democratic institutions such as popular initiatives, by which citizens can make direct input into the policy process.

For public choice theorists on metropolitan governance, these findings on the effect of democratic institutions on individual civic virtue (taxpayer honesty) and well-being (individual happiness) further corroborate their general view on the beneficial effects of metropolitan fragmentation. In small communities, they argue, the exercise of citizen control over politicians and policy choices tends to be more extensive and effective than in larger institutions (Parks and Oakerson 2000). Moreover, their argument also leads to the idea that, in order to reduce spillover problems, *voluntary* cooperation between autonomous localities in metropolitan areas is better than *forced* cooperation. The latter, as an external intervention, would decrease the intrinsic motivation of localities to cooperate and make them behave badly, whereas the former would increase their intrinsic motivation and facilitate coordination. Taking these arguments further, Frey and Eichenberger have come up with the concept of *Functional Overlapping Competing Jurisdictions* (FOCJ) (Frey and Eichenberger 2001) as the ideal form of metropolitan governance from a public choice point of view. FOCJ are functional networks through which different autonomous localities voluntarily cooperate in order to produce specific urban services, and which – in contrast to contemporary practice – include extensive participation rights for the services' clients.

Democracy and citizenship in new regionalist thinking

Reflecting on the issue of democracy and citizenship in metropolitan governance has led both metropolitan reformers and public choice theorists to reinforce further their point of view. There is undoubtedly something of a – rather unhelpful – dialogue of the deaf. As new regionalist thinkers have argued, the two traditional schools of thought are inadequate to debate contemporary issues of metropolitan governance. It is thus plausible that they may also provide little guidance for discussing questions of democracy and citizenship in contemporary metropolitan areas.

But what does new regionalism have to say in this realm? Like the other two schools of thought on metropolitan governance, most of the work in the wake of new regionalism has concentrated on economic arguments, particularly on territorial competitiveness and the imperative to attract external capital investment in the context of economic globalisation (Brenner 2003). True, questions about the implications of new regionalism for democracy and citizenship have been raised. Some scholars argue that new forms of governance contribute to a 'recomposition of the political' (Le Galès 1998: 501) and to a 'transformation of democracy' (Heinelt 1997), whereas others have accused new regionalism of a 'democratic deficit' (Heinz 2000) or of lacking in 'democratic quality' (Benz 2001). A first overview has identified two main lines of reasoning: a pessimistic and an optimistic view (Kübler and Wälti 2001).

The pessimistic view

The first line of reasoning rests on the classic argument of democracy theory, according to which advanced democratic political systems are structured by an intrinsic tension between *authenticity* and *effectiveness* of state action, that is, the democratic quality of inputs versus the quality of policy outputs (Scharpf 1999), or citizen participation versus system effectiveness (Dahl 1994). This line of reasoning can be termed pessimistic, given the extent to which it focuses on the decline of representative institutions in self-governing networks. More precisely, it argues that new regionalism is mainly concerned with 'making things happen', that is, to increase effectiveness of policy on the output side, and that it does so at the expense of the input side. Whilst increasing the capacity to produce effective metropolitan problem solving, new regionalism may reduce the importance of procedures which allow for the transmission of citizens' interests into the process of governing through voting and systems of territorial representation.

Drawing on the 'overhead democracy model' (Redford 1969),[4] advocates of this view argue that elected local or regional councils as well as other representative institutions and public arenas are disadvantaged by new regionalism. This position is informed by the argument that policy networks pose accountability problems, since non-governmental actors within these networks typically lack democratic legitimacy, and that horizontal cooperation and negotiation in functional networks can be no substitute for 'traditional' representative democracy.[5]

The optimistic view

The second line of reasoning with respect to democracy and citizenship in new regionalism focuses on two other key features of democracy: inclusiveness and deliberation. The aim is to identify the potential of new regionalism for the enhancement of these two democratic qualities. In this sense, this view can be portrayed as *optimistic*.

First, in this line of reasoning, the heterarchical nature of new regionalism is emphasised. Due to the high number of participating actors and the interdependencies between them, majority decisions are unlikely. Instead, decisions must be reached through compromise after negotiation, or through consensus after deliberation. Especially in the latter case, heterarchical networks can thus be seen as an important vector of 'deliberative politics' (Habermas 1996: 283ff.), where decisions are based on intersubjective understanding over the best arguments rather than on the representation of interests, thereby enhancing the option of creating 'good governance' through free, open and public debate or dialogue. Thus, it is assumed that new regionalism relying on heterarchical networks of cooperation increases the deliberative qualities of metropolitan policy-making.

Second, it is argued that area-wide networks that include not only state agencies but also varieties of non-governmental organisations and associations are an important vector of pluralism and civic culture. Based on the tenet of 'associative democracy' (Hirst 1994), the recruitment of the energies of citizen's organisations into public governance is seen as a step away from an oppressive state and towards a more egalitarian-democratic order (Cohen and Rogers 1992: 465). Because of associational involvement in public policies, transitions from government to governance are presented as an opportunity for empowering the citizen and pluralizing the state (Bang and Sørensen 1998). Consequently, it can be argued that metropolitan governance built on networks of non-governmental actors as well as public agencies strengthens the position of civil society actors in metropolitan policy-making, thereby extending citizens' influence upon it.

To sum up, three tenets flow out from these two lines of reasoning, namely that an assessment of the democratic quality in metropolitan governance must consider factors related to (1) the accountability of the instances who make decisions; (2) the ways in which these decisions are reached (deliberation, negotiation or majority vote); and (3) the relations between state agencies and non-governmental actors that are established within metropolitan governance. In comparison to the two classic schools of thought, new regionalism hence implies a widening of the focus for the reflection on the democratic question related to metropolitan governance. Metropolitan reformers and public choice theorists both limit themselves to the relationship between citizens and political authorities to argue about democracy in metropolitan governance. The new regionalist perspective additionally focuses on modes of decision making as well as on associative channels of influence as two supplementary features of a democratic polity. It argues that democratic metropolitan governance is not only a matter of accountability, but also of decision modes and associational involvement. However, no stable grid of arguments has yet emerged that could provide clear guidance for the reflection on the democratic question(s) posed by new regionalism. In particular, it is unclear how the three factors identified above combine in various national contexts.

Analysing metropolitan democracy: a comparative framework

Based on these premises, the remainder of this chapter endeavours to develop a framework whose intention is to specify the democratic question within metropolitan governance in a way that is suitable for cross-national comparison. As a first step, we suggest that an assessment of the democratic quality of metropolitan governance needs to start with considering the ways in which the tension between closeness and openness of area-wide governance networks is resolved. In a second step, we will concentrate on those factors that condition the coming about of various closeness/openness mixes, that is, contextual factors that vary across countries, sites or policy fields and therefore need to be taken into account in comparative analyses of democratic metropolitan governance. Finally, we suggest that a focus on 'place' may be useful in order to acknowledge the locally specific combinations of these different conditioning factors.

A general model of metropolitan governance: segments of steering and the openness/closeness of policy networks

Metropolitan governance – be it organised according to 'old' or 'new' regionalisms – can be considered as a mixture of different segments of steering (as shown in Figure 2.1).[6] According to this general model, a *core segment* of metropolitan governance consists of parliamentary and governmental institutions (including the bureaucracy). This core segment is embedded in four segments of interest intermediation that function according to different *decision modes* (majority decisions, hierarchy, bargaining/political exchange and arguing/debate) and that rely on different types of actors (as intermediators) and characteristics of citizenship (see Table 2.1). They are surrounded (as a 'peripheral context') by locally based associations, pressure groups and movements, which are seen as the *infrastructure* of civil society.

The segment of *territorial interest intermediation* – with parties as the crucial 'intermediators' and the option of majority decisions as the dominant decision mode – covers the sphere where input legitimisation can be produced. The segment of *administrative interest intermediation* is where output legitimisation can be achieved. Although this segment is characterised by the use of hierarchical interventions by public authorities to enforce binding decisions and to achieve coordination of interactions, it may well be very important that public authorities (as a 'bargaining administration', Benz *et al.* 1992) do interact with those affected by a policy in order to achieve their acceptance and compliance with policies. This can be achieved by addressing their motives and by finding ways to safeguard their willingness to comply as well as by investigating their relevant knowledge and taking it seriously. The *pessimistic view* developed above clearly focuses on these two segments of metropolitan governance, since they refer to conventional perceptions of government-related policy-making in the input and output realms of a political system.

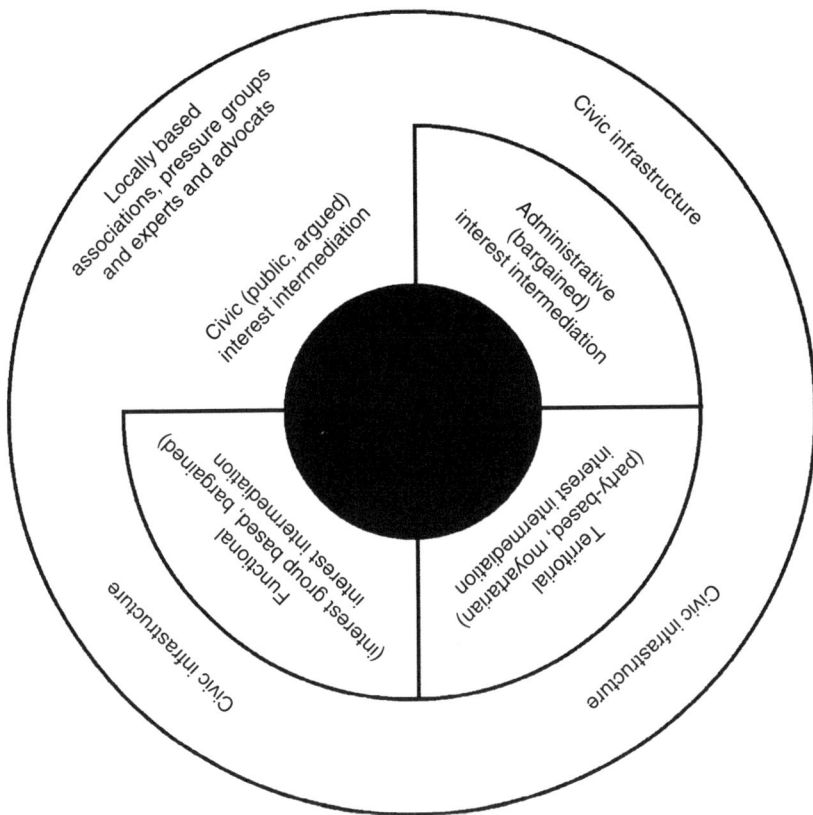

Figure 2.1 Segments of metropolitan governance.

The segment of *functional interest intermediation* relies on corporate actors (associations such as trade unions and chambers of commerce) as 'mediators' and on bargaining and political exchange as decision modes. The latter implies that the societal actors involved have 'bargaining power', as the binding nature of a decision depends on mutual agreement and can be questioned by way of disagreement or non-compliance, or by 'dropping out' ('exit'). This is different from the segment of *civil society related interest intermediation*. Here, the actors involved do not have such 'bargaining power'. They have to rely on 'voice' and public reasoning. This seems to be weak, but in so far as a common under-standing ('frames') of *problem definitions and patterns of action* can be brought about through public debate on urban issues (Akerman 2001), the debating style (mode) of interest intermediation can be crucial for every sector of interest intermediation, that is, for the whole governance system. These two segments of interest intermediation refer to the state–(civil-)society relations emphasised by the *optimistic view* developed above.

Table 2.1 Segments of interest intermediation, decision modes, types of actors and characteristics of citizenship

Segment of interest intermediation	Decision modes	Types of (collective) actors	Characteristics of citizenship
Territorial interest intermediation	Majority decisions (in parliaments/ councils or by referenda)	Parties	Vote
Administrative interest intermediation	Hierarchical administrative interventions	Local and regional authorities, quangos	Voice (including protest, direct action)
Functional interest intermediation	Bargaining/ political exchange	Corporate actors (associations, chambers, professional representation, trade unions)	Right to organise/ to form/join a collective/ corporate actor
Civil society related interest intermediation	Arguing/debate	Civil society actors (citizen initiatives, social movements, NGOs)	Voice (including protest, direct action)

What are the *new regionalist* specifications of this general model? First, it is clear that, in the absence of metropolitan territorial reforms, the *core segment* is more or less fragmented, and so are the segments of *territorial* and *administrative interest mediation*. New regionalism implies a number of formally independent jurisdictions with their own parliamentary and administrative bodies. In this respect, these segments of the general model of metropolitan governance represent the focus of two traditional schools of thought on metropolitan governance. What is of interest at this point is the *decision modes* found in these segments. It could be argued that the decision modes found in these segments depend on their degree of fragmentation. Majority decisions can occur only where a representative territorial body has been established (mainly task-oriented and sectoral) and where the individual jurisdictions are subordinated to this organisation. Hierarchical decisions can be made where a territorially integrated organisation has also been made the (mainly task-oriented and sectoral) ultimately responsible authority. Thus, in the context of new regionalism, where there are neither (integrated) territorial-representative bodies nor public authorities with a clear ultimate responsibility, *bargaining* and *deliberation* can be expected to be the typical decision modes in the segments of territorial and administrative interest intermediation.

Second, estimating the effect of new regionalism on *functional* and *civic interest intermediation* is less straightforward. New regionalist thinking implies that networks built on horizontal interactions between state agencies, corporate actors (e.g. business associations, chambers of commerce, trade unions, etc.) and civil society associations are increasingly important in these segments. However, the scholarly debate on policy networks has shown that there are important distinctions to be made between various types of network, involving specific state–society relations and therefore also specific effects on the variables of interest here. As van Waarden (1992) has suggested, policy networks can be classified and the state–society relations they institute can be summarised by considering characteristics such as the number and type of actors, power relations and the degree of institutionalisation, etc. The general argument flowing from such analyses of policy networks is that, on the one hand, for purposes of effectiveness, policy networks need to a certain extent to be closed. Otherwise, bargaining type solutions relying on package deals, side payments or 'tit for tat' arrangements cannot work. On the other hand, a certain degree of 'openness' and transparency is a condition for the solutions reached to be accepted. Developing this argument, we can say that – as is the case with network-based policy-making in general[7] – the segments of functional and civic-society-related interest intermediation in new regionalism are characterised by a tension between 'closeness' and 'openness' of policy networks. However, the question of the exact extent to which new regionalism leads to open or closed policy networks cannot be answered in general terms, but needs to be assessed empirically.

Conditioning factors: reflections on a comparative framework

As Savitch and Vogel (2000) have argued, there are various paths towards new regionalism, and they also bring about different types of policy networks. One can thus consider that these network types play an important role in explaining the impact of certain new regionalist arrangements on metropolitan democracy and citizenship. In other words, we would argue that metropolitan democracy and citizenship are not only strongly affected by territorial institutional fragmentation – as the classic debate between metropolitan reformers and public choice theorists suggests – but equally by the openness/closeness of policy networks that emerge within new regionalist arrangements.

However, empirical evidence on this topic (Kübler and Schwab 2006) suggests that the chosen paths towards new regionalism cannot provide a full explanation of when there is a shift from input to output legitimisation (the pessimist view), nor when involvement of civil society actors is increased or deliberation emerges as the main mode of decision mode (the optimist view) in individual metropolitan areas. This causal link is corroborated in some cases, but not in others. In other words, scrutinising the functioning of metropolitan governance networks in an isolated way does not take us very far in answering the question whether different paths to area-wide governance affect metropolitan democracy and citizenship, and if they do, in what way. Rather, it seems that there are conditioning factors that influence this causal relationship and that should be taken into account in comparative analyses of metropolitan governance and democracy across countries, sites or policy fields.

Input and output legitimisation in different local
government traditions

As Hesse and Sharpe (1991: 606–607) have shown, key characteristics of local government vary between countries. They identified three major types of local government systems. The first type follows the Napoleonic model and is called the *Franco* group. Here, the essence of local government is political rather than functional. Local governments are considered to embody territorial communities and office holders are expected to represent the interests of this community, especially in relation to higher levels of government. This 'political localism' (Page 1991) is found in countries such as France, Italy, Belgium, Spain, Portugal and Greece.

A second type is the *Anglo* group, where local governments have little legal and political status, but enjoy a high degree of autonomy and discretion from higher levels of government where day-to-day operations are concerned. The emphasis here is functional rather than political and the main role of local government is to shape and deliver public services. According to Hesse and Sharpe, this type of local government is to be found in the United Kingdom, Ireland, Canada, Australia, New Zealand and, with some qualifications, the USA.

The third group is the *North and Middle European* variant. As in the Anglo group, emphasis is placed on the functional capacity of local government to shape and deliver public services, but in addition, equal emphasis is placed on local democracy *per se*. This group is the most formally decentralised of the three types, and, reflecting the operation of the subsidiarity principle, sees local governments enjoying a strong constitutional status and a relatively high degree of policy-making autonomy and financial independence. The Scandinavian countries belong to this group, as well as Germany, the Netherlands, Austria and Switzerland.

National traditions of local government thus play an important role in shaping the relationship between input and output legitimisation at that level. Political localism as a reflection of community, found in the Franco group, can be seen as placing a strong emphasis on input legitimisation ('democracy'). The emphasis on functional capacity that is found in the Anglo group supports the case for output legitimisation ('efficiency') (Goldsmith 1996: 177), whereas the Northern or Middle European type represents an attempt to emphasise input as well as output legitimisation.

Based on this general argument, several specific suggestions can be made. We would expect, for example, the environment of political localism of the Franco-type tradition to be rather resistant to the shift from input to output legitimisation supposedly inherent in new metropolitan governance structures. In contrast, the Anglo type environment, where the functional capacity of local government institutions is central, can be expected to favour a shift from input to output legitimisation. No such development can be hypothetically predicted, however, for the Northern and Middle European local government type. Here, the emphasis on both local democracy and functional capacity could mean either that such an environment is quite resistant to a shift between these two principles, or that there is a (fragile) equilibrium which can quickly become imbalanced as a result of the impact of new metropolitan governance.

State–society relationships in different national and local contexts

The study of national differences in the relationship between the state and society is as old as the idea that there has to be a separation between the two.

Badie and Birnbaum (1979), in their historically comparative perspective, distinguish between *weak and strong states*. In a strong state, 'civil society' (consisting of civic society actors such as NGOs and social movements as well as corporate ones like unions and chambers of commerce) is dominated and organised by autonomous state agencies, whereas in a weak state, 'civil society' resists domination by state agencies and tends to organise itself (Badie and Birnbaum 1979: 171). From this point of view, the relationship between society and the state has to do with the degree of state autonomy from influence by social forces on the one hand, and the capacity of societal actors to exert control over state institutions on the other hand.

Some authors have argued that the degree of state autonomy towards societal actors can to a large extent be measured by the openness of its formal institutional structure (Kriesi *et al*. 1992: 222). They have put forward four operational criteria for comparative empirical measurement of the openness of an institutional structure across countries (Kriesi *et al*. 1995) or between localities in an individual country (Kriesi and Wisler 1996): First, the degree of centralisation is important, in the sense that decentralisation (e.g. federalism) implies a multiplicity of state actors and, hence, a wider range of formal channels of access for societal actors. Second, there is a state's separation of powers, that is, between the legislature, the executive and the judiciary. The greater the independence between these, the greater are the possibilities for people to access decision making. Third, a proportional electoral system is also supposed to increase the possibilities for influence on the part of societal actors: a large number of parties makes it easier to find allies within the party system. Fourth, formal access is also a function of the degree to which direct democracy procedures are institutionalised (i.e. referenda, popular initiatives).

However, the degree of openness of a formal institutional structure does not predict the extent to which the various access points are effectively used. This issue has been addressed by other work on the role of civil society organisations in the mobilisation and aggregation of individual demands and preferences, showing that engagement in voluntary associations increases the capacity of civil society to act.[8] In this respect, large-scale comparative surveys on levels of associative engagement have shown that strength and activeness of civil society – its 'vibrancy' as Putnam calls it (1995: 65) – can vary substantially across time and space.

The strength of civil society can therefore be defined as a product of its own vibrancy and the possibilities for accessing the formal government structure. Both of these elements vary a great deal between and within countries, and – especially the first element – across policy fields. Drawing on this argument with respect to metropolitan governance, we would expect that in the context of a 'strong civil society environment', the various types of metropolitan governance arrangements have a modest impact on the extent to which civil society actors are involved in metropolitan policy-making, since this is largely independent from the ways in which metropolitan governance is organised. As a corollary, in the context of a 'weak civil society environment', the impact of the characteristics of various metropolitan governance arrangements can be expected to be considerably greater.

Combining contextual factors: a focus on place

While local government traditions set an institutional structure for a whole country, state–society relations and especially the 'vibrancy' of civil society can differ between metropolitan regions. This points to a further factor whose importance becomes evident when we have to explain differences between cases within a country and between individual policies as well (see John and Cole 2000). This factor can be subsumed under the notion of '*place*' insofar as space-specific or space-related aspects are concerned.[9] On the one hand, this refers to the particular features of a divergence between functional and institutional urban space and the political challenge to cope with functional networks, cutting across institutionally defined territorial boundaries. This is, in other words, the 'objective' problem of governing a given metropolitan area in concrete terms. On the other hand – and more importantly for developing a framework for analysing metropolitan democracy – one has to consider place-specific actor constellations. As the growing literature on social capital emphasises (based on Coleman 1991; and Putnam 1993), concrete networking/relations of actors as well as the creation of trust and shared norms among them are historically determined and socially and culturally embedded in a territorial context. *Specific state–society relations and a particular 'vibrancy' of civil society socially and culturally embedded in a territorial context* are the main reasons why, against the background of globalisation, the importance of 'place' is highlighted for concrete features of societal and political developments (see Swyngedouw 1997).

Besides these particular characteristics of political space, place also matters in another respect. Indeed, *place-related events* can play a crucial role in opening 'windows of opportunities' (Kingdon 1984) for metropolitan governance building by altering the political agenda and stimulating new linkages and relationships between actors. These 'events' cover a broad spectrum – from the Olympic Games over decisions of crucial corporate actors to external political decisions emanating from higher government levels.

Conclusion

To sum up, three main arguments flow from our attempt to outline a comparative framework for an analysis of the 'democratic question' within metropolitan governance in the era of new regionalism.

First, the study of governance in metropolitan areas should broaden its focus beyond formal institutions (and their reform) in order to include cooperative arrangements that stabilise networks of policy-relevant actors be they public or private, local, regional or national. In the construction of area-wide governance capacity through cooperation, crucial factors are actor behaviour

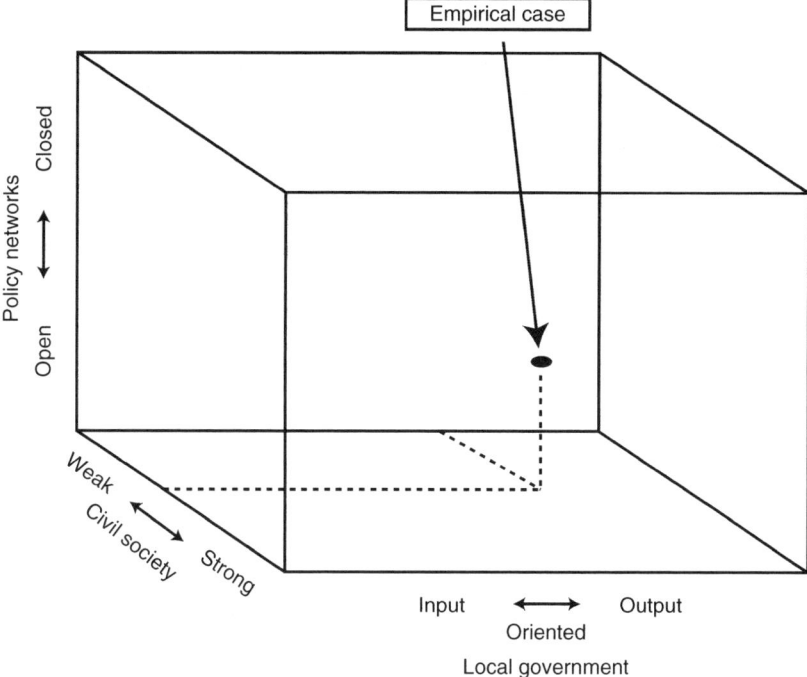

Figure 2.2 Cube of democratic metropolitan governance.

(conflict-avoiding or not), incentive structures set by higher level institutions, as well as political leadership.

Second, an assessment of democratic quality in metropolitan governance should not only consider the lines of accountability of decision-making bodies that are crucial to area-wide governance, but should also consider the ways in which these decisions are reached (majority vote, negotiation or deliberation), as well as the relations between state agencies and non-governmental actors that are established for the purpose of achieving area-wide governance.

Third, for a cross-national comparison of the democratic quality of governance in metropolitan areas, case studies should focus on the ways in which networks combining various segments of area-wide governance balance the tension between closeness and openness, and consider, as contextual conditioning factors, the extent of input-/output-orientation of the national local government tradition, as well as the relative strength or weakness of civil society. Based on these three elements (i.e. the characteristics of (1) policy-networks, (2) local government systems and (3) civil society), we can construct a comparative 'cube of democratic metropolitan governance' (Figure 2.2), wherein empirical examples can be placed for an assessment of their democratic quality.

Notes

1 The literature produced in this tradition is huge. Significant works are Studenski (1930), Wood (1958), and Committee on Economic Development (1970).
2 The most influential writings in this tradition are Tiebout (1956), Ostrom *et al.* (1961) and Bish (1971).
3 For an overview of reform projects and a review of scholarly work pertaining to these two schools of thought, see Ostrom (1972), Dente (1990), Lefèvre (1998) and Lowery (1999).
4 In this model, accountability is considered as a two-step process: electoral accountability (citizens control elected officials) and bureaucratic accountability (elected officials control bureaucrats). This model has been heavily criticised by commentators who have shown that not only electoral accountability, but also bureaucratic accountability are highly problematic (Jones 1995) and that it tends to draw far too rosy a picture of 'traditional' accountability procedures (Papadopoulos 2003: 486ff.).
5 This contention is put forward particularly by those who see procedures of accountability being threatened by new modes of governance. Among others, see, for instance, Mayntz (1998), Duran and Thoenig (1996), Leca (1997), Gaudin (1998) or Rhodes (1996, 2000).
6 This model has been elaborated in Heinelt (1997) based on Schmitter's idea of a 'regime composition' of political systems (1992) and work by Peters (1993: 330–340).
7 Schmitter (2002) tries to address this balance between closeness and openness (or even transparency) of policy networks with his 'generic design principles for (European) governance arrangements'.
8 The literature on this subject is huge. It includes not only classics in political sociology such as de Tocqueville's 'De la démocratie en Amérique', but all the research on associationalism (see Hirst 1994; Cohen and Rogers 1995) and 'social capital' initiated by James S. Coleman (1991) as well as Robert Putnam (1993).
9 For these issues, see the interesting UK debate in the 1980s about 'space' and 'locality'; see Gregory and Urry (1985), Savage *et al.* (1987).

Bibliography

Akerman, T. (2001) 'Urban Debates and Deliberative Democracy', *Acta Politica*, 36: 71–87.
Badie, B. and Birnbaum, P. (1979) *Sociologie de l'Etat*, Paris: Grasset.
Bang, H.P. and Sørensen, E. (1998) 'The Everyday Maker: A New Challenge to Democratic Governance', *ECPR Joint Sessions*, University of Warwick.
Baraize, F. and Négrier, E. (eds) (2001) *L'invention politique de l'agglomération*, Paris: L'Harmattan.
Benz, A. (2001) 'Vom Stadt-Umland-Verband zu "Regional Governance" in Stadtregionen', *Deutsche Zeitschrift für Kommunalwissenschaft*, 40: 55–71.
Benz, A., Scharpf, F.W. and Zintl, R. (1992) *Horizontale Politikverflechtung. Zur Theorie von Verhandlungssystemen*, Frankfurt: Campus.
Bish, F.P. (1971) *The Public Economy of Metropolitan Areas*, Chicago: Rand McNally.
Brenner, N. (2003) 'Standortpolitik, State Rescaling and the New Metropolitan Governance in Western Europe', *DISP*, 152: 15–25.
Cohen, J. and Rogers, J. (1992) 'Secondary Associations and Democratic Governance', *Politics and Society*, 20: 393–472.
—— (eds) (1995) *Associations and Democracy*, London: Verso.
Coleman, J.S. (1991) 'Social Capital in the Creation of Human Capital', *American Journal of Sociology*, 94: 94–119.

Committee on Economic Development (1970) *Reshaping Government in Metropolitan Areas*, New York: Comittee on Economic Development.

Dahl, R.A. (1994) 'A Democratic Dilemma: System Effectiveness versus Citizen Participation', *Political Science Quarterly*, 109 (1): 23–34.

Dente, B. (1990) 'Metropolitan Governance Reconsidered, or How to Avoid Errors of the Third Type', *Governance*, 3: 55–74.

Downs, A. (1994) *New Visions for Metropolitan America*, Washington, DC: Brookings Institution Press.

Duran, P. and Thoenig, J.-C. (1996) 'L'Etat et la gestion publique territoriale', *Revue française de science politique*, 46: 580–623.

Elcock, H. (2001) *Political Leadership*, Cheltenham: Edward Elgar.

Freitag, M. and Vatter, A. (2000) 'Direkte Demokratie, Konkordanz und wirtschaftliche Leistungskraft. Ein Vergleich der Schweizer Kantone', *Schweizerische Zeitschrift für Volkswirtschaft und Statistik*, 136: 579–606.

Frey, B.S. (1997) 'A Constitution for Knaves Crowds out Civic Virtues', *Economic Journal*, 107: 1043–1053.

Frey, B.S. and Eichenberger, R. (2001) 'Metropolitan Governance for the Future: Functional Overlapping Competing Jurisdictions (FOCJ)', *Swiss Political Science Review*, 7: 124–130.

Frey, B.S. and Stutzer, A. (1999) 'Public Choice and the Public Sector', *Swiss Political Science Review*, 5: 108–114.

Frisken, F. and Norris, D.F. (2001) 'Reginalism Reconsidered', *Journal of Urban Affairs*, 23: 467–478.

Gainsborough, J.F. (2001) 'Bridging the City–Suburb Divide: States and the Politics of Regional Cooperation', *Journal of Urban Affairs*, 23: 497–512.

Gaudin, J.-P. (1998) 'La gouvernance moderne, hier et aujourd'hui: quelques éclairages à partir des politiques publiques françaises', *Revue internationale des sciences sociales*, 155: 51–60.

Goldsmith, M. (1996) 'Normative Theories of Local Government: A European Comparison', in D. King and G. Stoker (eds), *Rethinking Local Democracy*, London: Macmillan.

Gregory, D. and Urry, J. (eds) (1985) *Social Relations and Spatial Structures*, Houndsmills/Basingstoke: Macmillan.

Habermas, J. (1996) *Die Einbeziehung des Anderen. Studien zur politischen Theorie*, Frankfurt-am-Main: Suhrkamp.

Heinelt, H. (1997) 'Neuere Debatten zur Modernisierung der Kommunalpolitik. Ein Überblick', in H. Heinelt and M. Mayer (eds), *Modernisierung der Kommunalpolitik. Neue Wege zur Ressourcenmobilisierung*, Opladen: Leske & Budrich.

Heinz, W. (2000) 'Interkommunale Kooperation in Stadtregionen: das Beispiel der Bundesrepublik Deutschland', in W. Heinz (ed.), *Stadt & Region – Kooperation oder Koordination? Ein internationaler Vergleich*, Stuttgart: Kohlhammer Verlag.

Hesse, J.J. (ed.) (1991) *Local Government and Urban Affairs in International Perspective*, Baden-Baden: Nomos Verlag.

Hirst, P. (1994) *Associative Democracy*, Cambridge: Polity Press.

John, P. and Cole, A. (2000) 'When do Institutions, Policy Sectors and Cities Matter? Comparing Networks of Local Policy Makers in Britain and France', *Comparative Political Studies*, 33: 248–268.

Jones, B.D. (1995) 'Bureaucrats and Urban Politics: Who Controls? Who Benefits?', in D. Judge, G. Stoker and H. Wolman (eds), *Theories of Urban Politics*, London: Sage.

Jouve, B. and Lefèvre, C. (eds) (1999) *Villes, métropoles. Les nouveaux territoires du politique*, Paris: Economica.

Kingdon, J.W. (1984) *Agendas, Alternatives and Public Policies*, Boston: Little, Brown and Co.

Kooiman, J. (ed.) (1993) *Modern Governance. New Government–Society Interactions*, London: Sage.

Kriesi, H. and Wisler, D. (1996) 'Social Movements and Direct Democracy in Switzerland', *European Journal of Political Research*, 30: 19–40.

Kriesi, H., Koopmans, R., Duyvendak, J.W. and Giugni, M.G. (1992) 'New Social Movements and Political Opportunities in Western Europe', *European Journal of Political Research*, 22: 219–244.

——(1995) *New social Movements in Western Europe: Comparative Analysis*, London: UCL Press.

Kübler, D. and Schwab, B. (2006) 'New Regionalism in Five Swiss Metropolitan Areas: An Assessment of Inclusiveness, Deliberation and Democratic Accountability', *European Journal of Political Research*, forthcoming.

Kübler, D. and Wälti, S. (2001) 'Metropolitan Governance and Democracy: How to Evaluate New Tendencies?', in P. McLaverty (ed.), *Public Participation and Developments in Community Governance*, Aldershot: Ashgate.

Kübler, D., Schenkel, W. and Leresche, J.-P. (2003) 'Bright Lights, Big Cities? Metropolization, Intergovernmental Relations and the New Federal Urban Policy in Switzerland', *Swiss Political Science Review*, 9: 35–60.

Leca, J. (1997) 'Préface', in F. Godard (ed.), *Le gouvernement des villes. Territoire et pouvoir*, Paris: Descartes & Cie.

Lefèvre, C. (1998) 'Metropolitan Government and Governance in Western Countries: A Critical Review', *International Journal of Urban and Regional Research*, 22: 9–25.

Le Galès, P. (1995) 'Du gouvernement des villes à la gouvernance urbaine', *Revue française de science politique*, 45: 57–95.

——(1998) 'Regulations and Governance in European Cities', *International Journal of Urban and Regional Research*: 482–506.

Lowery, D. (1999) 'Answering the Public Choice Challenge: A Neoprogressive Research Agenda', *Governance*, 12: 29–55.

——(2001) 'Metropolitan Governance Structures from a Neoprogressive Perspective', *Revue suisse de science politique*, 6: 130–136.

Lowery, D., Hooglan DeHoog, R. and Lyons, W.E. (1992) 'Citizenship in the Empowered Locality. An Elaboration, a Critique and a Partial Test', *Urban Affairs Quarterly*, 28: 69–103.

Lyons, W.E., Lowery, D. and Hooglan DeHoog, R. (1992) *The Politics of Dissatisfaction: citizens, services and urban institutions*, Armonk (NY): M.E: Sharpe.

Marin, B. and Mayntz, R. (eds) (1991) *Policy Networks: Empirical Evidence and Theoretical Considerations*, Frankfurt: Campus.

Mayntz, R. (1993) 'Policy-Netzwerke und die Logik von Verhandlungssystemen', in A. Héritier (ed.), *Policy-Analyse. Kritik und Neuorientierung (PVS Sonderband 24)*, Opladen: Westdeutscher Verlag.

——(1998) 'New Challenges to Governance Theory', Florence: Robert Schuman Centre at the European University Institute.

Ostrom, E. (1972) 'Metropolitan Reform: Propositions Derived from Two Traditions', *Social Science Quarterly*, 53: 474–493.

Ostrom, V., Tiebout, C.M. and Warren, R. (1961) 'The Organization of Government in Metropolitan Areas: A Theoretical Inquiry', *American Political Science Review*, 55: 831–842.

Page, E. (1991) *Localism and Centralism in Europe*, Oxford: Oxford University Press.

Papadopoulos, Y. (2003) 'Cooperative Forms of Governance: Problems of Democratic Accountability in Complex Environments', *European Journal of Political Research*, 42: 473–501.

Parks, R.B. and Oakerson, R.J. (2000) 'Regionalism, Localism, and Metropolitan Governance: Suggestions from the Research Program on Local Public Economies', *State and Local Government Review*, 32: 169–179.

Peters, B. (1993) *Die Integration moderner Gesellschaften*, Frankfurt-am-Main: Suhrkamp.

Pommerehne, W.W. and Weck-Heckmann, H. (1996) 'Tax Rates, Tax Administration and Income and Tax Evasion in Switzerland', *Public Choice*, 88: 161–170.

Putnam, R.D. (1993) *Making Democracy Work*, Princeton: Princeton University Press.

——(1995) 'Bowling Along: America's Declining Social Capital', *Journal of Democracy*, 6: 65–78.

Redford, E. (1969) *Democracy in the Administrative State*, New York: Oxford University Press.

Rhodes, R.A.W. (1996) 'The New Governance: Governing without Government', *Political Studies*, 44: 652–667.

——(2000) 'Governance and Public Administration', in J. Pierre (ed.), *Debating Governance*, Oxford: Oxford University Press.

Rusk, D. (1995) *Cities Without Suburbs*, Washington, DC: Woodrow Wilson Center (2nd edition).

Savage, M., Barlow, J., Duncan, S. and Saunders, P. (1987) 'Locality Research: The Sussex Programme of Economic Restructuring, Social Change and the Locality', *The Quarterly Journal of Social Affairs*, 3: 27–51.

Savitch, H. and Vogel, R.K. (2000) 'Paths to New Regionalism', *State and Local Government Review*, 32: 158–168.

Scharpf, F.W. (1988) 'The Joint Decision Trap: Lessons from German Federalism and European Integration', *Public Administration*, 66: 239–278.

——(1999) *Governing in Europe: Effective and Democratic?*, Oxford: Oxford University Press.

Schmitter, P.C. (1992) 'The Consolidation of Democracy and Representation of Social Groups', in L. Diamond and D. Marks (eds), *Comparative Perspectives on Democracy: Essays in Honor of Symour Martin Lipset*, Newbury Park: Sage.

——(2002) 'Participatory Governance Arrangements: Is There Any Reason to Expect it will Achieve "Sustainable and Innovative Policies in a Multilevel Context?" ', in J. Grote and B. Gbikpi (eds), *Participatory Governance: Political and Societal Implications*, Opladen: Leske & Budrich.

Schmitter, P.C. and Lehmbruch, G. (eds) (1979) *Trends Towards Corporatist Intermediation*, London: Sage.

Sørensen, E. (1997) 'Democracy and Empowerment', *Public Administration*, 75: 553–567.

Stoker, G. (1998) 'Cinq propositions pour une théorie de la gouvernance', *Revue internationale des sciences sociales*, 60: 19–30.

Stone, C. (1995) 'Political Leadership in Urban Politics', in D. Judge, G. Stoker and H. Wolman (eds), *Theories of Urban Politics*, London: Sage.

Studenski, P. (1930) *The Government of Metropolitan Areas*, New York: National Municipal League.

Stutzer, A. (2000) 'Stärkere Volksrechte – zufriedenere Bürger: eine mikroökonomische Untersuchung für die Schweiz', *Schweizerische Zeitschrift für Politikwissenschaft*, 6: 1–30.

Swanstrom, T. (2001) 'What we Argue about when we Argue about Regionalism', *Journal of Urban Affairs*, 23: 479–496.

Swyngedouw, E. (1997) 'Neither Global nor Local: "Globalisation" and the Politics of Scale', in K. Cox (ed.), *Spaces of Globalisation: Reasserting the Power of the Local*, New York: Guilford Press.

Tiebout, C.M. (1956) 'A Pure Theory of Local Expenditures', *Journal of Political Economy*, 44: 416–424.

van den Berg, L., Braun, E. and van der Meer, J. (1997) 'The Organising Capacity of Metropolitan Regions', *Environment and Planning C: Government and Policy*, 15.

van Waarden, F. (1992) 'Dimensions and Types of Policy Networks', *European Journal of Political Research*, 21: 29–52.

Wood, R.C. (1958) 'Metropolitan Government 1975: An Extrapolation of Trends. The New Metropolis: Green Belts, Grass Roots or Gargantua?', *American Political Science Review*, 52: 108–122.

3 The new French dice

Metropolitan institution building and democratic issues

Emmanuel Négrier

Introduction

The French case presents two contrasting profiles of local governance.[1] The first one reflects its large number of communes (36,700, as many as in the 14 other member states of the European Union before the last enlargement put together; see Négrier 1999). The second refers to the fact that, in order to address this fragmented administrative-political landscape, around 18,000 structures of inter-communal cooperation have been created – an overcrowding solution for solving overcrowded patterns of government. These structures are generally under local political control, so territorial cooperation has largely depended upon political agreements between local politicians who, for the same reason, have been unable to face the problems induced by metropolisation and urban sprawl. This phenomenon is generally explained as the result of 'jacobinism', where the central state seeks to keep cities politically weak in order to preserve its monopoly of power. Such an explanation can be only partially true, for even a Gaullist government in 1971 tried to reduce the number of communes by amalgamation (although it failed dramatically). This problem of amalgamating communes in order to adapt local political boundaries to new policies and urban life goals is not particularly French: extensive reform of local government structures has been successfully implemented only in Northern European countries and Greece (Négrier 2001; Hlepas 2002). Moreover, even in these countries, the amalgamation of municipalities has not achieved convergence between the scale of problems and institutions in metropolitan areas.

In France, inter-communal cooperation has been implemented through a range of legal formulas such as *Syndicats intercommunaux à vocation unique* (single-purpose inter-communal associations), *à vocation multiple* (multi-purpose inter-communal associations), districts, *Communautés de communes* (communities of communes), *communautés de ville* (urban area communities), *syndicats mixtes* (mixed associations), *chartes intercommunales* (intercommunal agreements), and other structures, which were invented (and never abolished) at various times. All these cooperation schemes represent attempts to compensate for failing to amalgamate communes. This piling up of structures of cooperation has often been denounced as inefficient, expensive and politically impenetrable.

Against this background, the objective of the Chevènement Law of 12 July 1999 was to 'reinforce and simplify' this cooperative landscape by distinguishing between three demographic categories: the *Communauté de communes* (communities of communes) formula for functional regions of under 50,000 inhabitants; the *Communauté d'agglomération* (CUA) formula for small and mid-sized metropolitan areas of between 50,000 and 500,000 inhabitants; and the *Communauté urbaine* (urban community) for large metropolitan areas above 500,000 inhabitants.

The conditions for the creation of these new bodies were simple but radical:

- two-thirds of municipal councils needed to represent more than 50 per cent of the population of the metropolitan area;
- or 50 per cent of municipal councils needed to represent two-thirds of this population.

For the first time, a French law allowed the prefect to force a commune to integrate within a supra-communal cooperative body. In order to encourage this process, the government provided financial support to local authorities.

Formed under these conditions, a CUA can have two types of competencies:

1   Compulsory powers: economic development, urban planning, social housing, urban regeneration and the fight against social exclusion, prevention of petty criminality.
2   Optional powers: sewage infrastructures and facilities, road infrastructures and parking facilities, environment, waste treatment, water provision, culture and sporting facilities (three at the minimum).

In addition, a CUA may opt for other powers that are not listed in these two categories. For each competence, the CUA has to agree on a relevant 'community interest', which must then be approved by two-thirds of the CUA representatives, and must define the boundary (in each policy field) between municipal and CUA powers. Levels of state financial support vary with the number of integrated policies. Thus, the CUAs have a clear incentive to accumulate the maximum number of competencies. But this interest runs against the will of individual municipalities to keep their own autonomy. This makes agreement rarely easy. In addition, the law stipulates that the right of individual communes to raise corporate taxes (one of four French local taxes) is transferred to the CUA, in order to ensure a stable financial base.

These are the essential rules of the game for the creation of a CUA. The convergence of these two instruments (a financial bonus and the capacity to impose membership on reluctant communes) has been considered the main explanation for the success of this new tool of urban cooperation. In a period of two and a half years, 120 CUAs were created. Given that such institutions could have been created in around 145 urban areas, this means that 82 per cent of those areas have taken the opportunity to do so. Given the whole range of cooperative institutions (communities of communes, CUAs and urban communities), it is possible that a 'new France' is emerging, built on around 140 CUAs, 15 *Communautés urbaines* and 3,500 *Communautés de communes*. Another indicator of this trend is that the total financial capacity of the CUAs has already exceeded the entire budgets of the regional councils. Taken together, these cooperation schemes now employ more than 30,000 people.

Paradoxically, this success does not undermine the argument that a structural gap exists between functional spaces and institutional territories. Even if the new cooperative bodies have been extended, they remain 'inefficient'. For example, the CUA cover only 39 per cent of the communes in their metropolitan areas (the *Communautés urbaines* cover only 29 per cent). In addition, they incorporate less than 50 per cent of the population found in the respective metropolitan areas. In other words, these new bodies are to be seen primarily as political units, but not as functional institutions.

How can such a revolution be explained? In the theoretical Chapter 2 of this volume, Kübler and Heinelt put forward three potentially explanatory factors for improving metropolitan governance: governmental framing (i.e. the impact of legal and financial incentives for cooperation set by higher state levels); incremental adaptation of local cooperation networks (i.e. institutional learning); and political leadership. The objective of this chapter is to discuss these factors in the light of the creation of the CUA in France. In the first part of the chapter, I discuss the effect of financial incentives on the development of cooperation projects and institutions. I argue that, in the French case, their impact is not very strong, even if conventional wisdom often considers them as the 'magic tool'. In the second part, I explain how previously existing cooperation networks and practices play an important role in building metropolitan institutions, taking us away from the argument based on a strictly functionalist approach to institutions or institutional learning. In the third part, I detail the role played by political leadership in such a development. This leads on to more general lessons about the transformation of the French model of local government. In the last part, I discuss issues related to the democratic questions that are central to the emerging debate about metropolitan governance in France.

The myths and realities of financial incentives

The financial incentives envisaged by the Chevènement Law have provoked many commentaries. They have contributed to simplistic explanations for the widespread success of the law. For many observers, financial incentives are the principal criterion for explaining the dynamics observed. The protagonists themselves popularise this idea and its immediate consequence: the production of a political requirement. An elected official who would neglect such a godsend of a source of finance would be irresponsible. However, taking into account the success, but also the obstacles which the law has encountered in several urban territories, the list of communal irresponsibles is rather long. Therefore, one must be very careful in interpreting the effects produced by the financial incentives. Indeed, there are several elements that limit the constraining effect of these incentives.

To assume that the DGF allowance[2] would be enough to create a CUA suggests a view of local politicians as foolish. First, and most basically, the question that such a supposition raises is: money to do what? As an elected official of Seine-Saint-Denis said to us: 'It is one thing to evaluate the financial benefit of the operation, it is another to make legitimate use of it.' And these are not just the scruples of a rich man or an accountant. Indeed, besides several advantages, there are also costs associated with the creation of a CUA, such as surrendering autonomy over certain policy domains. Second, the financial benefit does not offer long-term guarantees. Over the last few years, regional and local elected officials have witnessed so many examples of unilateral backtracking on financial commitments by their state partners that they are unlikely to be taken in by such an attractive promise. Moreover, the funds earmarked by the ministry for this purpose have been used up much more quickly than expected because of the success of the law as a whole. After two years, the amounts allocated as financial incentives have started to decrease. Lastly, their attractiveness remains real only if the CUAs do actually integrate their policies. A 'cosmetic' community, where the rate of tax integration remained low could even transform the benefit into a problem by forcing the communes to lose resources through having to pay money back. Acceptance of the material benefit thus leads potentially reluctant actors to enter a system of heavy and irreversible commitments. It would be an error to believe that they are not conscious of these constraints when engaging (or not) in such projects.

The 'financial carrot' is thus not the most important predictor of success. Nevertheless, it fulfils several roles. Its first role is symbolic. For public opinion in the metropolitan areas it is one of the most popular elements of the law. It is thus extremely easy to present the creation of a CUA positively, and hard to oppose it directly. The leader of such a project is in position to make the community save money; its opponent to make it lose money. The second role is transactional. The carrot is a resource at the leader's disposal to negotiate cooperation or to deprive opponents of a material argument to justify its refusal. Third, collectively, the bonus of DGF allows actors 'to neutralise' the initial adjustments and costs associated with the creation of the CUA structure. It means that nobody loses during this initial phase. In particular, it puts off the true costs (and the political transactions) of community integration (until the point when the CUA is fully established and legitimate). Finally, it should be noted that this 'carrot' obviously discriminates against the cities which cannot or do not want to follow the formula. French metropolitan areas, because of their varied cultures and institutional training, are far from able to benefit equally from the law. One can thus assume that for a long time the number of CUAs will be lower than the demographic optimum. What will happen to the areas without a CUA? Can one imagine a brutal closing of the window of opportunity created by the state itself? Conversely, can one envisage its continuity in time through other official means? Another equilibrium point between carrot and stick? In both cases, the selectivity brought about by a law introduced by the 'new republican' Jean-Pierre Chevènement comes as a considerable surprise.

If the impact of financial incentives is anything but magical or automatic, it is due to the fact that the implementation of these new frameworks is highly dependent on more and more specific territorial contexts. The incremental adaptation of the tools for cooperation and territorial political leadership are the two major elements that are developed in the next two sections.

Institutional learning and territorial political culture

At first glance, everything seems to justify the salience of a new-institutionalist approach to the process of institution building in metropolitan areas. The role played by institutions appears to confirm Peter Hall and Margaret Taylor's assessments (Hall and Taylor 1996): new institutionalists highlight the importance of the relationships between institutions and political behaviour, the asymmetry in power generated by institutional developments, and their capacity to steer the subsequent developments (path dependency). From this perspective, the creation of the CUAs has to be considered as a process of institutionalisation, thereby influencing analysis towards pre-existing forms of cooperation and bureaucratic arrangements. Institution building hence appears as an answer to internal (organisational) and external (social) pressures and demands, so that the CUA may be seen to be a more rational development from previous institutional interactions. We can define this way of interpreting this process as 'institutional learning'.

In 2001, only 14 of the 90 newly created CUAs were built *ex nihilo*, that is, without being preceded by an already existing institution. The creation of such an institution thus often appears to be the result of an institutional process itself. This is confirmed by the fact that even where CUAs appeared *ex nihilo*, there had always been some form of technical cooperation, although perhaps weak and limited, which preceded the new step. Thus there is, as predicted, a certain kind of path dependency, which provided a set of practices, mutual acquaintances, reciprocal trust and settled agreements for cooperation. However, even if such institutional sequences are the rule, their impact can be disputed. For some scholars, it is precisely these stages that produce the new institutions. Institutional learning thus constrains political invention. For others, the conditions of institutionalisation, far from being independent, rest on territorial political cultures. More precisely, assessing the relevance of cultural features means that the impact of standardisation, and thus the virtues of comparison, are not neglected.

The institutional building of a cooperative culture

In many instances, the history of cooperation mechanisms is one of step-by-step construction of an 'institutional culture' (Guéranger 2001). This culture prescribes identifiable roles, which are very difficult to refuse to play. It also constitutes a functional arena for seizing new opportunities, which can be endogenous (a sectoral project for instance) or exogenous (the implementation of the Chevènement law). Finally, this culture is imposed upon political actors who do not have much room for manoeuvre within the rules of the game. Only marginal changes can be made, and only as long as they do not disrupt traditional practices. This was true for all the cases studied. In the case of Bordeaux, the CUA strictly conformed to previous practices and inter-institutional exchanges. This kind of structuring of innovation leads Arpaillange *et al.* (2001) to identify a lack of ambition, through the perpetuation of a 'confederal' logic, limiting the extension of CUA integration.

This lack of ambition has extremely interesting consequences. On the one hand, it leads to the reproduction of arrangements which are not really compatible with the orientation and the letter of the law. On the other hand, actors develop their own expertise to check the conformity of the suggested innovation with respect to inherited routines of political exchanges. Each protagonist brings in professional advisers whose role it is to validate institutional situations. They note that actors who promote a political strategy which would be a departure from the old ways (integrating more powers, extending the territory of cooperation, reinforcing the capacities of the structure) all become politically marginal (e.g. the Chamber of Commerce and the representatives of the Green Party). In such cases, preceding institutional routines can be weighted in a 'positive' way (preliminary existence of agreements, arrangements and a culture of cooperation). But existing routines may also induce 'negative' elements, and here the 'political representation' debate is vitally important. For example, the Urban District of Mantes-La Jolie has been transformed into a CUA (Poupeau 2001). This institution has based its dynamics on the progressive increase of its set of powers. But the rule which actually cements actors together is, as in Marseilles, the core city's voluntary self-limitation in the collective assembly. The institutional condition of the rapidity with which the CUA in Mantes was implemented lies in the neutralisation of this question, and the safeguarding of the original political equilibrium. In addition, this 'rule' deprives the prefect of any unilateral capacity to impose a more logical or functional boundary. In the case of Voiron, Anne-Cecile Blanc (2001) also detects, throughout the former phases of inter-communality, the establishment of a typical culture of cooperation, which paved the way for the introduction of a CUA. This culture of cooperation, juggling flexibility and solidarity, prevents the 'politicizing' of issues. Institutional practices are considered as a means (albeit fragile) of avoiding political cleavages. And this is a general feature of nearly all CUAs, where political cleavages do not play an important role.

Finally, another element in favour of the idea that pre-existing institutions force choices is the fact that there is not a single French CUA whose perimeter is equal to its functional metropolitan area. The institutional paths of CUAs thus highlight a persistent gap between functional spaces and 'projectable' institutional territories. Moreover, if CUAs have not been able to extend beyond these political spaces, it is because this would call into question other territorial institutions, other communities of communes, the power of the *conseil general* and departmental boundaries.

Institution building and local political culture

In contrast to this (not always glorious) institutionalisation process, another explanatory factor is suggested by our case studies: the influence of local political culture. In short, we can define local political culture as a set of political representations and practices, whose reproduction is specific to a local space, and can be identified in the long term.[3] Indeed, in certain local situations in France, researchers cannot ignore such a tool to provide a complete and coherent explanation of the process. Escaffit (2001) has analysed the case of Béziers, in southern France, one of the rare cases of failure in building integrated cooperation. She offers the following elementary lesson: with similar institutional constraints, some cities succeed in driving forward such a project of urban governance, and others do not. In the case of Béziers, there were disparate forms of inter-communal cooperation schemes (charters, *Pays*, development contracts) which, elsewhere, would have paved the way for a future CUA. However, not only was the Chevènement Law invoked, but it also appears to have been an instrument that amplified local political conflicts. Thus, in this political configuration, the emergence of a new resource led to preventive manoeuvres: each actor tried to deprive the others from eventual political gain. Political mistrust existed between political factions, for example, in the economic and social circles of the city. Such mistrust increased concern about anything that could modify the fragile balance of local political exchanges. Other studies have emphasised the importance of local political culture (Olive and Oppenheim 2001; Pontier 2001; Poupeau 2001). The case of Montpellier highlights an additional feature, namely the importance of its urban leader, George Frêche (Baraize and Négrier 2001b). The economic and social characteristics of Montpellier are very particular. But an analysis of the process shows some similarities: the role played by conflict, the predisposition to treat partners as adversaries, and the use of institutions to continue the fight through other means.

Hence, inherited forms of institutional cooperation sometimes cannot explain the success or failure of the institution building process and do not indicate any path dependency. Even the Administrative Court, which has frequently been called upon to mediate in the process of metropolitan institution building, is involved in political conflicts. This alternative interpretation of the political acceptability of the new national legal framework could be summarised as an opportunity to feed political identity and cleavages, to continue a struggle in which institutions, far from constraining, are privileged instruments.

Whereas in the first approach, institutional learning is perceived as providing a culture of cooperation, through an incremental process, in the second it is quite the opposite: local political culture can support or undermine innovative capacities for institution building. The divergences resulting from these two kinds of interpretation should, however, not be exaggerated. The two analytical models may well be complementary, as they both reject simplistic, functionalist or fatalistic explanations. Talking about local political culture does not prevent us from focusing on the indefinite progression of cooperation. And focusing on institutional dynamics does not prevent us from taking other political or electoral motivations into account. It is on the question of leadership that both analytical models can be best combined.

Metropolitan leadership

One of the major political conditions for implementing CUAs is the presence of political leadership which can be extended into a new space (when this differs from the pre-existing boundary of cooperation). Moreover, it is one of the most obvious rules of the political game (Michel 1999; Smith 2000; Baraize 2001; John 2001). The most common lesson learnt from the case studies is that the question of leadership is not only useful for looking at narrowly political and electoral dimensions, but is also an appropriate analytical tool with which to understand the role of the prefects.[4]

What kind of political leadership ?

In situations marked by very uncertain changes of scale, leadership obviously plays a plurality of roles. Its capacity to embody a project simplifies situations which may be more complex in reality. Its intermediate position means that it becomes the focal point for requests for political guarantees. However, not all leaders behave similarly in comparable situations. In this respect, the academic distinction between transactional leadership and transformational leadership (Burns 1978) is useful. In the first case, the leader restricts himself or herself to ratifying an inherited structure of political exchanges, without having sufficient resources to allow them to evolve in time and space. Consisting of arrangements and conflicts, this structure is generally found in 'neutral' zones which are not suitable for negotiation or evolution. However, in the case of inter-communal cooperation, the existence of such zones is generally incompatible with the dynamics of reinforcing integrative institutions. These neutral zones indeed are often limited to key elements of the law: corporate tax, autonomy in management and water treatment, strengthening of cultural policies or the separate development of complementary or competing industrial zones. Such spaces collectively considered as neutral appear very frequently. Le Havre (Condé 2000) and Béziers illustrate the structural difficulty of such cooperation. Bordeaux is a case that illustrates the existence of a neutral zone in the corporate tax debate, or through the rejection of any discussion on the transfer of cultural policy to the community level. Marseilles experienced this over the boundary debate, and Montpellier, over the problem of sewage.

Unsurprisingly, the majority of 'innovating' leaderships are related to transformational leadership. In this case, the leader not only assumes long-term transactions between political actors, but also has the capacity to introduce new arenas for action and new fields of transaction. Moreover, such leaders can propose new partners who are better adapted to new issues. The challenge is also one of widening the spectrum of resources that can be negotiated and exchanged: for example, a political agreement about a CUA may be exchanged for support of the electoral ambitions of a key protagonist. To make these political transactions possible, the leadership must be well established. This is why the Chevènement Law, where implemented without major difficulty, is a factor of power centralisation. This does not necessarily lead to challenging personalised leadership. But it establishes or reinforces the role of a tightly knit group, who controls the relevant interactions, has a collective memory of its adversaries and secures access to a widened range of political resources. The capacity to force a hostile commune to join the CUA, by trading off the benefit of regrouping initiated by the core city, contributes to this concentration of political resources. Highlighting the importance of leadership does not mean reintroducing a psychological and personalised design of the 'chief'. In territorial policies, such a conception remains empirically aberrant. The analysis of the role of leaders is never void of an appreciation of territorial and collective configurations. It is thus intrinsically relational, even if 'the individual character' of the leader may be important: charisma (Hanoun in Voiron-Voreppe), style of authority (Frêche in Montpellier), imitation of another historical leader (Gaudin in Marseilles) or the problem of the 'age of the captain' (Ralite in Aubervilliers).

Models of prefectoral leadership

Dealing with prefectoral leadership does not fit in with the items of strict institutionalists. In theory, a prefect cannot be considered as a political leader. He or she is only supposed to transmit an impersonal and politically neutral discourse. Over the last few years, the theme of 'the return of the prefects' to local politics has been developed in France. But it was to characterise less a personalisation of their role than an extension, through them, of the capacity of the central state to control its territory. This kind of assessment has been criticised. The idea of a return of the central state as master of the territorial game is generally contradicted by the facts. Its modest capacity to force or direct change around Paris, Marseilles or Bordeaux is sufficient evidence. This capacity increasingly depends on context. The toolbox of prefectoral prerogatives depends on political configurations, and the intensity and nature of such a role consequently vary. Three models of prefectoral 'leadership' are briefly compared.

The contractor

This first model, in which urban partnerships are marked by high levels of stability and political leadership, is not really particularly salient, since the issues often focus on technical aspects of implementing the law. In these situations (e.g. Chambéry or Rennes; see Usannaz-Joris and Caillosse 2000), the role of the prefect seems to be that of a facilitator whose work concentrates on the centre–periphery relationship. Solving practical problems entails the classical technique of interpreting legislative provisions plus the capacity to adapt them to local reality. Voiron and Mantes-La Jolie correspond well to this first type. Bordeaux also does, since the room for manoeuvre of the representative of the state in this city is limited by the presence of a strong local politician and by the rigidity of political arrangements.

The entrepreneur

In the second model, relationships are conflictual, and leadership is criticised locally but recognised as legitimate, even if conditions for successfully implementing projects are present. In these situations, amongst which the case of Montpellier is typical, the prefect is forced to penetrate into the political arena in much more depth. His or her activity is less directed towards centre–periphery relations than towards the complexities of the territorial balance between political forces. The work is extensive: the prefect increasingly has to intervene in order to negotiate deals that have to remain secret, to find political partners, and to discuss publicly the strategies of elected officials who are opposed to the projects. The prefect must both exploit the 'authoritative' dimensions of his or her mandate (rejection of inefficient community projects; forced integration of reluctant communes; fixing of a boundary without political consensus), and behave like a full political actor. The prefect is one amongst many protagonists in territorial political exchanges. His or her status, as the representative of the central state, does not give him or her any unique room for manoeuvre, except the use of certain specific resources (a certain autonomy in the delimitation of a boundary; a certain ability to block some strategies). But these resources are part of the local political game, so this model is one of extended interdependence, within a polycentric political territory.

The saver

In the third model, contrary to the others, the local context is marked by full-frontal conflict, inexperience with integrated cooperation and the presence of a radically conflictual leadership. In these situations, for which Béziers provides a good illustration, the projects, when they exist, hardly reach the level of political feasibility. The 'authoritative' instruments of the prefect prove to be weak. The representative of the central state then tries to safeguard future opportunities that may arise following elections. From this perspective, far from getting politically involved as a stakeholder, the prefect acts to preserve a possible future, biding time for when the law might be implemented. The prefect may encourage certain initiatives towards functional cooperation if he or she considers they could lead to a model of a CUA. The prefect also tries to prevent the establishment of 'cosmetic' communities around a core city, whose only effect would be to hinder any larger project in the mid- and long term. His or her role is thus much more defensive than in the first two models, and his or her capacity to use resources likewise differs.

These three models are ideal types. In reality, prefects can borrow elements from each. But the case studies unfailingly reveal a dominant trend. Only the case of Marseilles illustrates a true mixture (between the model of the contractor and that of the saver). In any case, the prefect in action, who is generally motivated to implement the policy promoted by his or her own administration, does not conform to the image of the strategic state as many would predict. In spite of the prefect's new instruments, political context largely influences their operational use. The prefect's room for manoeuvre has not become greater because of the Chevènement Law, and is also circumscribed by limited expertise. Where cooperative institutions already exist, prefectoral expertise is always in competition with that of existing structures. In the future, prefectoral administrations may gain a certain autonomy of influence and an ability to intervene in taxation and policies cross-financed by the central state and CUAs. Such autonomy might emanate from the prefect's position in territorial policy networks. The prefect is the actor at the crossroads of territorially heterogeneous agreements: quality agreements for air, water, urban areas, employment areas, community zoning, CUA, localities, etc. This convergence of heterogeneous political maps could become the basis of his or her local influence. One could deduce from this that a prefect has an objective interest in maintaining a certain spatial inconsistency within his or her territory. The prefect is ultimately the actor towards whom the greatest number of actors turn. It is their centrality, and their consequent control of the greatest number of territorial political interactions, which is a permanent aspect of their influence on the territory. But this is by no means always the case, and thus the return of the state is not necessarily to be seen as a firm analytical conclusion from the impact of the Chevènement Law.

The democratic deficit

The Chevènement Law provoked a debate on the non-democratic character of the CUA. During these debates, members of the Communist Party, together with several other members of Parliament (both majority and minority), denounced this 'technocratic drift' of local government. To the absence of direct elections for officials of the CUA (the first democratic error) was added the possibility of forcing a hostile minority to integrate within an institutional boundary (the second). The law would thus have contained two provisions which would betray the spirit of decentralisation and, more seriously, even the holy writ of the Constitution. A counter-argument can be found in looking at the history of inter-municipal dynamics over the last decade. The inter-communal structures have not ceased to develop. The number of inter-communal syndicates rose from 15,940 in January 1988 (among which 12,900 were SIVU – Syndicat intercommunal à vocation unique, 2,290 SIVOM – Syndicat intercommunal à vocation multiple and 750 Mixed Syndicates) to 18,051 in 1999 (14,614 SIVU, 2,221 SIVOM and 1,216 Mixed Syndicates), while the number of the EPCI (Établissement public de coopération intercommunale) with full powers of taxation (urban communities, communities of communes, communities of city, districts and SAN)[5] grew from

192 to 2,679 during the same period. This trend illustrates a crucial fact. The persistence of a formal democratic system for the three traditional levels of French administration (commune, department, region) went hand in hand with a massive delegation of power to non-directly elected structures, and this had been going on for a long time. The law is thus in line with existing practices, themselves largely due to local government policies. However, the issues involved this time in the new institutional formula for metropolitan areas exceed the consequences of the earlier laws. It is thus possible to identify a real metropolitan power shift. For example, the possibility of setting a differential mechanism of equalisation between communes, through the Community Solidarity Grant, is sometimes regarded as an alarming instrument of political feudalism. The extent and the nature of CUA powers are the other aspect of this shift: development zones, cultural, environmental or transport policies could merge to bring about an increasingly powerful leading body. Social housing and the fight against social exclusion are among the greatest concerns. Indeed, they touch on core municipal powers (and *ipso facto* urban social discrimination strategies).

In contrast to the freely shared solidarity which has hitherto prevailed, direct elections would combine wishful thinking and a new step in integrated policies. Local elections would legitimate public decision making at the municipal and metropolitan levels. The gap between the electoral territory and the policy territory testifies to the difficulties of reconciling legitimacy and effectiveness in public action (Duran and Thoenig 1996; Duran 1998). However, this argument should be questioned, in particular because, in the majority of the case studies, it is underpinned by interests which have little to do with the democratic question. Indeed, the argument of the democratic deficit is often used in order to legitimate power positions. For example, there is a small communist city around the CUA of Mantes-La-Jolie. But its hostility to the CUA is less related to high politics (the pro-democratic position of the Communist Party) than to the material interest of remaining isolated. In the same way, the appeals to sacrosanct communal freedom by peripheral cities in the Montpellier metropolitan areas, which were amplified by the use of local referenda, testify more to the hope of preserving the status of financial and social 'islands' than they reflect some kind of democratic avant-garde. The occasionally successful attempts to avoid metropolitan integration in Bordeaux, Marseilles and Béziers appear to be founded on the defence of the commune, the threat to which is seen as the first stage of a threat to the Republic as a whole. It hardly disguises the real motivations of this discourse, namely:

- to protect the windfall effects produced by urban development on their own periphery;
- to refuse to participate in metropolitan structured policies in which these communes do not take part, and which they do not feel able to influence;
- to maintain the fiction of the capacities of the mayor, however eroded they may be by multiple public and private regulations, rather than to surrender authority to an urban leader and his or her 'technocratic' CUA teams.

Beyond this criticism of political justifications, there are also several latent functions of the so-called 'democratic deficit'. At least three can be identified. The first latent function is related to a kind of routinisation of adaptive constraints. CUAs have to face numerous problems whose treatment is politically risky, and have high political costs. This is the case for social housing or economic development for which the CUA has, in many cases, to take responsibility, such as the effects of the fragmentation of more or less efficient zonings. Environmental policy is also likely to involve high material and political costs: restoration or extension of networks of sewage, of water, or the control of pollution. In short, the first steps of CUAs' policies generate heavy responsibilities for which the single financial bonus is not enough to compensate. Consequently, the maintenance of the political marginality of this structure (through indirect elections) can protect the local politician from the political effects of unpopular decisions by shifting responsibility to the CUA.

The second latent function of the democratic deficit is that it facilitates the emergence of territorial political projects which transcend political cleavages. This phenomenon has already been observed in almost every CUA. They generally function, if not consensually, at least distantly from party political cleavages. This 'apolitical attitude' may reflect a genuine convergence of action and political exchanges related to a modern form of clientelism.

The third latent function is to preserve territorial political identity. According to regular data from opinion surveys, mayors are a rare breed of political men and women amongst elected politicians in that they still benefit from a strong level of satisfaction on the part of the electorate. Local elections (along with presidential ones) are those which best resist the rising tide of abstentionism. To maintain the urban monopoly of the commune, direct representation preserves a small political patrimony whose effectiveness is increasingly threatened by developments such as multi-level governance and private pressures (in particular in the field of the construction industry). This is why small municipalities hardly ever accept any proposal to give direct legitimacy (through elections) to a CUA, fearing to lose their last autonomous resource.

Beyond these latent functions, the gap between the local electoral space and the metropolitan policy area is likely to face increasing criticism. The progressive visibility of metropolitan policies will pose the problem of distance from the citizen. In parallel, mayors will have more and more difficulty in basing their election campaigns on projects for which their own responsibility is neither independent nor important. If such a gap remains, it would indicate that voting would only be justified for 'inefficient' policies and that, consequently, voting for 'great' policy and politics would not be any more valid. That is why the direct recruitment of metropolitan leaders seems politically inescapable and democratically necessary.

Conclusion

The CUA is a device which favours metropolitan institution building in areas where former cooperative practices exist. These are related to institutional trajectories or to local political cultures. Thus *ex nihilo* creations are both rare and difficult. Among the ingredients of a project's success or failure, the existence of a territorial leadership, its nature and its intensity, appears essential. Far from reflecting a revolution in the relationship between the state and 'its' territory, the implementation of the Chevènement Law confirms, on the contrary, the establishment of a polycentric territory, where the state government, through its prefectoral representative, undergoes an inflection by local political contexts. If financial incentives play a role in the success of this law, their longer-term effects should not be exaggerated. The shift between the new political centralities brought about by the law and the maintenance of the vote at a strictly communal level fulfils latent functions which can be seen as positive. Serious political accountability has not emerged so far – but the debate on it should not be further delayed. Such are the broad outlines of our argument.

To conclude, let us make a rapid inventory of the issues likely to arise in the medium term. The first relates to the institutional effects of policy learning to which the policy led, in general and in each case study. As has been emphasised, the problem of generalizing the Chevènement Law is posed by the success met by 1 or the other of the 3 community methods. Locally, analytical tools from new institutionalist and political culture studies would be useful to assess the successive implementation steps: definition of powers, identification of community interests, recruitment of personnel, suppression of the functional cooperative bodies, extensions of power and territories, etc. To these political and institutional analyses could be added a perspective centred on policy transfers (Radaelli 1999), policy learning and exchange of governmental subsidies. To these kinds of functional or management learning processes must be added social and political ones, in order to identify the sequential steps of regime changes (Stoker 1998). Will the community be attractive to the professionals of municipal technostructures, as well as to government officials, and perhaps to some prefects? What will the metropolitan political regimes evolve into (Le Saout 2000a,b)? Will they be parliamentary systems, technocratic systems, systems which separate executive and deliberative powers, or systems rooted in urban civil society? These questions are the institutional part of a broader interrogation on the urban regimes themselves.

Within the dynamics of urban political regimes,[6] the assumption is that new territories will become stronger. The best proof of this is undoubtedly the negative reaction of the Conseil Général whenever a CUA extends, even modestly, their boundary of integrated cooperation. The Conseil Général clearly lose influence when this happens. It is not obvious that in the future they can find new political and policy spaces. However, the decline of the departmental territory, an old story of administrative science, does not mean the triumph of 'functional territories'. On the contrary, we could hazard a guess that the gap between functional and political territories will be confirmed. CUAs are thus truly political territories. In the end, the democratic question remains completely open. Three issues arise:

1   The first involves the development of a political debate over CUA policies. The current situation is based on the following: political identification

remains at the municipal level, whereas the CUA level is built upon the negotiated compromises of public policy-making. The commune will find it hard to resist the extension of integrated policies and (popular and unpopular) policy results. The metropolitan area is already a policy body. It is becoming a political institution. Does this evolution suggest the disappearance of the commune? Some mayors are already preparing for the shift: removed from the need to make the public believe in their capacities, they could be working under the democratised authority of the metropolitan institution. All these processes are related to the analysis of urban political regime changes.

2   The second is related to metropolitan election. This trend is politically complex, because different dimensions are contradictory: representation of the people on a demographic basis or a recognition of municipal boundaries and interests? Abolish one level of voting or add a new level? This depends on the intensity of urban political regime change, and, in particular, on the progressive construction of a metropolitan identity (Cole and John 1998).

3   The third concerns the exclusive or non-exclusive representative dimensions of such a metropolitan democracy. Does the creation of a political metropolis open up an opportunity to question the limits of representative democracy? Such a debate did begin during the Montréal metropolitan reform (Latendresse 2002). It dealt with the role of participatory democracy and direct involvement of citizens in public affairs. In France, it mixes two different processes. The first one is the development of new devices for the 'democracy of proximity', based on local participatory structures. The second is the creation of Development Councils, allied to the CUA political assembly, to link civil society to decision making. It is too early to say much about these devices, which have been invented in a period of serious decline in electoral participation.

For the moment, we can only say that in metropolitan institutions, the rules of the political game remain to be invented. In such a political game, we can see that the contrasts noted throughout the building process of such institutions (i.e. more or less institutional capacities, different kinds of political leadership or cultural constraints) are likely to lead towards different metropolitan styles of governance. Referring to the 'cube of democratic metropolitan governance' (Chapter 2), this means that French metropolitan areas will be unlikely to converge to one single model, but rather present various different types, depending on a range of issues:

- the way in which territorial economic interests (absent or prudent in the early stages of institutional building) will be involved in the participative bodies (Development Councils), or linked to area-wide governance through policy networks;
- the way in which civil society representatives will be involved in these bodies, and, more generally, will define the new metropolitan territory as their major space of social and political mobilisation;

- the way in which the new institutions will manage on their own, or decentralise the management of their policies, through sectorial zoning (which appears to be the case in Nantes and Rennes), that is, the territorial designs of metropolitan spatial distribution;
- the kind of political compromise between the growth of metropolitan power and the claims for maintaining municipal political heritage and policy efficiency (i.e. proximity), and the invention of new forms of political participation (deliberative politics, neighbourhood councils...).

Hence, the French cube of democratic metropolitan governance will probably not look like a contemporary minimalist sculpture with just one stable point in the midst of a glass block. Rather, it will look more like a dice, where points are located differently, depending on the turn it has taken.

Notes

1 This chapter is a significantly revised version of an article published in *French Politics*, 1 (2003), pp. 175–198 (published by Palgrave Macmillan). It draws on case studies presented in Baraize and Négrier (2001).
2 DGF: Dotation Globale de Fonctionnement. This element of the state's financial contribution to local authorities is increased with the creation of CUAs CUs and CdCs.
3 This definition is close to that employed in the Italian sociology of regional development and politics (Trigilia 1981; Floridia 1996; Caciagli and Baccetti 1998; Caciagli 2001).
4 In political science in France, a number of scholars (including myself) are currently developing analytical approaches to political leadership. See, in particular, Genieys *et al.* (2000) and Smith (2000). They are well aware of the pitfalls of previous attempts that use leadership as an analytical tool. However, by using this term as an analytical framework rather than as a term on its own, the relationship between institutionalisation, territory and legitimation can be tackled more directly than has been the case in the past.
5 SAN: *Syndicat d'Agglomération Nouvelle*, a specific cooperation structure for new urban towns.
6 The term 'Urban Political Regime' is used to specify the notion of urban regime or governance. Such terms have led to a rich literature which cannot be discussed here. For an analysis, see Gaudin (1999), Jouve and Lefèvre (1999), Le Galès (1995), Borraz and Le Galès (2001), Stoker and Mossberger (1994).

Bibliography

Arpaillange, C., De Maillard, J., Guérin-Lavignotte, E., Kerrouche, E. and Montané, M.A. (2001) 'La Communauté Urbaine de Bordeaux à l'heure de la loi Chevènement: négociations contraintes dans une confédération de communes', in F. Baraize and E. Négrier (eds), *L'invention politique de l'agglomération*, Paris: L'Harmattan, *Logiques Politiques*: 67–98.
Baraize, F. (2001) 'Quel leadership pour les agglomérations françaises?', *Sciences de la société*, 52: 43–62.
Baraize, F. and Négrier, E. (2001a) *L'invention politique de l'agglomération*, Paris: L'Harmattan, *Logiques Politiques*.

—— (2001b) 'Quelle Communauté d'Agglomération pour Montpellier?', in F. Baraize and E. Négrier (eds), *L'invention politique de l'agglomération*, Paris: L'Harmattan, *Logiques Politiques*: 99–131.

Blanc, A.-C. (2001) 'La Communauté d'Agglomération du Pays Voironnais: un cas d'école pour l'intercommunalité intégrée?', in F. Baraize and E. Négrier (eds), *L'invention politique de l'agglomération*, Paris: L'Harmattan, *Logiques Politiques*: 193–220.

Borraz, O. and Le Galès, P. (2000) 'Gouvernement et gouvernance des villes', in J.P. Leresche (ed.), *Gouvernance urbaine et action publique en Suisse*, Paris: Pedone: 343–367.

Burns, J. Mc G. (1978) *Leadership*, New York: Harper and Row.

Caciagli, M. (2001) 'Toscanes rouges: du PSI au PCI, du PCI au PDS', in D. Cefaï (ed.), *Cultures politiques*, Paris: PUF, *La politique éclatée*: 299–316.

Caciagli, M. and Baccetti, C. (1998) 'Dynamiques électorales et forces politiques en Toscane', *Pôle Sud*, 8: 86–97.

Cole, A. and John, P. (1998) 'Urban Regime and Local Governance in Britain and France', *Urban Affairs Review*, 33: 382–404.

Condé, Y. (2000) 'La Haute-Normandie', in G. Marcou (ed.), *Les premiers mois d'application de la loi du 12 juillet 1999*, Paris: GRALE/CEP-Ministère de l'Intérieur: 379–404.

Duran, P. (1998) *Penser l'action publique*, Paris: LGDJ.

Duran, P. and Thoenig, J.C. (1996) 'L'État et la gestion publique territoriale', *Revue française de science politique*, 46(4): 580–623.

Escaffit, C. (2001) 'Le projet de Communauté d'Agglomération de Béziers: quel leader pour quel territoire?', in F. Baraize and E. Négrier (eds), *L'invention politique de l'agglomération*, Paris: L'Harmattan, *Logiques politiques*: 249–274.

Floridia, A. (1996) 'Le metamorfosi di una regione rossa: stabilità ed evoluzione nel voto del 21 aprile 1996 in Toscana', *Quaderni dell'Osservatorio Elettorale*, 36: 5–75.

Gaudin, J.P. (1999) *Gouverner par contrat. L'action publique en question*, Paris: Presses de Sciences-Po.

Genieys, W., Smith, A., Faure, A., Baraize, F. and Négrier, E. (2000) 'Le pouvoir local en débats. Pour une sociologie du rapport entre leadership et territoire', *Pôle Sud*, 13: 103–119.

Guéranger, D. (2001) 'Leadership intercommunal et stabilité institutionnelle: le cas chambérien', in F. Baraize and E. Négrier (eds), *L'invention politique de l'agglomération*, Paris: L'Harmattan, *Logiques politiques*: 221–248.

Hall, P.A. and Taylor, R.C.R. (1996) 'Political Science and the Three New Institutionalisms', *Political Studies*, 44: 936–957.

Hlepas, N. (2002) 'L'agglomération d'Athènes: Une capitale colonisée par la province', in E. Négrier (ed.), *'GouvernerMetropolis'*, *Les Annales des Ponts*, (102): 15–22.

John, P. (2001) *Local Governance in Western Europe*, London: Sage.

Jouve, B. and Lefèvre, Ch. (1999) *Villes, Métropoles. Les nouveaux territoires du politique*, Paris: Economica.

Latendresse, A. (2002) 'Réorganisation municipale sur l'île de Montréal: une opportunité pour la démocratie montréalaise?', in E. Négrier (ed.), *'GouvernerMetropolis'*, *Les Annales des Ponts* (102): 23–31.

Le Galès, P. (1995) 'Du gouvernement des villes à la gouvernance urbaine', *Revue française de science politique*, 45(1): 57–95.

Le Saout, R. (2000a) 'L'intercommunalité, un pouvoir inachevé?', *Revue française de science politique*, 50(3): 57–95.

Le Saout, R. (2000b) *Le pouvoir intercommunal*, Orléans: Cahiers du laboratoire collectivités locales.

Michel, H. (1999) *Intercommunalité et gouvernements locaux. L'exemple des départements de l'Ouest de la France*, Paris: L'Harmattan.

Négrier, E. (1999) 'The Changing Role of French Local Government', *West European Politics*, 22(4): 120–140.

——(2001) 'La fusion des communes en Grèce', in E. Négrier (ed.), *Intercommunalités, Les Annales des Ponts*, 100: 51–56.

Olive, M. and Oppenheim, J.P. (2001) 'La Communauté Urbaine de Marseille: un fragment métropolitain', in F. Baraize and E. Négrier (eds), *L'invention politique de l'agglomération*, Paris: L'Harmattan, *Logiques politiques*: 31–66.

Pontier, J. (2001) 'Politique communautaire en petite couronne: l'Agglomération Plaine Commune', in F. Baraize and E. Négrier (eds), *L'invention politique de l'agglomération*, Paris: L'Harmattan, Logiques politiques: 157–192.

Poupeau, F.M. (2001) 'La transformation du District Urbain de Mantes en Communauté d'Agglomération de Mantes-en-Yvelines', in F. Baraize and E. Négrier (eds), *L'invention politique de l'agglomération*, Paris: L'Harmattan, *Logiques politiques*: 131–156.

Radaelli, C. (1999) 'Idee e conoscenza nell politiche pubbliche europee: tecnocrazia o politicizzazione?', *Rivista Italiana di Scienza* Politica, 29(3): 517–546.

Smith, A. (2000) 'Leadership and Territory, a Conflictual but Crucial Couple. Examples from French Regionalization and European Integration', paper for *Leadership and Globalization*, International Seminar, University of Oslo, 16–17 June.

Stoker, G. (1998) 'Theory and Urban Politics', *International Political Science Review*, 19(2): 119–129.

Stoker, G. and Mossberger, K. (1994) 'Urban Regime Theory in Comparative Perspective', *Government and Policy*, 12: 195–212.

Trigilia, C. (1981) *Le subculture politiche territoriali*, Milan: Feltrinelli.

Usannaz-Joris, M. and Caillosse, J. (2000) 'Bretagne: analyse des conditions d'application de la loi relative au renforcement et à la simplification de la coopération intercommunale avant le 1er janvier 2000', in G. Marcou (ed.), *Les premiers mois d'application de la loi du 12 juillet 1999*, Paris: GRALE/CEP-Ministère de l'Intérieur: 141–160.

Waters, S. (1998) 'Chambers of Commerce and Local Development in France: Problems and Constraints', *Government and Policy*, 16: 591–604.

4 Building metropolitan governance in Spain

Madrid and Barcelona

Mariona Tomàs

Introduction

Following the analytical framework presented in Chapter 2, the aim of this chapter is to assess area-wide governance in the two largest Spanish metropolitan areas: Madrid and Barcelona. As examined in the first sections, both cases show different patterns of governance, even if they are embedded in a common political and territorial structure. In the following section of the chapter we analyse their specific characteristics in relation to the three dimensions of metropolitan democracy: the tension of policy networks (openness/closeness), the legitimisation of local governments (input/output oriented) and the relationships between the state and civil society.

Madrid and Barcelona present different strategies in the development of their metropolitan characteristics, based on place-specific combinations of the three dimensions. Since 1983, the city of Madrid has had a metropolitan structure (the government of the Autonomous Community) that has coordinated the relationships between actors and has legitimised the decision-making process and implementation of public policies in an orderly way. Barcelona, however, is characterised by metropolitan fragmentation and difficult relationships between governmental actors. Nevertheless, the coalition of several sectors of civil society (such as employers' organisations, chambers of commerce and representatives from the financial sector) with local and regional authorities has helped to avoid the 'joint decision trap' (Scharpf 1988) thanks to the challenge of hosting place-related events (specially the 1992 Olympic Games).

Madrid and Barcelona: metropolitan governance in the Spanish context

Spanish territorial structure and the metropolitan institutions

The Spanish case reflects some special features because its political system has recently changed to one of democracy after the Francoist dictatorship (1939–1975). The Spanish Constitution of 1978 changed the basic territorial structure. As in some other European countries, the decentralisation process has resulted in progressive rationalisation or the rise of stronger levels of sub-national government (Keating and Loughlin 1997). The territorial model adopted was the State of Autonomies, where seventeen Autonomous Communities (*Comunidades Autónomas*) have significant legislative and executive powers over a wide range of areas – housing, urban and regional planning, agriculture, transport, health, education, social welfare and culture – according to the terms of their individual autonomy statutes. The Autonomous Communities have progressively achieved more competences, demonstrated by trends in the distribution of public expenditure between central, regional and local governments.[1]

The treatment of local government in the 1978 Spanish Constitution was relatively brief, most of the articles being devoted to the new regions. The 1985 Local Government Law (LBRL) specified only general principles regarding the territory, internal organisation and functions of local government; the more concrete details were left to regional legislation. Spanish local government fits into the *Franco* group (Hesse and Sharpe 1991), its basic political entity being the municipality. The structure is based on two levels: 50 provinces (supra-municipal political bodies) and 8,108 municipalities, following the Napoleonic model.

Nowadays, Spain has 'an urban society in a preponderant rural territory' (Rodríguez Álvarez 2002b: 108). Of the population, 40.5 per cent lives in 57 municipalities with more than 100,000 inhabitants (representing 0.7 per cent of the municipalities). Densely populated areas on the coast and in Madrid contrast with a pattern of low density in the central zones of the country. There are 12 cities with more than 300,000 inhabitants, whereas more than 85 per cent of the municipalities count less than 5,000 inhabitants (Rodríguez Álvarez 2002b).

This urban society developed in the main in two periods: 1960–1975 and 1975–1995. The first period, from 1960 to 1975, saw major urbanisation analogous to the economic development of the country. It brought rapid industrialisation, massive rural exodus and high levels of urban growth, specially in the metropolitan areas of Madrid (increasing from 2.3 to 4.05 million inhabitants) and Barcelona (2.5 to 4 million) (Nel lo 1997). The main cities and their metropolitan areas lacked the instruments for urban planning, suffering from deficits in essential public services and infrastructure in education, health, transport, housing and social welfare. The uniformity of the legal framework that set the conditions for the structure and functioning of the municipalities was not helpful for the management of big cities, which is why two special laws for Madrid and Barcelona were passed in 1960 and 1963. As we see, this tendency towards homogeneity is still a matter of debate between local and national authorities (Rodríguez Álvarez 2002b).

Prior to the 1960–1975 period, the approval of the General Urban Plan for Madrid (*Plan Bigador*, in 1946) and the creation of the Commission of Urban Planning brought about the amalgamation of thirteen municipalities close to Madrid,[2] its size growing from 66.2 to 607 km^2 in the period 1948–1954. The next step was to organise the area of influence around the capital. The General

Plan of the Metropolitan Area of Madrid (*Plan General de Ordenación del Area Metropolitana*) was written in 1961 and approved in 1963. In 1964, the Metropolitan Area of Madrid was created, comprising twenty-three municipalities. The Plan established two main areas for expansion that transformed Madrid into one of the most important centres for economic development in Spain. In the north-west, it was planned to build a residential area and also a large university campus, whilst the south-east was devoted to the location of industry (mainly of the electronic and chemical sectors) (Bahamonde and Otero 1999).

The history of Barcelona and its metropolitan area can be understood in terms of the gap between the functional area and the administrative boundaries. While it was an important centre of the industrial revolution in Spain, the city remained within its fortified medieval boundary until the second half of the nineteenth century (with the implementation of the Cerdà Plan in 1859). The most recent change in administrative boundaries was in 1921, when the last nearby village (now 1 of the 10 districts) was amalgamated with the city. With the growth of the city and its area of influence, successive territorial plans were implemented, like the *Pla Comarcal* (1953) and *Pla Provincial* (1959), which embraced twenty-seven municipalities. The city of Barcelona obtained in 1960 a specific law (Municipal Charter), which resulted in the reform of municipal finances and the substitution of the previous Urban Development Commission with the Urban Development and Common Services Commission (adding collective responsibilities in transportation, water supply and waste collection in the twenty-seven municipalities). In 1966, a new Master Plan for the Metropolitan Area for 163 municipalities and more than 3,000 km^2 was designed, representing a change in perspective as it covered a much larger area. This plan was revised and approved in 1976 as the General Metropolitan Plan (for Urban Development), integrating 27 municipalities and 476 km^2 (López 2002).

The second phase goes from 1975 to 1995 and is characterised by a slower pace in the process of urbanisation, a decentralisation of the population and activities in the metropolitan areas, the decay of industry and the growth of the services sector. Central cities started losing population in favour of the newer rings of development, increasing the mobility of inhabitants and spreading the urban style of life around the territory. This process had significant impacts on the environment, such as the construction of transport infrastructures, a high level of land consumption and the enlargement of the ecological footprint of cities.

In this phase, the design of a new political scenario following forty years of dictatorship proved a good opportunity to face the challenge of the governance of metropolitan areas such as Madrid and Barcelona, as well as others such as Bilbao and Valencia. The political transition focused on the process of regional decentralisation, which left the responsibility for facing metropolitan governance to the Autonomous Communities. This is one of the factors that explains the different strategies in the two main metropolitan areas, Madrid and Barcelona.

For Madrid, there was a debate on the need to create a specific region, since the area did not have any special identity. It was suggested that the area could belong to the adjacent Autonomous Community of Castilla-La Mancha (but its leaders did not favour this idea) or that Madrid could be a federal district (which was thought to be too complicated). In 1983, the Spanish Parliament decided to create the Autonomous Community of Madrid,[3] with 5 million inhabitants and 179 municipalities, covering an area of 8,028 km[2] (García de Enterría 1983).

The creation of the Autonomous Community of Madrid had some legal and political consequences. First of all, the boundaries of the new region covered the same territory as the province of Madrid (second level of local government). Following constitutional law, the Provincial Council was absorbed by the Autonomous Community in order to avoid duplication and overlapping of institutions. The responsibilities of the province (such as the coordination of municipalities and the fire fighting service) were assumed by the regional government.[4]

Second, the regional government dissolved the Metropolitan Area created during the dictatorship, as happened in other big cities (Bilbao in 1980, Valencia in 1986 and Barcelona in 1987). The levels of government were reduced to two: the regional government (with an elected assembly, executive and president) and local government (with 179 municipalities). There are also 37 inter-municipal structures (*mancomunidades*), and the municipalities manage 70 agencies and 51 public sector companies (Rodríguez Álvarez 2002a: 111).

Fifty-four per cent of the population of the region of Madrid lives in the city of Madrid, which has a high density of population (data from 2001; see Table 4.1). However, this percentage has been decreasing in the last two decades of the twentieth century. In 1975, it represented 75 per cent of the population, and in 1981 the proportion was 67.4 per cent. The inhabitants of Madrid have been leaving the city in favour of the municipalities on the outskirts,[5] accelerating the process of decentralisation in the metropolitan area (Castillo and Casado 2000).

Similarly, the city of Barcelona had 1,745,000 inhabitants at the end of the 1970s, which progressively decreased as a result of moves to the periphery. However, as shown in Table 4.2, the city has a high density, and its metropolitan area represents almost 75 per cent of the Catalan population.[6]

In relation to the metropolitan institutions, the creation of the Municipal Metropolitan Entity of Barcelona (*Entitat Municipal Metropolitana de Barcelona*)[7] in 1974 was based on the area covered by twenty-seven municipalities. After the Franco dictatorship, its name became the Barcelona Metropolitan Corporation

Table 4.1 Basic data for Madrid and the Autonomous Community of Madrid (2001)

	Madrid (city)	*Autonomous Community*
Area (km[2])	607	8,028
Inhabitants	2,938,723	5,423,384
Density (population/km[2])	4,841	676

Source: National Institute of Statistics (INE) (2001).

Table 4.2 Basic data for Barcelona, its metropolitan area, the province of Barcelona and the Autonomous Community of Catalonia (2001)

	Barcelona (city)	*Barcelona (metropolitan area)*[a]	*Barcelona (province)*	*Autonomous Community of Catalonia*
Area (km²)	99	3,235.6	7,719.0	31,895.3
Inhabitants	1,503,884	4,390,390.0	4,805,927.0	6,343,110.0
Density (population/km²)	15,175	1,356.9	622.6	198.8

Source: National Institute of Statistics (INE) (2001).

Note
a This is the broad definition of the metropolitan area, with 164 municipalities and seven *comarques*.

(*Corporació Metropolitana de Barcelona*, CMB). It consisted of a Metropolitan Council with important economic resources (drawn from the twenty-seven municipalities) and competences in urban planning (such as implementing the General Metropolitan Plan), public transportation, water supply and waste treatment. During the 1980s, the budget increased thanks to regional and state funds, and the CMB implemented several plans (such as those for the coastline and for Collserola's mountain) (Artal 2002).

The CMB suffered from two political problems. On the one hand, there was a conflict between the left-wing political parties that governed the municipalities of the metropolitan area. The communists rejected the predominant role of the socialist mayor of Barcelona, Pasqual Maragall, while the socialists accused the communists of not supporting the project. On the other hand, the regional government, run by the Catalan nationalists (*Convergència i Unió*) and headed by Jordi Pujol, feared the power of the CMB. Taking advantage of both the powers that the Spanish Constitution gave to the Autonomous Communities and the political majority in Parliament, the Catalan regional government abolished the Metropolitan Corporation in 1987, as part of a general reform of the territorial structure in Catalonia.

Four laws on territorial organisation (*Lleis d'Ordenació Territorial*) were implemented and set up the current administrative structure of the Catalan region: 4 provinces, 41 counties (*comarques*, a traditional supra-municipal division) and 946 municipalities. Moreover, there are multiple public sector companies and associations of municipalities to provide some services, as well as consortiums (of different levels of government and also between public bodies and private enterprise).

The CMB was replaced by two metropolitan bodies based on voluntary association. The first metropolitan body is the Metropolitan Authority for Transport (*Entitat Metropolitana del Transport*), formed by eighteen municipalities. It provides joint public transport services for its area. Second, the Metropolitan Environmental Authority (*Entitat Metropolitana del Medi Ambient*) covers thirty-three municipalities and is responsible for water supply, sewage disposal and urban waste treatment. Finally, most of the municipalities governed by the Metropolitan Corporation of Barcelona created a third body in 1988: the Association of Municipalities of Barcelona (*Mancomunitat de Municipis de l'Àrea de Barcelona*), which brought together thirty municipalities and tries to encourage cooperation between municipalities (MMAMB 1995).

Then, in 1997 the Authority for Metropolitan Transport (ATM) was created. The function of the ATM (which is a public consortium) is to organise the public transportation system in the Metropolitan Region, covering 7 *comarques*, 164 municipalities, more than 3,000 km^2 and 4.5 million inhabitants. The integration of the system of transport fares has been its main achievement.

Metropolitan governance patterns in Madrid and Barcelona

In this section, we cover the differences and similarities in the building of governance in the metropolitan areas of Madrid and Barcelona. To do so, we analyse the significance of the three crucial factors identified by researchers of new regionalism (see Chapter 2). In a context of interdependence between a variety of actors and conflicts raised by their interaction, the combination of these three factors is argued to be place-specific. This offers an alternative approach to the traditional conceptions of metropolitan governance (the metropolitan reform tradition and the public choice school) (Hoffmann-Martinot 2002).

The first factor relates to cooperative behaviour between territorially relevant actors, basically political parties. In Madrid, cooperation seemed to be easier to achieve, given that the same political party has been governing more or less at the same time at both the municipal and regional levels (and also at the national level). From the 1980s to the mid-1990s, there was a left-wing majority. More recently, it has shifted to the right, the Popular Party having governed at the national level since 1996, at the regional level since 1995 and at the local level since 1991 (not in all the 179 municipalities but in most, including Madrid).

However, there have been some political disagreements between the Autonomous Community and the city of Madrid. On the one hand, there have been different styles of leadership between the mayor of the city and the president of the regional government.[8] On the other hand, the distribution of competences between the two levels of government have resulted in disagreements. Being the capital of Spain, it is argued, the city of Madrid should have a special status (including more powers), as stated in the law of 1983. In spite of this, the recognition of the special status of the city has not been supported by either the Autonomous Community or the central government, showing that the distribution of powers and the model of national and sub-national decentralisation is partly independent of political convergence (Rodríguez Álvarez 2002b).

In Barcelona, political interests led to the dissolution of the metropolitan authority, as the ideological cleavage was a factor that structured the debate on metropolitan governance.[9] Recent changes in the political profile, with the socialist Pasqual Maragall as the president of the Catalan Autonomous

Community (since December 2003) and the socialist Joan Clos as the mayor of Barcelona (since 1997), question the relevance of political disagreements as the main reason for the lack of cooperative behaviour by actors in the same territorial areas.

Like Madrid, the claim for a special status for the city of Barcelona (the Municipal Charter approved by the Catalan Parliament in 1999)[10] is an ongoing matter of debate. However, in this case the regional government supports the charter (in part because it does not deal with the metropolitan question) (Colomé and Tomàs 2002). The fight for specific legislation for big cities led in the beginning of the 1990s to a combined lobby by the seven biggest cities in Spain (G-7: Madrid, Barcelona, Bilbao, Valencia, Seville, Zaragoza and Malaga). The activity of this network lessened in the mid-1990s, and the recent changes in legislation (*Proyecto de Ley de Medidas para la Modernización del Gobierno Local*, June 2003) have not satisfied the demands of the biggest cities (see Rodríguez Álvarez 2002b).

A second factor in relation to metropolitan governance building is the incentive structures set by higher level institutions. In both Madrid and Barcelona, regional governments (the level of government that has the relevant competence) abolished metropolitan structures. From a similar starting point, the history of the two cases has been significantly different. Madrid is an exception in the Spanish context, since the Autonomous Community has become the promoter and leader of the metropolitan region of Madrid, whose boundaries already correspond to those of the regional territory.[11] The regional government, with elected representatives, has a range of competences (enlarged since 1998) including territorial and urban planning, housing, transportation (the metro), economic development, social services, as well as fire fighting services and water management (the public agency Canal de Isabel II). Some scholars have referred to such a model as a 'meso-level type of metropolitan governance' (Jouve 2003), and it is exceptional due to its legitimacy, and its legal and financial autonomy (Rodríguez Álvarez 2002b).

For Barcelona, the abolition of the metropolitan authority resulted in a fragmentation of the metropolitan area between different bodies. The only incentive structure set by the regional government has been the creation of the Authority for Metropolitan Transport. The revision of the General Metropolitan Plan of 1976, which is a regional government competence, is still on the agenda and is an obstacle for the urban planning of the large metropolitan area (Nel lo 1997).

Finally, political leadership is a crucial element for metropolitan governance capacity. In the case of Madrid, the regional government has played the role of a facilitative leader since 1983, with the former socialist president, Joaquín Leguina, from 1983 to 1995, followed by the next president, the conservative Alberto Ruiz-Gallardón, from 1995 to 2003. If we adopt the two dimensions of urban governance developed by Le Galès (1998), it can be argued that under the leadership of Leguina the internal dimension (or integrative capacity of urban governance) was emphasised, while Ruiz-Gallardón has also developed the external dimension (the strategy towards the external world). New strategies of city marketing, such as the candidature for the 2012 Olympic Games, demonstrate this approach.

In the case of Barcelona, political disagreements as well as the institutional fragmentation of the metropolitan area have been obstacles to building an integrated vision of the metropolitan area. However, the model of urban governance has succeeded in avoiding the 'joint decision trap' (Scharpf 1988) and has enhanced both internal and external dimensions.

In the internal dimension, political blockage on the metropolitan issue has been overcome under the leadership of the mayor of Barcelona and through the complicity of civil society (an important instrument has been strategic planning, discussed further in the next section). The need for collaboration is regularly renewed on the basis of a high-profile project, usually place-related events. This cooperative pattern was followed in a similar way in the past, when the EXPOs of 1888 and 1929 took place in Barcelona. In the democratic context after the era of Franco, the motor for the development of the metropolitan area was the 1992 Olympic Games.

The 'Barcelona model' for organising the Olympics was based on large urban projects combined with small operations in the neighbourhoods, the decentralisation of the city into ten districts and the modernisation of public administration. At the same time, the need to collect funds encouraged the representatives of the city to negotiate with other levels of governments and different international organisations (such as the International Olympic Committee). In order to ensure the investment of private actors, the strategy adopted was focused on public–private partnerships (Borja 1995).

At present, the same model of cooperation is being repeated with a new place-related event, *Fòrum 2004*.[12] On this occasion, cooperation has been more problematic due to the uncertainty surrounding a new international event to be held for the first time in Barcelona. However, the alliance has been sustained through the leadership of the city, the support of the regional government and the main actors from civil society. They all believe that it represents another opportunity for the city to stimulate economic development and catch the attention of millions of potential visitors and investors (Négrier and Tomàs 2004).

The external dimension of urban governance has been enhanced since the 1992 Olympic Games. Barcelona has promoted its own foreign policy based on leadership and membership of pan-European urban networks (such as Eurocities and Metropolis). The use of strategic planning has also been an instrument for city marketing since it has been exported all over the world (Le Galès 2002), a practice followed by the mayor who followed Maragall (the socialist Joan Clos).

Comparing the three dimensions of metropolitan democracy

In this section, the democratic quality of the metropolitan governance of Madrid and Barcelona is analysed on the basis of the three dimensions proposed by Kübler and Heinelt in Chapter 2.

Openness and closedness of policy networks

This dimension reflects the decision modes found in the four segments of interest intermediation described in Chapter 2: territorial, administrative, functional and civil society related. We see how the tension between openness and closedness of policy networks is different in the two cities.

As the capital of Spain, Madrid is the seat of the national administration and a wide range of different institutions and public agencies, that is a large number of actors from the administrative and the political segments. Moreover, the city not only contains several institutions belonging to the corporatist or functional segment (trade unions, chambers, professional associations, employers' organisations) but also the headquarters of associations from civil society, companies and financial groups. To this complexity can be added all the institutions and bodies of the regional and municipal levels of government.

Rodríguez Álvarez (2002a) has analysed the mode of interest mediation between the public and the private spheres in the Autonomous Community of Madrid. He argues that metropolitan governance in Madrid works on the basis of a regional neo-corporatist system that has been stable since 1983. Policy networks have been based on the territorial, administrative and corporate actors, being less open to members from civil society.

Among these actors, Rodríguez Álvarez emphasises the role of representatives from the Autonomous Community of Madrid, the Confederation of Enterprises of Madrid (Ceim) and the two main trade unions (*Unión General de Trabajadores*, UGT and *Comisiones Obreras*, CCOO). For instance, these actors have formal representation on the main consultative bodies at the regional level such as the Economic and Social Council (a consultative body that has influence on the economic development plans of the region) as well as on the main public agencies (related to education, employment and public health). Another actor from the private sector, the Chamber of Commerce and Industry of Madrid (CCIM), runs the important Fair of Madrid (Ifema), and is also member of several institutions and assemblies representing different sectors (design, industry, transportation).

According to Rodríguez Álvarez (2002a), these corporate actors are content with this mode of metropolitan/regional governance, while other actors such as the professional associations (of economists, engineers, lawyers) are under-represented and want to play a larger part in the system of mediation. Other key actors (trade unions, Ceim) are less satisfied with their relationships with the city of Madrid, where policy networks (in their opinion) are more closed than at the regional level. They would like to see a real participative process of strategic planning and would like the city to try innovative initiatives.

In Barcelona, the model of cooperation between public and private actors is renewed on the basis of specific events. The use of strategic planning has become the instrument of creating a collective vision and designing the main guidelines for the city's development over a ten-year term. It works through cooperation between different commissions that analyse important sectors (economic development, housing, environment and urban planning, culture, education), and the way that they can contribute to the future of the city.

During the 1990s, three Strategic Plans were approved (1990, 1994, 1999) based on the city of Barcelona. These were successful, so following metropolitan dynamics, the city council decided to go one step further and started working on the first Strategic Metropolitan Plan (approved in March 2003).

In respect of territorial interest intermediation, the first Strategic Metropolitan Plan is different from the other plans because it includes representatives from thirty-six municipalities of the metropolitan area of Barcelona (628 km^2 and 3 million people). The leadership comes from the mayor of Barcelona (who is the president of the general council of the plan, which includes 300 represen- tatives from different sectors) and also from members of his team (who lead different commissions). This plan has also enabled the participation of other local leaders (and mayors from other political parties) for the first time. One of the collective demands that was supported by the majority was the need to simplify the institutions of the metropolitan area and create a new body to coor- dinate the thirty-six municipalities. Furthermore, this plan has provoked a reaction from municipalities in the metropolitan region that were not included. Seven medium-sized municipalities have argued for participation in the plan, raising the question as to whether the limits of the metropolitan area are too small (Colomé and Tomàs 2002).

In relation to the participation of other local and regional authorities, this plan integrates all the municipalities that belong to the three different metro- politan bodies created in the 1980s (Environment, Transport and Association of Municipalities). It also includes the bodies in charge of the port and the airport of Barcelona, as well as representatives from the two supra-local levels (counties and the province of Barcelona). The plan also has three commissions which work with the regional government (through meetings four times a year), with other big cities such as Madrid and Valencia (through meetings twice a year), and with other European cities that have expertise in strategic planning such as Lyon and Milan (through annual meetings). This plan has opened up the debate on the future of the metropolitan area to a larger number of actors from the administrative segment of interest mediation (Strategic Metropolitan Plan of Barcelona 2002).

The corporate actors are represented in several commissions such as those centred on tourism and economic development. They include the Chamber of Commerce, Industry and Shipping, the Fair, the trade unions (CCOO and UGT, and also the unions of farmers, hospitals, metallurgic sector), employers' organi- sations (*Foment del Treball*), financial groups, hotel groups and the utility companies.

Finally, a wide variety of actors from civil society participate in the general council of the plan, including NGOs, private foundations, centres for research, universities, the mass media and several associations (ranging from arts, crafts and sports to automobiles). There are also some individuals who participate as experts on specific issues. To sum up, the representation of collective actors is quite substantial in the four segments of interest mediation, so we would conclude that there is some degree of openness in this process.

Input and output legitimisation: trends in Spanish local government

During the 1970s, there was a rise of highly organised protest movements in many of the large towns, mobilised around urban issues. Neighbourhood associations, students, trade unionists and regionalist movements demanded both the restoration of democracy and an improvement in living conditions in cities. The first local democratic elections after the dictatorship took place in April 1979. The newly elected municipal councillors had difficulties meeting the demands of local residents because most of them were in debt and their internal organisation was in crisis. It was a period characterised by the active role of municipalities and local elites, whose objectives were focused on solving basic demands. In big cities such as Madrid and Barcelona in particular, there were neighbourhoods that needed a lot of investment in infrastructure (water, transport).

In spite of the lack of economic resources and expertise, towns experimented with important transformations that improved the living conditions of citizens. Barcelona tried to implement its policies more efficiently through decentralisation into ten districts associated with the idea of providing room for community involvement. One of its main achievements was the establishment of the Citizen Information Offices which were set up in each district not only to give information to the citizens but also to make it unnecessary for them to go to the city council for bureaucratic procedures such as the handing over of documents or making changes in the register. Madrid did this through the decentralisation of its municipal organisation into twenty-one districts, although they lacked the participatory dimension. To sum up, municipal legitimisation was mainly measured by output, whereas there was a progressive demobilisation of urban social movements, both because some of their leaders were co-opted for local, regional and national politics and because demands were being gradually met (Brugué and Gomà 1998).

During the 1990s, local government had to face different challenges as circumstances changed. First, whilst basic services had been covered, new demands concerning employment, environment and particularly immigration emerged, as well as other demands linked to a post-materialist society (such as leisure and culture). Second, the idea that local government was more than local administration started taking hold. The city councils tried to improve communication with and involvement of the population in public affairs through some experiments to strengthen local democracy (consultative committees, strategic plans, citizen juries). Catalonia initiated the use of citizen juries, discussion forums and consultative citizen committees. The aim of these initiatives was to involve citizens in discussion on policy-relevant issues such as the Local Agenda 21 or public spaces. All these developments made local government rethink its role and its relationship with citizens, making input legitimisation the priority (Font 2002).

At present, the two orientations are combined, both in Barcelona and in Madrid, which illustrates that democracy and efficiency are not two opposed concepts but complementary (Hoffmann-Martinot 2002). On the one hand, the discourse on the need to reinforce local democracy is present in both cities, although the city of Barcelona has gone further in practice. For instance, the New Regulatory Norms for the Organisation of the Districts and Citizen Participation were approved in November 2002. The new regulation allows more mechanisms for the participation of citizens (through the associations or individually), such as citizen juries or public meetings. On the other hand, the implementation of instruments of benchmarking, the externalisation of some services and the use of public–private partnerships have also been happening.

The new law approved in June 2003 by the Spanish Parliament (*Proyecto de Ley de Medidas para la Modernización del Gobierno Local*) reflects this duality. In relation to efficiency, two main reforms have been introduced. First, several elements characteristic of the New Public Management (such as instruments of benchmarking and evaluation) have been introduced. Second, it reinforces the role of the mayor and the executive committee by differentiating more clearly their functions and those of the assembly. At the same time, the new regulation introduces some measures to enhance the participation of citizens (such as popular initiatives and the use of new technologies). The law requires the creation of Social Councils in cities of over 250,000 inhabitants to represent economic, professional and neighbourhood groups that will make reports and be consulted on big urban projects. We can conclude, then, that both input and output orientations are present in the metropolitan governance of Barcelona and Madrid (Rodríguez Álvarez 2002b).

State–society relationships

For Madrid, we have characterised the model of metropolitan governance as neo-corporatist, with active participation by corporate and administrative actors. The role of civil society organisations in the mobilisation and aggregation of individual demands and preferences is therefore less strong and active (Rodríguez Álvarez 2002a). However, the Autonomous Community of Madrid is a political structure with legal and financial autonomy, with a directly elected assembly and a president. This institutional structure offers more opportunities to citizens to have an influence on public decisions (essentially, through voting) and guarantees the accountability of elected members. Compared with the fragmentation and lack of opportunity for citizens to express their views in other metropolitan areas, in Madrid there has been an institutionalisation of state–society relationships based on metropolitan/regional government.

In Barcelona, we have seen that its model of governance is renewed on the basis of regular events that require the involvement of civil society. Challenges to organise place-related events such as the 1992 Olympic Games serve to reinforce the coalition of several sectors of society, confirming its 'vibrancy'. The instrument through which the interaction is organised has been strategic planning. Even if it is not a regular form of participation (since it depends on the will of the city councils) it is a mechanism to activate state–society relationships and give voice to the main actors of the four segments of interest mediation. However, it does not allow for the participation of 'ordinary' citizens.

To avoid this bias, the city council of Barcelona changed its arrangements for participation both at the municipal level (2002) and at the district level (2001). Among the new mechanisms, there are classic instruments such as consultative councils based on single issues (environment, economy) and cross-cutting groups (youth, old people, women). There are also innovative instruments such as citizen juries which combine representation by collective actors (associations) with individuals.[13] To sum up, it is an institutional arrangement limited to the municipality of Barcelona, but it can encourage new forms of dialogue between the municipality and civil society in the rest of the metropolitan area.

Conclusions

In the first section of this chapter we analysed the patterns of metropolitan governance in Madrid and in Barcelona. To understand how the modes of metro-politan governance work in a specific context we have taken into account the combination of three factors: actor behaviour, incentive structures and political leadership.

In the case of Madrid, the Autonomous Community (a sub-national authority with autonomy and legitimacy) governs roughly within the same boundaries as the metropolitan area of Madrid. With the leadership residing with the president at the regional level, as well as with strong cooperation between corporate actors, the mode of metropolitan governance has been quite stable since 1983 (when the regional level was created).

In contrast, Barcelona provides a more complicated and difficult scenario because of the administratively fragmented metropolitan area and political conflicts between levels of government. Nevertheless, the consensus reached between the major actors from the public and private sectors has been achieved through successive commitments, encouraged by place-related events such as the 1992 Olympic Games. In this instance, leadership has naturally come from the mayor of the city of Barcelona, who has tried to encourage support through strategic planning.

In the second section of the chapter we assessed the quality of metropolitan democracy referring to the three dimensions of the 'cube of democratic metro-politan governance' (see Chapter 2). The first dimension refers to the openness and closedness of policy networks, which follow different patterns in the two cases. In Madrid, a stable alliance between the regional representatives and a few corporate actors has been the predominant model, while actors from the civic sphere (NGOs, professional associations) have been under-represented. Analysis of the first Strategic Metropolitan Plan of Barcelona showed a higher degree of openness due to the variety and large number of actors involved.

The second dimension relates to the legitimisation of local governments (input or output oriented). In both metropolitan areas, there is a combination of the two elements, since the need to ensure efficiency in the delivery of services is linked with efforts to enhance citizen participation. This particular state of affairs is understandable if we consider the evolution of local government in Spain after the dictatorship. We can identify an initial period during which municipalities had to resolve basic problems, and a second period during which the accent was put on the need to increase communication with citizens and provide them with more opportunities to encourage their involvement in public affairs.

Finally, the quality of metropolitan democracy is also measured by the strength of the civil society. The case of Madrid is atypical given that there is a political framework (the Autonomous Community) that allows citizens to participate in a formal institutionalised way. However, ways other than elections are less usual. In the case of Barcelona, different mechanisms for citizen participation have been put into practice to allow collective actors as well as individuals to get involved. At the metropolitan level, the means for orchestrating state–society relationships has been strategic planning, where civil society has proved its 'vibrancy'.

To sum up, we have identified two strategies of metropolitan governance that result from a combination of different factors. The examples of Madrid and Barcelona confirm the importance of space-specific and space-related aspects. In other words, this chapter reinforces the argument that an assessment of the 'democratic question' within metropolitan governance has to consider particular political structures as well as place-specific actor constellations that play a role in functional policy networks that operate beyond institutionally defined territorial limits.

Notes

1 In 1981, the distribution of public expenditure was, in percentages, 87 per cent by the state, 3 per cent by the Autonomous Communities and 10 per cent by local government. In 2000, the State spent 48 per cent of public expenditure, the Autonomous Communities 36 per cent and local government 16 per cent (MAP 2000).
2 Madrid amalgamated thirteen nearby municipalities: Aravaca, Barajas, Canillas, Canillejas, Chamartín de la Rosa, Fuencarral, Hortaleza, El Pardo, Vallecas, Vicálvaro, Villaverde, Carabanchel Alto and Carabanchel Bajo.
3 Law of 25 February 1983.
4 Except for the fire services of the city of Madrid, which were the responsibility of the municipality.
5 This is shown by the fact that 6 other municipalities have more than 100,000 inhabitants (Getafe, Fuenlabrada, Leganés, Móstoles, Parla and Alcalá de Henares).
6 The geographical delimitation of the metropolitan area of Barcelona is a controversial issue: some take the first ring (twenty-seven municipalities), some consider 164 municipalities (as the area covered by the Authority for Metropolitan Transport and the Territorial Plan of 1976) and, according to the Metropolitan and Regional Studies Institute of Barcelona, the whole province of Barcelona could be seen as the metropolitan region.
7 Law 5/1974 of 7 August.
8 Until May 2003, Alvarez del Manzano (who represents the most conservative wing of the Popular Party) was the mayor of Madrid and Ruiz-Gallardón (who is more liberal), the president of the Autonomous Community of Madrid. However, the new scenario after the local and regional elections in 2003, with Ruiz-Gallardón as the

new mayor of Madrid and Esperanza Aguirre as the president of the Autonomous Community, may lead to new patterns of governance.

9 One example that illustrates the partisan influence on local politics is the existence of two different organisations of municipalities according to the political party that runs the city council. The Catalan Association of Municipalities groups the nationalist local governments, while the Federation of Municipalities of Catalonia represents the left-wing local governments. In contrast, the Autonomous Community of Madrid has a single organisation for the municipalities, the Federation of Municipalities of Madrid.

10 The Municipal Charter argues for more powers in urban planning, infrastructure, education, social services and culture, as well as more financial resources. It also strengthens the control mechanisms of city management and emphasises the delimitation of functions between the city council and the executive organs (Longo 1999).

11 Adding the corridors of Toledo and Gualadajara (Rodríguez Álvarez 2002b).

12 The 2004 Universal Forum of Cultures is a new international event that took place between April and September 2004. It is conceived as a meeting to exchange ideas about peace, sustainable development and cultural diversity.

13 See http://www.bcn.es/participacio/catala/pdf/normesparticipacio.pdf (of the city) and http://www.bcn.es/participacio/catala/pdf/nrfd2001.pdf (of the districts).

Bibliography

Artal, F. (2002) 'Articulació i desarticulació de la metròpoli, 1953–1988', *L'Avenç*, 272: 50–56.

Bahamonde, O. and Otero, L.E. (1999) 'Economía de las Comunidades Autónomas: Madrid', *Papeles de Economía Española*, 18: 18–30.

Borja, J. (ed.) (1995) *Barcelona, un modelo de transformación urbana*, Quito: PGU-LAC.

Brugué, Q. and Gomà, R. (eds) (1998) *Gobiernos locales y políticas públicas. Bienestar social, promoción económica y territorio*, Barcelona: Ariel.

Castillo, F. and Casado, C. (2000) *Perfil socioeconómico de los municipios madrileños en los noventa*. Madrid: Instituto de Estadística de la Comunidad Autónoma de Madrid.

Colomé, G. and Tomàs, M. (2002) 'La gobernabilidad metropolitana: el caso de Barcelona', *Revista Gestión y Análisis de Políticas Públicas*, 24: 141–146.

Font, J. (ed.) (2002) *Public participation and local governance*, Barcelona: Institut de Ciències Polítiques i Socials.

García de Enterría, E. (1983) *Madrid: Comunidad Autónoma Metropolitana*, Madrid: Instituto de Estudios Económicos.

Hesse, J. and Sharpe, L.J. (1991) 'Local Government in International Perspective: Some Comparative Observations', in J. Hesse and L.J. Sharpe (eds), *Local Government and Urban Affairs in International Perspective*, Baden-Baden: Nomos: 603–621.

Hoffmann-Martinot, V. (2002) 'Democracia y gobernabilidad de las grandes ciudades en Europa: una comparación internacional', *Revista Gestión y Análisis de Políticas Públicas*, 24: 7–16.

Jouve, B. (2003) *La gouvernance urbaine en questions*, Paris: Elsevier.

Keating, M. and Loughlin, J. (eds) (1997) *The Political Economy of Regionalism*, London: Frank Cass.

Le Galès, P. (1998) 'Regulations and Governance in European Cities', *International Journal of Urban and Regional Research*, 22: 482–506.

——(2002) *European Cities: Social Conflicts and Governance*, New York: Oxford University Press.

Longo, F. (1999) *La Carta Municipal*, Barcelona: Aula Barcelona.

López, M. (2002) 'Per l'autonomia i sense democràcia. Vers una carta municipal. 1924–1960', *L'Avenç*, 272: 40–48.

Mancomunitat de Municipis de l'Àrea Metropolitana de Barcelona (MMAMB) (1995) *Dinàmiques metropolitanes a l'àrea i la regió de Barcelona*, Barcelona: MMAMB.

Ministerio de Administraciones Públicas (MAP) (2000) *La regionalización y sus consecuencias sobre la autonomía local*, Madrid: MAP.

Négrier, E. and Tomàs, M. (2003) 'Temps, pouvoir, espace: la métropolisation de Barcelone', *Revue française d'administration publique*, 107: 357–368.

Nel lo, O. (1997) 'Les grans ciutats espanyoles: transformacions i polítiques urbanes', *Papers*, 27: 9–70.

Rodríguez Álvarez, J.M. (2002a) 'Madrid: le pilotage politique par la région', in B. Jouve and C. Lefèvre (eds), *Métropoles ingouvernables*, Paris: Elsevier: 107–124.

——(2002b) 'La política sobre grandes ciudades y áreas metropolitanas en España o el temor a la diversidad', *Revista Gestión y Análisis de Políticas Públicas*, 24: 107–126.

Scharpf, F.W. (1988) 'The Joint Decision Trap: Lessons from German Federalism and European Integration', *Public Administration*, 66: 239–278.

Strategic Metropolitan Plan of Barcelona (2002) *Strategic Metropolitan Plan of Barcelona (Perspective 2007)*, Barcelona: Strategic Metropolitan Plan of Barcelona.

5　The emergence of metropolitan governance in Athens

Panagiotis Getimis and Nikolaos Hlepas

Introduction

By the beginning of the nineteenth century, Athens has been described as a 'tiny oriental town with some of the most magnificent European monuments on its castle'. Being aware of the city's worldwide fame, as well as of its symbolic potential for Greek national identity, the Bavarian regents of the New Greek State have chosen (1834) Athens to be the royal residence (Clogg 1983). For the first time in the Near East, a university has been established (1837), since Athens is not only supposed to become the political and cultural centre of the Greek nation, but also a kind of 'European Lighthouse' at the Balkan Peninsula. This double role of the city, neglected for a long period, seems nowadays to be emerging again, after several decades of national antagonism and political rift within the wider south-east European region (Koliopoulos and Veremis 2002). Several Balkan countries and also Turkey are seeking to join the European Union, following the Greek example of democratic consolidation and EU membership, while political turbulence in the Middle East is turning the city into a very attractive place for businesses and immigrants from a wider area.

Economic recovery and an unprecedented mobilisation due to the city's nomination for the Olympic Games (in 1996) gave new hope to the population of a metropolitan area that has been characterised by citizens' dissatisfaction and alienation, growing social segregation and a fragmented civil society. While the acceptance of top-down policies is fading, the need to conceptualise a 'modern' scheme of metropolitan governance has become a part of the political debate.

Different opportunities and threats combined to alternative scenarios of metropolitan reform in major Athens (Region of Attica) are analysed in this chapter once the previous organisational restructuring and the socio-economic environment have been presented. Finally, the concrete form and real perspectives of a major change towards metropolitan governance are evaluated. The core argument of this chapter is that especially in a state characterised by non-Weberian administration and inefficient regulations, the main way to mobilise and integrate different actors within a system of metropolitan governance is a combination of effectiveness as well as efficiency-oriented schemes ('acceptance through success') with strong democratic legitimacy ('acceptance through votes').

The competitiveness of metropolitan Athens and its dynamism

During the second half of the last century, the population of Athens tripled. In 2001, the population of the region was 3,764,348 people, making up a significant percentage (35 per cent) of the country's population and an even higher percentage of industrial, commercial and banking activities. One should not leave out the role of Athens for the Greek diaspora (i.e. the Greek communities all over the world) and its lively cultural scene, nor its importance for international shipping. The economic competitiveness of this region is a crucial factor for the economic development of the whole country. It is not surprising, then, that nearly every major metropolitan issue is regarded as a matter of national interest.

In addition, a significant factor for the agglomeration of economic activities in the area is the fact that the bulk of national government offices and organisations are situated here. The increasing percentage of employment in the tertiary sector of the metropolitan region in comparison with that of the rest of the country demonstrates the dominance of the Athens region over the whole country (see Table 5.1).

Consequently, metropolitan Athens concentrates a number of conditions for being not only a national but also an international developmental and cultural centre (economic growth, flexible high-skilled personnel, cultural heritage, infrastructure). In the context of European enlargement into Eastern Europe, Athens has significant opportunities to become the main metropolitan centre of south-eastern Europe. It scores far higher in terms of GDP per capita and labour productivity compared with the other Balkan capitals. The role of the Attica region in the eastern Mediterranean is also strategic as it demonstrates better standards of life, ongoing development and a stable political environment.

However, this relative success should initially go along with a responsive public sector, effective public–private partnerships and a concept of metropolitan governance, which are still pending. The endogenous potentials of this metropolitan area together with the opportunities that have arisen from exogenous factors (the process of Europeanisation, political stability, global economic development) are threatened due to a lack of effective public policies carried out by adequate, well-organised administrative structures (state and local). For a long time, rising socio-economic complexity, combined in the growing deficit of social capital and urban identity, as well as in several

Table 5.1 Basic data for Greece and the metropolitan area of Athens

Indicators	Metropolitan Athens (%)	Country (%)
Employment in the tertiary sector (1997)	73.7	57.7
GDP per capita (% of EU average in 1996)	77	68
Productivity (% of EU average)	74	72

Source: Operational Program of Attika 2000–2006.

self-referential organisations and particularistic interests (Papadopoulos 1995), has led to a series of failures and blockades of top-down, sectoral, fragmented policies for this metropolitan area. The governability problems of Athens have been legendary for many years (Makrydimitris 1994).

The plague of being the capital of an extremely centralist country

The search for an adequate administrative structure in Athens has a history of some decades: a first scheme of metropolitan administration was established in an authoritarian manner during the 1930s, just after the area's population had doubled within a few years due to the influx of Christian refugees from Anatolia. The 'administration of the capital region' was a state-controlled entity directed by a minister that tried to concentrate planning, public transport and infrastructure responsibilities while it intensified state supervision over the numerous municipalities of the region. This entity was abolished during the war and was not re-established in the following years, since the ongoing political instability, as well as the opposing sectoral and territorial interests, would not allow the formation of a metropolitan entity. In 1985, a law introduced a strategic 'regulatory plan' that included the whole metropolitan territory of Attica, while a specialised planning entity was established. The results of this attempt were far from satisfactory, since this new entity was deprived of the necessary resources, as well as the adequate institutional tools, to put into effect the strict implementation of this strategic plan for Attica.

Just as in the postwar era, the driving force within the metropolitan area was still a certain kind of greedy private business that was destroying the environment and had taken over housing, a large part of health and educational services, as well as a major section of transport activities. At the same time, state-controlled entities and agencies were engaged for water and sewage, public transport and spatial planning. These entities were (and still are) integrated into the respective administrative sectors (ministries or independent institutions), being supervised by the minister responsible. The lack of trans-sectoral coordination, complementarity and synergy has been pointed out for many years, but a consequent effort to change this situation would affect the core of politics within central government, which is sector-bound, top-down, inflexible and strictly regulatory.

It should be pointed out that various plans and policies for the metropolitan area have been frustrated by local blockades. To date, local government structures are extremely fragmented in the region of Attica. The first tier consists of 116 municipalities, but it should also be taken into account that important municipal responsibilities are undertaken by no fewer than 150 municipal enterprises and approximately 400 municipal public entities. Several issue-based associations of municipalities try to cope with local problems, while the 'unified association of municipalities of the Attica Region' (ESDKNA, with eighty-nine municipal members) is the oldest (established in 1970) institutional agency for planning and management of waste in Attica. During the last decade, however, this 'unified association' has faced vehement local opposition and has failed several times to build and operate the waste disposal units that had been planned in close cooperation with central government.

A second tier of local government was established in 1994. The Attica region, subdivided since 1970 into 4 prefectures, included 3 second-level local government agencies. The Athens–Piraeus 'unified prefecture' was established in order to cover a major part of the metropolitan area, where nearly 80 per cent of the population and an even higher percentage of the socio-economic activities of the region are concentrated. Although the territorial borders of this 'unified prefecture' have been criticised for being too narrow (making up only 12 per cent of the total surface area of the Attica region), the directly elected prefect of Athens–Piraeus could theoretically have played a crucial role as a local leader, if this new entity had obtained some important metropolitan responsibilities and, of course, the necessary resources. But neither happened. Reformers built up the subdivisions of this 'unified prefecture', the so-called 'sub-prefectural departments', which became stronger than the prefectural level. No resources and no metropolitan responsibilities have been delegated to this new entity. It seems that neither the responsible ministers, nor the country's political elite in general would be willing to allow the emergence of a new pole of political power within the over-sized centre of an extremely centralist country.

Despite being a deconcentrated unit of state administration, even the Attica region established by law in 1986 has been deprived of a series of responsibilities (especially in the sectors of physical planning and transport) which are exercised in the rest of the country by regional administration. In addition, the indirectly elected 'regional council', which consists mainly of representatives of several local authorities and some corporate interests, does have a certain influence on development planning but is not accountable and visible enough to become an arena for transparent public deliberation on metropolitan strategies (Hlepas 2003). This is an important deficit, since no other institutionalised bodies and forums of public deliberation by and for Athens exist, for the time being.

The highly fragmented administrative and political structures of Attica obviously impede the creation of a metropolitan political identity among the citizenry, while the constituencies for parliamentary elections (which, in most parts of the country, constitute a solid base for local identity and political bargaining) are, in the case of Attica, both too numerous and too large to serve as groundwork for building up a metropolitan political identity (Hlepas 2002). Finally, one should not leave out the fact that the citizenry is, to a great extent, of rural origin and is more mobilised for the problems of its places of origin (as is indicated by the numerous and influential associations of Cretan, Peloponnesian, etc. 'compatriots') than for those of Athens (Tsoukalas 1996). Younger Athenian families, who do tend to develop a kind of 'imaginary identification' with the city, move to the suburbs, while foreign immigrants, deprived of voting rights, take their place within the central city boroughs (Hlepas 2002); social segregation is getting rapidly worse (Maloutas and Economou 1992).

How a 'hopeless case' becomes an 'Olympic challenge'

Treated as a 'hopeless case' by the major part of the Greek political elite, Athens gained international interest after its nomination for the Olympics of 2004. Decision makers and stakeholders were faced with the unprecedented challenge of organising the Olympic games in a quite chaotic major agglomeration of a small country. It was agreed that, for the time being, no major territorial reforms would take place, and this is the reason that the region of Attica was excluded from the ambitious national programme for the amalgamation of municipalities that in 1998 reduced the number of municipalities from a total of 5,700 to 1,033 (Hlepas 2003). Neither did the government follow the advice of the International Olympic Committee, which suggested the establishment of a new ministry for the Olympic Games.

A new entity named 'Athens 2004' took primary responsibility for coordination and promotion of several projects. Due to 'Olympic pressure', several issue- and project-based mechanisms of coordination were established, in most cases including social and private organisations as partners. It should be pointed out, however, that this newly built arena of policies and politics had a limit of time and scope: the Olympics of 2004. This means that there is still a lack of policies, and from a certain point of view also a lack of politics, for the Athens metropolitan area as a whole, and not only with reference to the concrete Olympic projects. A great part of the investments in the region have focused on high-quality sporting infrastructure that will prove to be extremely expensive to maintain in the near future. A lot of public and private capital has been locked up in projects connected to the Games, while important long-term needs (such as an underground system) have been neglected. In addition, influential politicians and stakeholders from other parts of the country, especially from the 'rival' metropolitan area of Thessalonica, have been loudly protesting against 'too much public spending for Athens' and have been strongly demanding financial support for themselves after the Olympic Games.

On the other hand, there is no doubt that in Athens public awareness for the metropolitan problems of the region has grown a great deal in comparison with the past. This is not only due to the Olympics as a mobilising mega-project, but also to the fact that the implemented modes of metropolitan governance, although structured by single issues and projects associated with the Olympics, promoted ties between sectors and agencies and also between these and the citizens. In addition, within the region the Olympic project seems to have activated several modernisation efforts at all levels of governance. Their success is interlinked with the enhancement of the competitive advantage of the city to the European and the global space. These challenges have also revitalised an ongoing debate on the emergence of a new form of metropolitan governance in Athens (Getimis and Kafkalas 2003).

Through participation to mobilisation?

What is of particular interest in the case of Athens is the fact that a visible, persistent and multiple deficit of effectiveness in metropolitan government now seems to bend the reforming efforts towards the democratic legitimacy of a new system of metropolitan governance. In the past, several metropolitan projects (such as the location and operation of waste disposal units) have been frustrated because the respective decision making lacked transparency and public acceptance. Strong protests, long-lasting litigation and inter-sectoral blockades were, to a large degree, the result of uncoordinated top-down policies for the region. Nowadays, democratic legitimacy, political accountability, transparency and public deliberation are regarded as necessary preconditions in order to achieve a satisfactory level of consensus and acceptance, efficiency and effectiveness within a metropolitan system of governance.

The concrete institutional design, however, of this new scheme of governance is still something to be invented. Of course, alternative scenarios (see below) are being discussed, mainly from a constitutional or a party politics point of view, but many actors are not eager to expose themselves as holding a clear position. Nevertheless, an unprecedented level of consensus will be necessary during the next few years, since the new institutional settings and territorial reforms need to be carefully planned, while the delegation of power and resources to the new metropolitan level in particular will certainly take some time: the metropolitan reform will prove to be a long-lasting, continuous task of high difficulty that will have to be carried out by several actors in close cooperation with each other.

Furthermore, although the necessity of a metropolitan reform is generally recognised, it is obvious that neither the decision makers nor Athenian public opinion realise the kind of changes that a new scheme of metropolitan governance would bring. After all, a new, metropolitan level of administration could mean less freedom, influence, blockading abilities, etc. for a series of local, sectoral and corporate interests as well as for other actors. Furthermore, the long centralist tradition of sectoral dependency and non-transparent bargaining, in conjunction with a majoritarian and non-consensual representative and non-participatory political culture could undermine, in the near future, the success of a metropolitan reform.

On the other hand, new chances of participation, public bargaining and deliberation that could lead to transparent and coherent decision making for the metropolitan area has the potential to empower and mobilise a series of actors and stakeholders that were disappointed and had simply 'retreated' in the past. In particular, if democratically legitimised organs are to be introduced, an obvious improvement in the learning and steering capacity at the metropolitan level could occur which would attract additional support for metropolitan reform. Furthermore, the institutionalisation of new bodies of deliberation and bargaining (especially an 'economic and social committee' from and for the metropolitan area; see below) would systematise and make public, transparent and visible what nowadays only occasionally, informally and invisibly happens. A new scheme of metropolitan governance could visibly articulate policy-making and politics for the metropolitan area, foster socio-political integration and identification, and improve knowledge and information sharing.

What will happen after the Olympics? The debate on alternative scenarios

Since the perspective of metropolitan reform has become more and more realistic, the debate has ceased to be a merely academic issue and members of the concerned political elite are now trying to position themselves. Ambitious local leaders (i.e. the mayors of Athens and of some other major municipalities) have claimed to have 'new ideas' about this reform, while the major political parties actually promised metropolitan reform in view of the parliamentary elections (in spring 2004). But few leaders have been eager to expose themselves with concrete plans in detail. Scientific expertise has again been mobilised by some of the main future debaters, who have ordered policy studies of metropolitan reforms:

- the local association of municipalities: mainly focusing on the future role of local government within a scheme of metropolitan government,
- the Ministry of Environment, Spatial Planning and Public Works: mainly focusing on questions of strategic and spatial planning for the whole metropolitan region,
- the Ministry of Interior, Public Administration and Decentralisation: this has ordered a major, trans-sectoral study of present metropolitan needs and future scenarios for the design of a new system of metropolitan governance in Athens. The latter is briefly presented in this chapter.

Despite different approaches, all three studies found remarkable resonance among decision makers and also in the media, because they proposed three major alternative scenarios regarding the form of future metropolitan governance in Athens. These scenarios are:

1 The establishment of a 'metropolitan regional authority' with appointed general secretary and a directly elected metropolitan council (mixed form).
2 The creation of a 'metropolitan government', with elected mayor and council (second tier of local government).
3 A strong 'metropolitan association of local authorities'.[1]

Finally, all three governance scenarios have been assessed, while a 'hard core' of metropolitan functions that should be fulfilled under any scenario has been worked out and some central questions about the meaning of broader implications of these newly proposed metropolitan schemes in terms of governance have been faced. In this context, it can be argued that the impact of this procedure has not only been the production of a study of three scenarios but also the first major attempt to establish an informal horizontal network of dialogue between the key-holders of the metropolitan region of Athens.

Scenario 1: metropolitan regional authority

This scenario is based on the acknowledgement that, taking into consideration the relation between the size of this metropolitan area and the size of the whole country, most of the metropolitan governance arrangements in Athens would create implications of national range. On this view, the fact cannot be avoided that central government and national leadership exercise strong influence on metropolitan policies and politics. On the other hand, the weak performance of central government and government-controlled agencies and entities is often due to local or other social reactions, revealing the fact that there is not only a problem of policy implementation within the administration but also a problem of policy acceptance within the Athenian population.

Instead of the present authoritarian, but also ineffective centralistic approach, this first alternative scenario is based on a 'mixed' form of metropolitan governance, embodying the central state as well as local representatives. According to this scenario, the region of Attica is to obtain special status and become a 'metropolitan region'. The head of the administration of this region, the general secretary of the Attica region, a person of 'general acceptance and authority', is to be elected by the national parliament (from three candidates proposed by central government) for a period of five years. The citizens of the metropolitan region should directly elect a metropolitan council for a period of four years. This council would have the general competence, control the administration and build thematic or local committees. The general secretary should appoint 5–11 members of the council as his assistants. A second body, called the 'Economic and Social Committee of Athens', would be composed of representatives of different social groups (private sector, chambers, labour associations, NGOs, etc.), as well as of local government agencies, experts and government officials. This second body would be able to make proposals, formulate opinions and in general be consulted before the metropolitan council takes decisions.

This institutional design would foster the emergence of a metropolitan political elite and increase acceptance of decisions and policies by the population. Through the directly elected metropolitan council, the citizens' vote could influence the agenda-setting for resolving metropolitan problems, while for the first time some elements of metropolitan political identity could be created among the citizenry. For the first time, politicians with important metropolitan competence would be elected by the citizens of the metropolitan area, for the metropolitan area. At the same time, a second body combining sectoral, corporatist, social and expertise elements could create an important metropolitan sphere of deliberation, before the metropolitan council takes the final decision. The metropolitan region would act as a main junction for several networks that nowadays act separately or even conflictually. The new metropolitan region would concentrate several responsibilities now belonging to central government, some specialised state-controlled entities and the regional level of state administration, as well as some responsibilities that cannot be faced by the fragmented local government authorities and their associations.

Nevertheless, it should be pointed out that this new scheme should not be over-loaded with competence, because this would lead to the building of 'a new state within the Greek state' and to a well-known pathology of administrative and political congestion. For this reason, some of the specialised entities dealing (in part or in total) with metropolitan issues should not be formally integrated or even put under the supervision of the metropolitan region. Coordination and synergy could also be achieved when the region appoints some members of the boards of these entities (acting as 'antennae'), when constant information sharing is introduced and when regular joint sessions take place.

The transfer of responsibilities to the metropolitan region can, of course, only succeed if the proper resources are also transferred. Several state agencies would hand over their know-how and their specialised, experienced personnel to this new authority. From a macro-organisational point of view, this reform should be framed with the abolition of the existing 'unified prefecture of Athens–Piraeus' and the creation of more (8 instead of today's 6) local government agencies on the second tier, as well as the establishment of a number of territorial and thematic associations of municipalities combined with some amalgamations that would stretch the weak organisational structures of the first tier, now consisting of 118 municipalities. An overall reorganisation of territorial government structures would help create flexible balances within the new system of metropolitan governance, inhibit tendencies of a new 'inner-metropolitan centralism' and enhance planning, as well as escalating the performance of administrative duties.

Nevertheless, questions arise with regard to financing this new form of governance. Since, according to the Greek Constitution, regions are not allowed to raise their own taxes, this metropolitan region will depend on grants coming from the central state, or on taxation that has been approved by the national parliament. Another important disadvantage would be the trend to overload and congest this new form of governance, since there are many unsolved problems and vacuums left by the central state (and state-controlled entities), which will also try to transfer many difficult or costly duties to the new metropolitan organisation, while it will try to retain resources and influence. Reform blockades could also arise when sectoral and/or corporate interests feel that their position is threatened by new overall governance arrangements within the core region of the country.

Scenario 2: metropolitan government

The establishment of a metropolitan government seems to be a solution that ensures citizens' participation, 'authentic' democratic legitimisation of the metropolitan organs and their choices/decisions through universal suffrage and direct election, as well as accountability through the concentration of political responsibility for the solutions that have been chosen. There is no doubt that this scenario would promote the creation of a (nowadays nearly non-existent) metropolitan political identity among the citizenry and foster the emergence of a metropolitan political elite.

In Greece, the constitution safeguards the existence of two tiers of local government (Art. 102 I). For this reason, metropolitan government can be established on the second tier of local government. This new entity would be, in a way, a new form of the unified prefecture of Athens–Piraeus initially inaugurated in 1994. But the latter included only 60 out of the metropolitan area's 118 municipalities and less than the half of the whole surface area of the Attica region, while its responsibilities and its resources were extremely poor.

This second scenario proposes the establishment of a metropolitan prefecture of Athens that would cover the whole Attica region, concentrate important responsibilities and command important human and financial resources. The metropolitan prefect and the prefectural council should be directly elected. Also this scenario could be combined with the establishment of a certain kind of metropolitan economic and social committee, which would include members representing sectoral, corporatist, social (NGOs etc.) interests and institutions with technical expertise. This new body would offer important expertise and create a new different sphere of deliberation before the directly elected prefectural council takes the final decision. Since the territory of the metropolitan prefecture and the one of the region of Attica would be identical, the indirectly elected regional council of Attica could fulfil this role of a metropolitan social and economic committee.

This new entity ('metropolitan prefecture') would be subdivided into 6–8 departments (or sub-prefectures) in order to facilitate citizen-friendly services and local citizen participation. On the first tier of local government, a number of territorial and thematic associations of municipalities would be formed, probably combined with some amalgamations. This overall reorganisation of territorial government structures would have, within the new system of metropolitan governance, the positive effects already mentioned with regard to the first scenario.

Among the responsibilities that could be transferred to this new metropolitan entity, planning would be of great importance. It would be the first time that a directly elected local government agency would be responsible for development planning, spatial and urban planning, as well as 'sectoral' planning (location of hospitals, social services, waste treatment plants, etc.) in the area. Compared to the centralised way of planning that is practised today (where citizen participation is so weak that local blockades are the rule), this new metropolitan planning would certainly be more democratic and more easily accepted by the concerned citizens and agencies. Nevertheless, when single sectors or single territories are affected, a majoritarian decision by a metropolitan council could also provoke blockades and strong reactions from those who are directly concerned. Redesigning the planning procedures in favour of citizen participation could be one tool – strengthening deliberative metropolitan forums could be another – to cope with or solve these problems.

The scenario of metropolitan local government would definitely affect the political system of the whole country in an essential way, since the directly elected prefect of Athens could even compete with the political authority of the prime minister, since this metropolitan prefect would be the leader of an area concentrating no less than 35 per cent of the nation's citizenry. For this reason it is quite unlikely that the country's political elite would favour such a scenario.

On the other hand, taking into account the clientelist tradition of Greek politics, it is quite probable that those who will be directly elected in order to govern the area will be vulnerable to many different kinds of pressure and will tend to build up their political career using clientelist practices. This would reproduce the well-known patterns of non-solution, non-existence of long-term strategy, non-effectiveness, inefficient public spending and majoritarian arbitrariness. It is doubtful whether the regional council, as an official forum of metropolitan deliberation and state supervision, would be able to set a bar against such practices.

Financial constraints could be more effective against such clientelist tendencies: although local government agencies are now allowed to impose local taxes, it is quite unlikely that these revenues could be sufficient for the responsibilities undertaken by this metropolitan local government agency, which will certainly depend on state grants. Furthermore, many sectoral and infrastructure policies can only be elaborated and implemented in close cooperation with state and, in many cases, private agencies.

Scenario 3: metropolitan association of local authorities

Metropolitan associations of local authorities constitute (in their multitude) a well-tested variety of solutions for the problems of metropolitan areas (Getimis *et al.* 2003). In Greece, such a solution seems now to be facilitated by the new Article 102 of the constitution, which explicitly allows even the compulsory establishment of 'municipal associations that undertake responsibilities of local government'. These municipal associations cannot, however, replace the two constitutionally safeguarded tiers of local government: they are supposed to fulfil a complementary function that could include coordination in the case of metropolitan areas.

According to this scenario, the proposed metropolitan association (which would cover the whole Attica region) should have an assembly, whose members would represent both tiers of local government in Attica, some thematic or smaller territorial associations of local authorities, as well as members of sectoral, corporatist, social (NGOs etc.) or 'expertocratic' (state or private agencies' officials, etc.) origin. This assembly would elect the executive committee and the secretary general of the metropolitan association.

This association would concentrate responsibilities for planning and appoint an important number of representatives in the boards of state-controlled entities dealing with metropolitan problems such as public transport, or even supervise some of the now state-controlled entities dealing with tasks such as water supply. Also under the scenario of a metropolitan association, an overall reorganisation of territorial administration within the metropolitan area is suggested. The existing thematic and smaller territorial associations would be maintained, while the unified prefecture Athens–Piraeus would be abolished and the whole Attica region would be divided into 6–8 (instead of the current three) prefectures. In addition, some amalgamations of municipalities are recommended.

This scenario raises the question of the relation between this new entity and the Attica region. There is no doubt, that the indirectly elected regional council could play the role of a social and economic committee as forum of metropolitan deliberation, while some of its members could at the same time act as representatives of corporate, sectoral, social, non-governmental organisations within the assembly of the metropolitan association. This third scenario seems to favour the creation of horizontal networks beyond sectoral, social and territorial borders. Further, it is quite possible that the establishment of a metropolitan association would face less local reaction than any other scenario, since local authorities would be represented in the assembly.

On the other hand, the danger of everlasting and paralysing conflicts within the association should not be underestimated, since no stable majority can be formed within an only indirectly elected assembly in which majoritarian decision making is always a result of *ad hoc* bargaining. This could turn the identification of a common metropolitan interest into a quite difficult (if not impossible) undertaking. Moreover, it is possible that decisions will not be turned into practice, either because they will be blocked by other agencies or the directly concerned citizens (who could not influence the decision of this association by voting directly), or because the decision itself may be the result of a faulty compromise.

Finally, it should be mentioned that the problem arising from the clientelist culture in Greek politics mentioned with regard to the second scenario would also apply to this scenario. However, this third scenario would not lead to the emergence of a new metropolitan political elite, since the members of the assembly have already been elected somewhere else. On the other hand, the creation of a metropolitan identity among the citizenry could hardly be promoted, since it would not be possible to vote directly for metropolitan leaders that could lean upon their area-wide democratic legitimation and their popularity in order to articulate and symbolise such an identity. Last but not least, this scenario could frustrate metropolitan leadership, because the members of the assembly would be particularly vulnerable towards local and sectoral pressures.

Perspectives and evaluation

From non-government to governance? Some guidelines for institutional design

The research procedure identified pressing needs for exercising metropolitan functions and building structures of decision making, political responsibility and policy implementation on a metropolitan level. The common point is the need for linking and coordination of the various policies exercised in (and for) the metropolitan area of Attica. Metropolitan strategic planning, coordination, supervision and implementation control, documentation and information sharing are the four main categories of metropolitan responsibility that were localised by all six sectoral research projects.

Several policy studies carried out recently within the context of the debate on a metropolitan reform of the Athens region pointed out the need for strategic planning as a core aspect of reform policy (Getimis and Kafkalas 2003). Institutional and administrative fragmentation, regulatory inflation, weak coordination and synergy, the lack of systematic documentation and information sharing, the culture of a clientelist, otherwise sectoral and corporate, approach within the administration and some extremely intricate distributive alliances seem up to now to have blocked or frustrated a strategic approach.

However, the establishment of a new scheme of metropolitan government should not mean the concentration of a great number of responsibilities from lower administrative levels. It is suggested that responsibilities are transferred from the central state or state-controlled agencies, or that new functions are taken over which are not currently fulfilled or which are exercised only haphazardly or in a non-effective manner. The new scheme should have a complementary character and not allow tendencies that would lead to overloading and congestion and finally undermine metropolitan governance reform.

No other way than efficiency combined with democratic legitimacy

The traditional 'sectoral federalism' within central government, combined with the fragmentation of local government structures, of democratic legitimacy and political responsibility, do not allow the formulation of coherent policies for the metropolitan area (Makrydimitris 1994). But even in cases where concrete policy options have been agreed among major stakeholders and promoted by the government and some specialised entities, the lack of visible democratic legitimacy and broad citizen participation have led to local resistance and, finally, the frustration of major projects such as the introduction of a new, rational system for waste management in Attica. In the case of Athens, higher efficiency would come to a dead-end if the social acceptance of concrete policy options could not be backed up by democratic legitimacy, accountability of the decision makers, citizen control and broader participation.

A new scheme of metropolitan governance should enable metropolitan leadership, political responsibility, efficiency and effectiveness, while at the same time broaden democratic legitimacy and citizen participation. The existing state and market mechanisms will not be replaced (Getimis and Kavkalas 2003) but complemented and partially restructured; new governance arrangements (Lefèvre 1998) should lead to early conflict resolution and deal with problems of governability, which are nowadays mostly visible at the local level but sometimes originate from the regulatory inefficiency of the state and an unrestrained market.

Of the three proposed scenarios for metropolitan governance in Athens only the first one, based on 'a mixed form' of governance, could be strongly supported by the party political system (politicians), public administration (public servants) and local government (elected local leaders). The establishment of a directly elected metropolitan council with powerful functions and competencies *vis-à-vis* the appointed general secretary and the regional state is the most acceptable balance of power between the dominant actors involved in the decision-making process: namely the central state, the political parties and local government in the Athens metropolitan area. In this sense, the perspective of the implementation of the first scenario is more realistic while at the same time it integrates principles of efficiency and democratic legitimacy. In fact, the first scenario is the only one that has officially been under discussion by the responsible Minister of the Interior, not only at the National Committee of Administrative Reform (which is an important consulting body) but also during the last (November 2003) annual congress of the national association of municipalities.

From fragmentation to integration? Political elite, political identity and civil society within the context of an emerging metropolitan governance scheme

Administrative fragmentation, growing social segregation (Maloutas and Economou 1992) and historical boundaries (Goldsmith 1995) constitute some of the main obstacles to any kind of metropolitan integration intended by a new scheme of metropolitan governance. In fact, the lack of a metropolitan identity and orientation in Athens does not only concern the political elite but also several pressure groups (trade unions, etc.), even the better part of the business community. Civil society remains fragmented (most activities are local or sector-oriented) and weak, while even the empowerment of traditionally input-oriented local government in Greece ('Franco-group', according to Hesse and Sharpe 1991) during the last decades seems further to have enhanced a sort of 'blindness to what is happening outside of my neighbourhood'. Under these circumstances, a kind of governance that would simply incorporate stakeholders would simply lead to further fragmentation and increase the possibilities of conflict that would paralyse the political system.

For these reasons, the creation of a metropolitan political identity among the citizenry would not be impeded by new modes of governance as long as the latter are combined with forms of citizen participation based on universal suffrage and direct election or, in some instances, forms of direct participation. If they do not decide by themselves, the citizens need visible and accountable representatives who will incorporate their 'choice through voting' for the metropolitan area. The main task of metropolitan reform should, therefore, be to build up, through participation and democratic legitimisation, a metropolitan political identity, and to foster the emergence of a metropolitan political elite. The emergence of a metropolitan civil society could be promoted by new forms of specific interest or engagement-oriented participation that would offer new channels of political influence to active citizens which secure that their activation counts (Stoker and Mossberger 1994).

All three proposed scenarios seem to foster the emergence of a metropolitan elite. In particular, the first and the second scenario offer new opportunities for political careers and could promote the renewal of the local political elite. The connection between territorially elected bodies and institutionalised forums of deliberation and participation for sectoral, corporate and social interests and expertise could lead to new modes of bargaining and common interest identification, so that the scope of this new political elite could change. Towards this perspective, the role of an economic and social committee at the metropolitan level, with representatives of the major economic and social groups, could be decisive.

Similarly, all three scenarios tend to create new deliberative forums and respective forms of citizen involvement. Since the main decisions for the metropolitan area of Athens should no longer be taken by central government but by elected bodies in cooperation with other forms of participation and interest articulation on a metropolitan level, it can be expected that new spheres of negotiation and deliberation will emerge.

Conclusion

Kübler and Heinelt's cube (see Chapter 2) in which a certain type of metropolitan governance can be placed has three dimensions: the dimension of policy networks ('openness' or 'closedness'); the dimension of local government (measured as 'input-oriented' or 'output-oriented'); and the dimension of civil society ('weak' or 'strong'). In the case of Athens, the fact that a major reform 'from metropolitan non-government to governance' is still pending leads to an assessment that is based on the comparison between today's realities and future scenarios.

Policy networks traditionally used to be rather 'closed' in Athens, while the respective corporate interests, party mechanisms and also a part of the business community kept privileges of informal access depending on organisational and bargaining skills, party politics and personal relations. Nowadays, large-scale projects (with pressing needs for private capital and expertise), a growing voluntary sector and self-confident local leaders create a tendency to open networks of metropolitan policies. Accessibility remains, however, strongly variable from case to case, so that an environment of non-continuity and disruption, distrust and non-transparency, persists. Metropolitan reform would certainly, therefore, increase the 'openness' of policy networks in and for Athens. But this 'openness' would differ depending on the reform scenario that would finally be put into action: The third scenario, of 'metropolitan association of local authorities', for instance, would improve the access of local actors and NGOs but policy networks dominated by this association could prove to be less open to big business and sectoral interests, or even to state authorities. The second scenario, of 'metropolitan government', could lead to similar results (besides improving access to big business). The 'mixed form' (first scenario) of metropolitan governance combines state power, a second body of institutionalised deliberation (the economic and social committee) and direct democratic legitimation, so that policy networks would be open to all kinds of actors. In this way the interaction of several actors could lead to the desired balance between the 'closedness' and 'openness' of policy networks.

Greek local government is traditionally 'input-oriented': the primacy of politics remains unchallenged and service performance is not a matter of top priority (Hlepas 2003). This input-orientation would probably not change much if scenarios 2 (metropolitan government) or 3 (metropolitan association) were put into practice. Only the establishment of an economic and social committee (in both scenarios) could cause a certain move towards 'output', since social and especially economic actors would rather focus on service performance. This move would be a little more powerful in the third scenario (metropolitan association), since the assembly of the association would not be as strong as a directly elected council (second scenario). The economic and social committee could, therefore, have a stronger influence inside a metropolitan association scheme. An even stronger shift towards 'output-orientation' could be expected if the first scenario (mixed form) would be put into action, since state organs and especially a general secretary of the Attica region would tend to pay more attention to the output – not least in order to promote personal careers.

Greek civil society was undermined through extreme party politicisation in the 1980s (Mavrogordatos 1993), while nowadays in Athens it suffers from extreme territorial fragmentation. The present weakness of civil society would change if a new scheme of metropolitan governance were to be implemented and all proposed scenarios would strengthen the Athenian civil society, since elected organs with metropolitan responsibilities and a second deliberative body (economic and social committee) would be established. The third (metropolitan association) and especially the second (metropolitan government) scenarios would rather tend to advance the dominant role of political parties, while the first scenario (mixed form) could lead to a more balanced division of influence that would facilitate the positioning of civil society at the metropolitan level: if central government, political parties and local leaders do not dominate everything, some civil society actors might become more self-confident and directly engage in metropolitan issues.

The final result is obvious: of the three scenarios, the first ('mixed form') is closer to the ideal point of democratic metropolitan governance characterised by a balance of input and output orientations of local government as well as openness and closedness of policy networks and a strong civil society (as is implicitly indicated by the 'cube of democratic metropolitan governance'; see Chapter 2). Being an institutional scheme that integrates several actors, this 'metropolitan regional authority' could bring the desired balance between 'openness' and 'closedness' of metropolitan policy networks, as well as between the input and output orientation of local government. Further, this new system of metropolitan governance could strengthen civil society in and for Athens.

Note

1 The research team that prepared the policy study for the Ministry of the Interior has been subdivided into two major groups. The first group (called the 'horizontal' group) would be responsible for coordination and all-embracing assessment, combined with

a comparative approach referring to the international experience of metropolitan governance. The second group (called the 'vertical' group) would consist of six groups of researchers specialising in six main sectors: (1) urban development and economic activities; (2) spatial planning; (3) social policy; (4) environment; (5) transport; and (6) civil protection, emergency and security. At a first stage these 'sectoral' groups should detect problems of a metropolitan dimension within 'their' own sector. This could be achieved through research and personal interviews with practitioners from each sector. It should be noted that more than sixty practitioners participated in the whole procedure, representing a wide spectrum of actors from public and private sectors, local authorities, social partners, NGOs etc. Several panel meetings (where members of the 'horizontal' group also participated) took place, so that researchers and practitioners could exchange experiences and arguments. At a later stage, practitioners were faced with alternative scenarios of metropolitan governance, in order to access the possible results of each scenario within their own sector. On this groundwork, each 'sectoral' (or 'vertical') group prepared studies and proposals (including concrete responsibilities, procedures and decision-structures) for its own sector with reference to each alternative scenario. There were joint sessions between each sectoral group and the coordination team, as well as plenary sessions, so that the vertical ('sectoral') perceptions and the 'horizontal' approach could be crossed and combined, leading to a comprehensive concept.

Bibliography

Clogg, R. (1983) *A Concise History of Modern Greece*, Oxford: Oxford University Press.

Getimis, P. and Kafkalas, G. (2003), 'European Metropolitan Areas and the Issue of Multi-Level REGIONAL Governance', in P. Getimis and G. Kafkalas (eds), *Metropolitan Governance: International Experience and Greek Reality*, Athens: Institute of Urban Environment and Human Resources: 13–31 (in Greek).

Getimis, P., Gregoriadou, D. and Marava, N. (2003), 'Metropolitan Governance: European and International Experience', in P. Getimis and G. Kafkalas (eds), *Metropolitan Governance: International Experience and Greek Reality*, Athens: Institute of Urban Environment and Human Resources: 33–61 (in Greek).

Goldsmith, M. (1995) 'Autonomy and City Limits', in G. Stoker and H. Wollmann (eds), *Theories of Urban Politics*, London: Sage: 228–252.

Hesse, J.J. and Sharpe, L.J. (1991) 'Local Government in International Perspective: Some Comparative Observations', in J.J. Hesse and L.J. Sharpe (eds), *Local Government and Urban Affairs in International Perspective*, Baden-Baden: Nomos: 603–621.

Hlepas, N. (2002) 'L' agglomération d' Athènes. Une capitale colonisée par la province?', *Les annales des ponts et des chaussees*, (102): 15–22.

——(2003) 'Local Government Reform in Greece', in A. Vetter and N. Kersting (eds), *Reforming Local Government in Europe: Closing the Gap between Democracy and Efficiency*, Opladen: Leske & Budrich: 221–239.

Koliopoulos, J. and Veremis, T. (2002) *Greece. The Modern Sequel. From 1831 to the Present*, London: Hurst & Company.

Lefèvre, Chr. (1998) 'Metropolitan Government and Governance in Western Countries: A Critical Review', *International Journal of Urban and Regional Research*: 9–25.

Makrydimitris, A. (1994) 'The Non-Governed City', in A. Makrydimitris and G. Papadimitriou (eds), *The Administration of Metropolitan Regions*, Athens: Ant. N. Sakkoulas: 87–109 (in Greek).

Maloutas, T. and Economou, D. (eds) (1992) *Social Structures and Urban Organisation in Athens*, Thessaloniki: Paratiritis (in Greek).

Mavrogordatos, G. (1993) 'Civil Society under Populism', in R. Clogg (ed.), *Greece 1981–89: The Populist Decade*, New York: St Martin's Press: 47–64.

Papadopoulos, Y. (1995) *Complexité sociale et politiques publiques*, Paris: Montchrestien.

Stoker, G. and Mossberger, K. (1994) 'Urban Regime Theory in Comparative Perspective', *Government and Policy*, 12: 195–212.

Tsoukalas, K. (1996) 'The Origin of the Athenian Urban Society', in: Technical Chamber, *A Vision for Athens*, Athens: 61–65 (in Greek).

6 The experience of metropolitan government in England

Michael Goldsmith

Introduction

With the creation of the London County Council in 1889, Britain was the first country to introduce area-wide metropolitan government. In the 1960s, London government was further reformed, and in the 1970s, six further area-wide metropolitan authorities were introduced to cover the conurbations of Birmingham, Leeds, Liverpool, Manchester, Newcastle and Sheffield. All seven of these new institutions were abolished in 1986, and the question of area-wide metropolitan government only came back onto the agenda in the late 1990s, culminating in the introduction of a new directly elected Mayor and Assembly for London.

This chapter seeks to review the English experience of metropolitan government in the light of arguments about desirable ways of governing metropolitan areas and the solutions adopted elsewhere. After a brief discussion of the old London County Council (LCC), the focus turns to the experience of the Greater London Council (GLC) and the former metropolitan counties; their abolition and the way in which metropolitan governance has operated after that event. It turns again to consider the recent reforms in London, and the chapter concludes with an assessment of England's metropolitan governance in the light of the Heinelt–Kübler cube (see Chapter 2).

What form of institutional structure?

It is fashionable today to talk about metropolitan governance rather than government, and fragmented institutional arrangements are a key characteristic of metropolitan areas. However, it is important to remember that the government of metropolitan areas has always involved large numbers of institutions and agencies. In this sense governance is not new: nineteenth-century cities were also recognisable as places based on systems of governance (Goldsmith and Garrard 2000). It was not until late in the nineteenth century that arguments began to be raised about the democratic and service efficiency that such fragmented systems appeared not to deliver, especially in relation to London.[1]

As London continued to grow in the early and mid-twentieth century, the limitations of the existing governmental system began to become more apparent. By this time both academic and professional thinking had become dominated by the attractions of area-wide metropolitan government, ideally involving a single tier responsible for all functions. Later, as Heinelt and Kübler demonstrate, arguments more in favour of a public choice approach also gained support.

Stated simply, there are essentially four approaches to the issue of governmental structures for metropolitan areas.

First, one can choose to do simply nothing, an option widely adopted in practice – at least in the short run. Politicians at all levels are well aware of the dangers of reforming local structures – the old adage that 'there are no votes in local government reform' still holds sway today. But because the problems driving the need for change are likely to persist, some action is likely – and the most favoured is often to create a special district or agency to deal with the problem.

A second approach much favoured in the nineteenth and early twentieth century was the promotion of a metropolitan area through annexation and amalgamation but it fell out of use by the early 1950s.

The third and most common approach involving institutional and territorial change is the adoption of either a two- or a single-tier system of government. Whilst some authors and official reports have argued for a single-tier area-wide government to cover a metropolitan area, such proposals have proved politically impossible to adopt. The result has been that where a top-down approach to structural reform has been adopted, governments have adopted a two-tier system. The top tier has been area-wide and responsible for a range of strategic services, such as planning and public transport, with the bottom tier responsible for the more personal services, such as education and welfare services, with some services being shared between the two tiers (e.g. housing). A number of such reforms were introduced in the 1960s and 1970s, including reform in England. As we see, one reason why these reforms failed was the lack of public support for the upper-tier institutions, or a general reluctance to accept change of any kind.

The final approach is one based on bottom-up voluntary cooperation, albeit generally encouraged by central governments. The success or failure of such voluntary schemes depends on a number of factors – the rules of the game; the financial sticks and carrots available; and the quality of local political leaders, especially their skill in building and sustaining coalitions and regimes (Stone 1989, 1995).

London's government has experienced all these different types of reform over the years. By the early nineteenth century, London was the world's first modern metropolis, far larger than Paris, the second largest city at the time. But a new institutional structure was a long time coming, arriving after the introduction of the new urban governments (boroughs) which encouraged the development of local government in cities such as Birmingham and Manchester, and after a new two-tier structure had been introduced to cover the rest of the country in 1888. The introduction of the LCC in 1889 represented a multi-purpose area-wide elected body covering much of the urban area of the time, replacing a number of single-purpose bodies such as the Metropolitan Board of Works, but leaving the powerful City of London intact and with vestry or parish governments still in existence, though with very limited powers (Young and Garside 1982). It would be a further ten years before the parishes would be replaced by a system of boroughs in 1900, by which time the continued growth of the metropolitan area already called into question the new structure. Over the next twenty years, public debate continued on the desirable structure of London government, but, fearful of the outright opposition further expansion of the LCC would produce, governments decided to retain the existing boundaries.

But the continued spread of the (Greater) London urban area up to the Second World War continued to pose problems in the metropolis, notwithstanding the modest success of the LCC under the leadership of Herbert Morrison (Labour), especially in promoting housing. The LCC faced constant conflict, especially with the boroughs to the west of London, and from the surrounding counties in which the LCC often sought to purchase land for housing purposes.[2] With private development, particularly along the transport networks out from the centre, Greater London had increased in size by an amount 'equal to the City of Manchester' by 1939, the LCC's jubilee year – a jubilee marked by renewed debate about the appropriate institutional structure for the metropolitan area. With the intervention of war, however, it was to be more than a further twenty years before reform was to occur.

In part, as Young and Garside (1982: 256–295) demonstrate, this immediate postwar period was one of mixed fortunes for London and its metropolitan government. Other priorities took precedence, and within the greater London area, the New Towns policy and the imposition of the Green Belt had the effect – temporarily at least – of constraining London's growth.

By the middle 1950s, however, infrastructure problems – housing, roads – together with continued planning failures posed a challenge to the existing structures. The 1951 Census showed how much the population of Greater London had grown, and the LCC continued to have difficulties in finding sites for new housing, both within and outside its boundaries, whilst growing traffic congestion threatened London with gridlock. Outside London, especially in Middlesex, population growth led to many towns reaching a size at which they considered themselves eligible to be single-tier authorities (county boroughs), threatening the very existence of the county. Overall, some hundred local government units were not surprisingly unable to cope with the interrelated problems of the great metropolis. In the light of these developments, the then Conservative government bravely established a Royal Commission in 1956 to consider the future of London government.

At the time, as authors such as Smallwood (1965), Rhodes (1970), and Young and Garside (1982) have shown, although most people were convinced something should be done about London's government, there was considerable academic, professional and political disagreement about what should be done and how extensive reforms should be. For example, two influential London university-based research groups offered contradictory advice on reform.[3] Politically, local government Conservatives feared the extension of London's administrative boundaries would mean extension of Labour control over much of the metropolis, especially in the surrounding counties, then Conservative controlled.

Reporting three years later, the Herbert Commission Report recommended considerable extensions to London's boundaries, with a two-tier structure in which the major functions, including land use planning, education and housing, were located with the strong upper tier. Its emphasis was very much on improving service efficiency rather than on new democratic initiatives – Mill's doctrine of representative government still holding sway. Though it could have buried the report, the then Conservative government under Harold Macmillan decided to introduce legislation in 1962 to implement the report's proposals, albeit somewhat watered down in the face of political opposition from within the party's ranks. In particular, although the Conservative government calculated that alienating the Conservative-controlled fringe counties was worthwhile if the Labour-controlled LCC could be broken up, it excluded parts of Surrey (a party stronghold), and it also severely reduced the GLC's powers in areas such as education and housing – in the latter case to make it largely ineffective as a housing body (Young and Kramer 1978).[4] Following further important changes in the legislation secured by opponents as the bill went through Parliament, the new GLC and the thirty-three new London boroughs came into existence in 1963.

Given that the new GLC was effectively a compromise institution, and additionally that it was something of an experiment at the time, the result was at best mixed. The GLC was not only a service provider, but also a strategic planning authority – and responsible for resource allocation to boot. Little thought had been given to how these different and somewhat conflicting roles could be performed. And over the next twenty years not only did London's needs change, but functions were added to and taken away from the GLC. And this difficult social and functional environment was further complicated by the differing political complexions of the two tiers covering London – many London boroughs (especially the outer ones) were Conservative controlled, and even the Labour controlled inner boroughs were not well disposed towards the GLC, which itself swung backwards and forwards between the two main parties in terms of political control.

Viewed with hindsight, the GLC was doomed to failure. However, whilst it was never popular, the structure adopted for London was also to be implemented in the other metropolitan areas of England (Birmingham, Liverpool, Manchester, Newcastle, Leeds-Bradford and Sheffield/South Yorkshire) ten years later, following yet another Royal Commission (Redcliffe-Maud) on local government, this time established by a Labour government. Here, however, the major institutional strain had been and was between the great cities – all single-tier county boroughs – at the centre of these conurbations – and the counties surrounding them, especially the conflicts between Manchester and Cheshire and Birmingham and Worcestershire over sites for new housing, battles which also reflected important party political differences. The cities were Labour strongholds, whilst the counties were heavily dominated by the Conservatives.

Like the Herbert Commission before it, the Redcliffe–Maud Report was stronger on service efficiency than democracy. It was also bolder in its recommendations than were the politicians when it came to implementing the report. The report laid more stress on what it deemed were 'objective' environmental factors – the interdependence of home, work and leisure activities in the conurbations and their surrounding countryside; the housing needs of the large cities; transportation issues and planning – which the Commission believed required a 'metropolitan tier' to tackle them effectively. Essentially, as Flynn *et al.* (1985: 25) note, both reports drew attention to the inadequacy of existing institutional arrangements to handle the increasingly complex economic and social environment of the metropolitan areas. And like its predecessor, but in an interesting departure from its basic preference for a unitary structure, Redcliffe–Maud Report advocated a two-tier metropolitan structure. But before the Labour government could implement the report, it was defeated in a general election – leaving the report's fate in the hands of a Conservative government less committed to the report's preference for a unitary system generally and to the kind of territorial extensions implied by its proposals for metropolitan reform, although its manifesto did give a commitment to reform of the local government structure.

In introducing the reforms in the metropolitan areas, the new Conservative government followed in the footsteps of their predecessors, with calculations of the political consequences an important element in the decisions. As with the GLC, the proposed boundaries of the new metropolitan counties were drawn much more tightly than in the original proposals, though two new metropolitan authorities (South Yorkshire and Tyne and Wear) were added; education was given to the lower-tier boroughs, as was the taxing power – thus loosening the tie at the metropolitan level between taxing and spending. Thus the metropolitan counties raised their finance to cover their expenditures effectively by levying a charge (precept) on the lower-tier authorities, something which was later to lead to accusations of profligate spending by the metropolitan counties. And as with the GLC, several last-minute amendments to the legislation weakened the territorial proposals still further.

Functionally, although they did not have responsibility for education, the metropolitan counties were responsible for police, the fire service, refuse disposal, trading standards and consumer protection, and for public transport. They shared responsibility with the metropolitan districts for land use planning – with the counties having the strategic responsibility, though the scope for interpretation of this provision often meant there was disagreement between the counties and districts over precisely what constituted a strategic matter. The counties also shared responsibility for cultural and leisure activities, and for local economic development.

The metropolitan districts were responsible for education, social services, libraries, housing, refuse collection and environmental (public) health. As a result the districts determined the bulk of the expenditure (around 74 per cent: Flynn *et al.* 1985: 77).

As with London, the system in the metropolitan areas outside London depended on willing cooperation between the two levels. Such cooperation was not always forthcoming, especially in the land use area, notwithstanding some improvements generally because transport, strategic planning and highways were all at the upper tier – which allowed, for example, some choice to be made in terms of public transport versus road building, something not easily achieved previously. Innovations in integrated public transport, for example, were noticeable in Tyne and Wear, Merseyside and West Midlands. The production of strategic structure plans proceeded to schedule, but generally lacked strong political commitment to their contents, which did not help decision making in relation to specific land use matters. Similarly, whilst some metropolitan counties took strong action in relation to policy areas such as culture, leisure and economic development, so did many of the metropolitan districts – again cooperation was not always forthcoming and proposals were not always compatible (Flynn *et al.* 1985: 82). But in those areas where the metropolitan counties had full responsibility for services, such as waste disposal, trading standards and consumer protection, there was certainly some improvement on what went before reform. Furthermore, whilst in accountability terms voters were no less supportive of the metropolitan counties than they were of the GLC, they lacked friends in high places. With conflict between the metropolitan counties and the districts increasing in the early 1980s, largely as a result of partisan and territorial differences, not surprisingly in the circumstances, change was on the way. The arrival of a new Conservative government in 1979, with Mrs Thatcher at its head, was to herald the eventual dismantling of metropolitan government in England, leaving the country as the only one in Western Europe without some form of area-wide government for its capital city.

In part perhaps this development was not unexpected. In London the GLC proved unable to produce a strategic plan quickly, if only because of the cumbersome planning procedures that were in place. The authority continued to be involved in constant struggles over such issues as housing and transport, where it lacked the powers necessary for it to have real impact. Education was given to a separate body, the Inner London Education Authority (ILEA – which operated in the same area as the old LCC had done) or to the lower tier. Political control swung too and fro between Labour and Conservative, with the latter less willing to push the GLC's strategic interests. Victory in the 1980s for a radical left Labour group in the GLC elections and the election of Ken Livingstone as the leader of the new GLC council, radically opposed to the Thatcher policies of the time, provided an excellent excuse for her to abolish the GLC – and the other metropolitan counties as well – removing what was seen as a 'wasteful tier' of government (Young 1986; O'Leary 1987), notwithstanding Sharpe's (1995b: 21) comment that 'GLC abolition is one of the most bizarre in the history of Western government'. Outside London, where the case was certainly less clear-cut, lack of political support, no widespread enthusiasm for the upper metropolitan tier and increasing conflicts between the two tiers and with central government made reform virtually inevitable, despite considerable anti-abolition campaigning by the counties themselves.

After abolition: no chaos, gentle decline?

The London experience

As Pimlott and Rao (2002: 45) note, 'the abolition of the GLC [...] left London's future in the hands of ministers, the 32 London boroughs, and a web of joint arrangements'. As a result decision making became highly fragmented, with

Whitehall increasingly becoming involved. Yet the system continued to function, as it did elsewhere in the English metropolitan areas, so the expected crisis did not arise. As required by the Local Government Act 1985, a London Coordinating Committee was established, chaired by the leader from Croydon, whilst responsibility for all policy and expenditure decisions rested with the London Boroughs Grants Committee (LBGC), a body set up effectively to take over as a funding source from the GLC, but funded by all the boroughs on a population basis. In order to avoid a possible funding crisis and further political unpopularity, the Conservative government gave London an unexpectedly generous grant settlement for the first year of operation of the new system, a settlement which effectively allowed funding levels to be maintained at GLC levels.

As elsewhere, the organisation of the former GLC functions was undertaken on a joint basis with one of the boroughs acting as the lead authority. Thus, for example, research was lead by Islington and the London Planning Advisory Committee (LPAC) by Havering. But one effect of reorganisation was to shift primary responsibility for planning away from the local authorities to Whitehall, so that the powers of LPAC were largely advisory and not executive. LPAC also revealed a weakness in the new system, in that its partisan political makeup largely prevented it from ever really presenting a London-wide perspective. In education, ILEA became an independent authority in its own right, with elected members responsible for education within the twelve inner boroughs and the City of London. Its penchant for high spending, together with criticisms of the quality of education provided, quickly attracted government attention, and ILEA was abolished in 1990, with the education function moving to the boroughs.

A third important body was the London Residual Body (LRB), an appointed agency charged with dealing with the GLC's loan debt and other legal liabilities. It also assumed responsibility for a number of other tasks not transferred directly to the boroughs, including pensions, but also for selling off the former GLC's assets.

By 1990, however, further change was afoot. John Major, Thatcher's successor as prime minister and leader of the Conservative party, was determined not to have a new GLC emerge, despite initial moves in that direction. He rejected a directly elected executive (mayor) in favour of having a Cabinet sub-committee responsible for coordinating the central government departments dealing with London, and appointed a minister to be responsible for London affairs. In 1994, as with the rest of the country, London received a new regional government office (GOL).

Notwithstanding these developments, which effectively served to place London further under the direct control of the central government, but which also increased the part played by the boroughs (Pimlott and Rao 2002: 52), concerns about the ability of London to remain economically competitive internationally continued to be expressed by many London businesses. In 1992, a collaborative body, London First, brought together borough leaders, leading private sector interests and the voluntary sector to act as a London-wide promotion and development organisation. Chaired by a leading businessman, the organisation quickly took the lead in the debate about the future of London government and in promoting a new vision for London, establishing the London Pride Partnership in response to the government's City Pride initiative.[5] Despite some internal divisions (the private sector seeking new development in the central part of London, the outer boroughs' concerns for their economic future), London First and the London Pride initiative gave a considerable boost to the promotion of London internationally, whilst also helping to push much-needed infrastructure developments up the political agenda. Despite this development, however, the continuing fragmentation of London's government continued to be seen as a problem – the need to tackle this fragmentation in a more coordinated fashion being increasingly recognised as the decade wore on.

By the 1997 election, the main parties were divided in terms of their view of how London should be governed. Whilst the Conservatives wished to maintain the status quo, Labour had been convinced since the early 1990s of the need for some form of metropolitan government for London but did not wish to return to a GLC. They wanted something more streamlined – and found it in the ideas which the Conservatives had rejected – a directly elected mayor plus an elected assembly.[6]

When the new Labour government was elected in 1997, events moved quickly. A consultation paper, 'New Leadership for London', was published ahead of a referendum on the question in May 1998. Despite heavy campaigning for the proposals, the turnout in the referendum fell below that for London local elections generally. Whilst over 70 per cent of those voting voted in favour of the idea of an elected mayor, turnout reached only 28 per cent. As Pimlott and Rao (2002: 70) put it, the result 'was a muted triumph for Labour'. Worse was to follow, as the government began to realise that Ken Livingstone, the old leader of the GLC at the time of its abolition, was the strongest candidate for the position of mayor – the one person Tony Blair did not wish to see in the post.

The legislation designed to turn the simple idea of a directly elected mayor into reality proved complex, particularly given the government's fear that a strong mayor might prove an embarrassment. In essence, the legislation provided for a mayor whose position is effectively quite weak. His main responsibility is for strategy – with planning and transport to the fore. He shares executive responsibility with a number of agencies (e.g. Transport for London, responsible for the London metro) and the boroughs. He is accountable to the Greater London Assembly, to whom he has to present a budget, but which requires a two-thirds majority to reject the mayor's proposals and budget. Above all the legislation provides for the Secretary of State (relevant government minister) to act if he or she considers the mayor's proposals contradict government policy or if he or she considers the budget excessive. This led the main opposition spokesman on London to claim that 'the first mayor of London is going to be John Prescott (then Secretary of State) because he is going to have more powers than the Mayor' (Hansard, 17 December 1998, quoted in Pimlott and Rao 2002: 73).

This situation did not deter Livingstone from running as a candidate for mayor. He first attempted to win the Labour party nomination, but was defeated. He decided to run as an independent candidate, despite having promised the

Labour party that he would not do so, and despite being thrown out of the party. For the government and the prime minister, the result was an embarrassment, equalled only by a similar degree of ineptitude on the part of the Conservative party.[7]

In the May 2000 election for mayor, on a 33 per cent turnout, Livingstone secured a convincing victory, polling almost as much as the Conservative and Labour candidates obtained together, with the Labour party candidate, Frank Dobson (a former Secretary of State for Health) beaten into third place.[8] As Pimlott and Rao comment:

> It was a reverse for Blair, who had done everything in his power to prevent it happening. Yet in a way it was also a vindication of the philosophy around the mayoralty idea, showing that the ideas of a well-known individual as the capital's leader appealed to the voters and indicating that Londoners took the powers seriously enough to decide for themselves.
>
> (Pimlott and Rao 2002: 94)

Elections to the twenty-five-member Greater London Assembly (GLA) took place at the same time, resulting in the Conservative and Labour parties each having nine seats, the Liberal Democrats four and the Greens three. With no clear majority, it seemed as if the Assembly would help build consensus and help it scrutinise and check the Mayor rather than be dominated by him – or indeed control him. Allowing for a transition period, the mayor and assembly duly took office on 3 July 2000.

Three years later, it is still too soon to pass a final judgement on the effectiveness of the new system. At best, the results are mixed, for a variety of reasons. Given that the mayor has only limited financial resources and given that he has to work with so many different agencies, there was never any real chance that Livingstone could adopt a strong mayoral role. His role is one essentially designed to develop strategy – which in turn has to be implemented by others. Three policy areas are significant in this respect: transport, crime and economic development.

Livingstone believed that transport was the major concern for Londoners. To date, he has met with one failure (largely over the modernisation of the Underground) and one unexpected success. The latter concerns the introduction of congestion charges early in 2003 – something his opponents believed would be immensely unpopular, administratively incompetent and doomed to failure. It has proved a great success, reducing congestion in the central areas, improving bus journey times, and has met with few administrative difficulties. As far as the Underground was concerned, however, Livingstone was unable to defeat the government over its proposals for modernisation. The latter preferred a major form of public–private partnership, along similar lines to those implemented in rail privatisation. Livingstone wanted a more public form of organisation, and for modernisation to be funded on the basis of bonds, similar to the way in which the New York metro has been revitalised. Despite opposing the government for months and winning several symbolic victories in the media and despite popular support (and that of several London parliamentarians) for his position, a judicial review of the process found in favour of the government – an almost inevitable outcome given the government's strong commitment to its original proposals. Only the future will tell whether or not the government was correct – the only clear outcome is that the delay and disagreements between the mayor and the government only served to frighten the private sector companies involved, to the extent that they raised the cost of their participation considerably.

Crime, and more particularly the fear of crime, has been a concern of Londoners for some time. In effect, this concern is a reflection of considerable economic differences between different parts of London (with areas of consider-able poverty and unemployment in the eastern part of the metropolis), suggesting problems of social cohesion. Here the mayor was in a more difficult position, having to work with another agency, the Metropolitan Policy Authority (MPA), only some of whose members were mayoral nominations, and whose chair was elected from amongst the members of the authority. The Metropolitan Policing Srategy set four key priorities – the first three to make the streets safer by reducing street crime; to reduce burglary rates; and to reduce the level of drug-related crime, particularly by reducing the supply of drugs. But it was the fourth priority which was to attract most attention, namely to reduce hate or race-related crime. Problems of institutional racism within the Metropolitan Police (and other agencies) made this more difficult, and the MPA tackled it by setting targets designed to deal with such discrimination issues as gender, disability, race and age. In addition, considerable weight was placed on more effective local working through the establishment of Community Safety Units.

Most of these moves were in line with the priorities for policing which the mayor himself had. But his influence is very much arm's length. In effect, he can be a stimulus for change or action – as he himself put it he was 'elected... to tell these people to get their act together and that is what I shall do' (*Evening Standard*, 30 June 2000, quoted in Pimlott and Rao 2002: 136).

The third policy area of importance for the mayor was economic development. Again his role is strategic, with implementation in the hands of other agencies. In essence, his strategy has been underlain by three priorities. First, maintaining London (i.e. the City) as an economically competitive centre. Second, concern for regeneration, especially to the east of the City, where de-industrialisation had meant severe job losses and plant closures; and, finally, the need to see that more affordable housing was made available, especially given the difficulty London has faced in attracting workers to key public sector jobs in areas such as educa-tion, social work and health. In practice, the mayor is responsible for producing spatial and economic development strategies (SDS/EDS), though the latter is under the effective control of the London Development Agency (LDA). The mayor's strategy (perhaps surprisingly given his background) has been effec-tively market led – strong on maintaining the competitive position of London, less clear on redistributive questions. In this he met criticism from the assembly in its scrutiny role – who believed that both the SDSs and EDSs should have a stronger role in planning and regulating for social purposes. In effect the mayor's vision ('Ken's plan', as the strategic document was known) favours growth, particularly in the City and its surrounding areas rather than in outer London – either east or west, and as such would also find support from some boroughs difficult to win. Perhaps such a conclusion is inevitable – as a mayor of a city with a larger population than New York and covering a wider area than Paris, Livingstone is likely to put world city concerns ahead of those of outer suburbs, recognising how much more difficult it is to represent areas less identifiable than the core city (Buck *et al.* 2002: 388–392).[9] But in terms of the mayor's capacity to influence change generally, he appears weak, still having to forge working relationships with the boroughs, the bureaucracy, numerous quangos and the central government. Whilst his readmission to the Labour party in early 2004 might help some of these relationships, his welcome by the party had more to do with considerations of its overall electoral chances in 2004/2005 than with any recognition of the continuing problems London's mayor and governmental institutions might face (Travers 2003: 182–210). The GLA, with limited powers which it has not used well, has not been an effective scrutinising body or really able to influence policy (Travers 2003: 193–194). Its experience does not augur well for elected regional assemblies elsewhere in England, should voters decide they want them. Overall, despite several attempts at reform, London still lacks effective governance capacity. London's government remains an oddity, and in the view of at least one observer, further reform is inevitable, though not in the immediate future (Travers 2002, 2003).

The experience outside London

Also far from descending into anticipated chaos, the metropolitan areas outside London generally managed to maintain service delivery and levels in the years following abolition (Leach *et al.* 1991). What one did see was what might best be considered a process of gradual decline, especially in London, where by the early 1990s there were already calls for the reintroduction of some kind of area-wide authority (Travers *et al.* 1991; Sharpe 1995b). Outside London, voluntary arrangements for cooperation made in advance of abolition largely remained intact, reflecting some policy areas where former metropolitan county initiatives had been appreciated by many districts, such as in economic development, public transport or in the provision of country parks and the management of derelict land. In other service areas, such as waste disposal, the districts quickly came to appreciate the difficulties of running such a highly interconnected service on anything less than the county scale (Leach *et al.* 1991: 56). And some of the district political leaders recognised the value of the county level, especially when political values were widely shared, as for example amongst leaders of a Labour persuasion. The 1985 Abolition Act required that districts' Coordinating Committees be established in each former county area, and Leach *et al.* (1991: 64) note that in each county significant leadership roles in such committees were played by politicians who came from districts other than the dominant core authority. In Greater Manchester it was the leader of Wigan who played this role, whilst in the West Midlands the task fell to the leader of Dudley, and in South Yorkshire it was played by the Rotherham leader. The willingness of local political leaders to cooperate for the common good of all the districts was a marked feature of much of the post-abolition period, as we see later.

By what might be seen as almost a chance turn of fate, an external development certainly helped to encourage this kind of political and administrative cooperation – namely the development of EU cohesion policy and the associated structural funds. Conservative government policies from the early 1980s onwards both severely restricted local government taxing and spending and at the same time contributed to the fragmentation of local government in the metropolitan areas by the introduction of special-purpose bodies and agencies (Davis 1996; Harding *et al.* 2000). Not without considerable difficulty, some cities (notably Birmingham and Manchester) began to exploit EU funding opportunities. Further reform of the structural funds at the end of the 1980s led to increased numbers of English metropolitan areas being eligible and able to exploit EU regional policy possibilities. Given, however, that EU cohesion policy required such programmes to be organised on a partnership basis (national – local as well as between different local agencies, local governments, the voluntary and private sectors), local level cooperation (especially amongst the political leaders involved) was essential (Harding 1997; GFA Consulting and European Institute of Urban Affairs 1998).

Manchester, in the north-west of England, provides an excellent example of how this process of cooperation worked to the advantage of the constituent local governments in the metropolitan area (Deas and Hebbert 1999; Hebbert and Deas 2000; Quilley 2000). The Coordination Committee (the Association of Greater Manchester Authorities, AGMA) established under the abolition legislation still exists today. Based in Wigan on the western periphery of the metropolitan area, it allows all the ten districts to speak with one voice, which has helped when making bids either to central government on matters such as transport (Manchester had the first of the recent crop of tramway systems, for example, and it is now being further extended) or to the EU for structural funds. AGMA is small – a group of five staff and with no technical responsibilities – it simply prepares the agenda for AGMA politicians, takes minutes. At the technical level, a number of working groups and specialist bodies have been created. In the case of the latter, this has meant that some former Greater Manchester units have been retained – for example, research and information, the transportation unit, county records, geology and archaeological units, etc. – and some new ones created – Planning Officers Group; Strategic Planning and Information Group etc. (see Deas and Hebbert 1999: 173–175). And most of these groups/ activities have their coordinating centre in a different local government in the metropolitan area. This lead authority approach has meant that only Salford, Rochdale and Stockport do not have some area-wide functional responsibility.

The result of this approach is that there exist strong area-wide political and professional networks which have been able to work together and, where necessary, solve differences and find solutions. It has also helped in permitting pragmatic approaches to be adopted when opportunities for action arise. Political leaders, particularly in Manchester and its neighbouring authorities Salford and Trafford, were prepared to compromise and cooperate, and as a result the Manchester authorities were able to exploit national and European funding opportunities which have led to the redevelopment of the old Manchester docks, the building of a new exhibition and conference centre, a concert hall, and new museum and art gallery, and to making (unsuccessful) bids for the 1996 and 2000 Olympic Games as well as a successful one for the 2002 Commonwealth Games.

Here the involvement of private sector elites, in partnership with the various local governments, was crucial, if largely opportunistic. Whilst Manchester exhibits many of the features of a classic regime in Stone's (1989) sense, most commentators would argue that in practice it was not as tightly knit or focused as such a regime requires (Peck and Tickell 1995; Harding 1997). What is clear is that business interests saw possibilities for profit by engaging with the relevant munici-palities, particularly in infrastructure projects such as the new light rail(tram)way and airport development, as well as the flagship projects already mentioned. Others saw the possibility of housing development through the conversion of old industrial warehouses into loft and apartment accommodation, especially, but not only, in the city of Manchester. Last but not least, the explosion of an IRA bomb in Manchester city centre provided an unwanted but willingly accepted opportunity to redevelop much of the commercial and shopping part of the city, including its prestigious Royal Exchange Theatre.

All of these examples provided business opportunities, but they occurred within a political environment which encouraged the private sector to work with public authorities. Whilst central government provided a legislative and policy framework within which such partnerships were encouraged, political leaders (especially in Manchester, Salford and Trafford) adopted a collaborative stance, not only with each other, but with the private sector as well. The success, for example, of the Manchester area under the City Pride initiative in 1994 and with the Olympic/Commonwealth Games bids allowed the area to develop a vision of itself and, for its core central city as the regional economic centre, a place of quality shopping, leisure and cultural activities as well as a major sporting centre designed to make it a rival to other European cities such as Barcelona, Milan, Frankfurt and Lyons (Peck 1995; Peck and Tickell 1995; Taylor *et al.* 1996; Deas and Hebbert 1999).

During this time perhaps only Birmingham and to a lesser extent Leeds were able to rival Manchester's success. Like Manchester, Birmingham set out to establish itself as a truly European city, also using structural funds to enable it to do so. It also adopted a Big Project approach. And again an adaptive, pragmatic political leadership was important in achieving these goals. And in many ways Leeds did the same, a city with a tradition of strong municipal government, often under the Labour party, but a tradition also based on pragmatism. Cole and John (2001: 102–117) argue that Leeds has always had a history of strong political leadership, based on the fact that Leeds City Council is a large authority which requires strong leaders to pull its somewhat unwieldy organisation together. They suggest its political culture is 'hierarchical, closed and deferential' (Cole and John 2001: 103).

This strong municipal culture was challenged by the abolition of the metropolitan counties in the mid-1980s and the further reforms introduced by the Conservative into the 1990s. Strong leadership is what allowed the authority to adapt and to work with others, especially with the local chamber of commerce, in the area of economic developments under what was known as the Leeds Initiative. And again, as Cole and John note (2001: 106), this kind of local partnership 'allowed the city to play the grants game more effectively'.[10]

Though the other metropolitan areas, such as Tyne and Wear, South Yorkshire/Sheffield and Merseyside/Liverpool, may not have achieved quite the same degree of change as Manchester, Birmingham or Leeds, even here the impact of strong political and administrative leadership, strengthening local partnerships across different sectors, and the benefits of EU funding under the regionally targeted structural fund's Objective 1 and Objective 2 have produced important developments. For example, Liverpool will be the European City of Culture for 2008; Newcastle and Gateshead in the Tyne and Wear area can boast several new economic and cultural facilities. In all cases willingness to work in partnership and in cooperation with others, but with a strong sense of political leadership, has been the key to success.

Nevertheless, there remain doubts about the extent to which such willingness to cooperate persists over time, and how long individual leaders with a commitment to partnership working remain in place. Private sector CEOs change, as do the heads of other public sector organisations, quangos and NGOs. Even relatively long-serving local politicians can be defeated in local elections, and both they and local bureaucrats can move on to other things. As these changes occur, the commitment to collaboration may weaken; the rules of the 'partnership game' may change, whilst national governments may introduce new legislation. Such has been the case in England, where legislation now permits the introduction of regional assemblies subject to a positive vote in a referendum. Such votes will occur in a number of English regions in 2004, particularly in the North-East and North-West. But the proposed regional assemblies have few powers, like the GLA, and also require a restructuring of local government at sub-regional level. Such a move is likely to involve the disappearance of county councils and county districts and their replacement by a smaller number of even larger unitary authorities. Whilst the current metropolitan unitary boroughs are not threatened, there are no proposals to strengthen the present system of metropolitan governance, for example by considering some kind of structure/institution to operate at the city region level. Unlike their counterparts in other West European countries, the British government is reluctant to allow diverse, multi-level sub-national institutions. Perhaps by not doing so the government not only threatens its own hopes of success for the introduction of regional assemblies, but puts at risk the continued adaptation of major city regions to the changing global environment in which they operate.

Conclusions

In their introductory chapter, Kübler and Heinelt set out an analytical framework within which one might assess the performance of metropolitan governance. They suggest the assessment takes place over three different dimensions. The first is a local government dimension in which institutional arrangements are assessed in terms of their input or output orientation. In effect this measure reflects the traditional criteria for assessing local government systems according to their democratic or efficiency characteristics.

The second dimension they call the civil society dimension, in which one is concerned to assess how strong or weak civil society actually is, as well as how far institutional arrangements encourage civil participation in the affairs of the metropolis. Where the civil society is strong and widespread citizen participation through forms of deliberative democracy is strongly encouraged, institutional arrangements may be less important than is the case where civil society is weak, and where the structure and processes may help strengthen civil society.

The third dimension concerns the policy networks of private, associational and public sector actors which emerge in the new metropolitan governance context. Here the concern is the extent to which such networks are open or closed, and how far a balance between these two extremes can be achieved.

How does metropolitan government and governance in England come out on these measures? Along with others, Kübler and Heinelt note the extent to which British local government has traditionally been concerned (and continues to be so) with service provision and efficiency, and less so with democratic concerns over and above a provision for some form of representative democracy. Changes associated first with the Conservative governments of the 1980s and 1990s saw a move from government to governance (Stoker 1999), though still with a stress on efficiency, whilst under the Blair governments since 1997 there has been some attempt at democratic renewal at the local level.

Despite these latter changes, as well as the introduction of an elected mayor and new assembly for London, and the possibility of elected mayors in other metropolitan boroughs, metropolitan governance in England is still more heavily output orientated. Even the London reforms reflect the government's concern with efficient service delivery, reflected in the strong powers which the relevant minister has to overrule the mayor's decisions.

In terms of the second dimension, the strength of civil society, the attempted moves to improve local democracy and to produce more accountable local leadership through elected mayors still leave civil society weak. Turnout in local elections remains amongst the lowest worldwide, and the reforms in London have not provided a significant boost to the numbers voting. Fragmented metropolitan governance outside London means civil society – especially in the form of voluntary associations – has great difficulty in engaging at the metropolitan-wide level. Even the reformed London, with its new elected assembly, remains weak in this respect.

Moves towards governance over the last twenty years or so have greatly improved the access of private sector bodies (especially big business) at the metropolitan level. The importance of the business-led London First campaign in leading to the introduction of an elected mayor and assembly for Greater London – in effect giving London back its area-wide institutions – has already been noted, as has the mayor's predilection for supporting business (and particularly City) interests at the expense of others. In the other metropolitan areas, a concern with infrastructure and large-scale projects stressing the (at least) European scale of the major cities involved also reflects the influence of business interests, as the Manchester case demonstrates. And whilst the voluntary sector has often been at the table, its presence has been as much the result of funding rules (European and national) as a reflection of the real interest local elites have shown in involving such groups. And given the division of local government functions, such groups are much more likely to find their interests best served by engaging with the metropolitan boroughs than with the wider-area coalition of interests. Thus, insofar as the policy networks are open, access is biased, mobilisation being towards the major business interests rather than towards smaller voluntary or territorial bodies.

Such a picture undoubtedly holds true when one takes a historical perspective on metropolitan government and governance in England. Such a finding is hardly surprising, especially when one remembers the strong role political parties have played in English local government since the early twentieth century – and before. With Labour and Conservative parties effectively reflecting the old class divisions of British society until the late 1960s and early 1970s, and given Labour's domination of much of England's metropolitan landscape even to today, issues of equality, equity and redistribution were part and parcel of metropolitan political life. But over the last thirty years class-based politics and parties have become less relevant to British political life, and the link between local and national politics more complex. In a political system where the centre dominates everything and has no real trust in the locality, in effect the forms and processes of metropolitan governance and government matter little. The result is that English metropolitan governance is far from the ideal position represented by the Kübler and Heinelt cube.

This review also importantly suggests two other things. First, as other authors have noted (John 2001; Le Galès 2002), there is the importance of political leadership in securing successful metropolitan governance. Whether it be Morrison in the case of the old LCC or Livingstone with the new Greater London Authority, or the emergence of important leaders in other metropolitan areas since abolition, the ability of key figures – political and economic – to work together to develop and implement a vision for their metropolis is a, if not the, key to ensuring that the continuing fragmented governance systems in English metropolitan areas actually work, delivering the policies and services which ensure successful economic development and social cohesion. Second, and in opposition to the first, there remains the overwhelmingly centralised British government which remains largely unwilling and unable to grapple with the institutional problems that modern metropolitan governance continues to pose.

Notes

1 Outside London the problem of city government was solved by the introduction in 1835 of municipal boroughs and later in 1888 of the county boroughs – single-tier bodies responsible for a wide range of services covering the then extant built-up areas throughout England. This system remained in place and served remarkably well until the reforms of the 1960s which are discussed below.

2 By the 1930s, the LCC was Labour controlled – a fact which did not stop some of the Labour-controlled London boroughs also opposing some of the LCC's housing plans. See Young and Garside (1982); Young and Kramer (1978).

3 The Greater London Group, led by the formidable Professor Robson, long-time critic of the existing system, favoured a two-tier structure. The other group, based at University College London and led by the sociologists Ruth Glass and John Westergaard, was less wedded to reform, making a case for the retention of the old LCC (Pimlott and Rao 2002: 26).

4 Interestingly, in a response to teacher organisation representations, the government also introduced an additional (elected) educational body – based on the old LCC boundaries – namely the Inner London Education Authority.

5 The Major government's City Pride initiative permitted a number of cities, including London, to develop a vision for their future development. Acceptance by the government meant extra funding could be available for specific projects within the City Pride document.

6 In adopting this policy, the influence of Tony Blair was crucial. He became convinced of the idea following the work of the Commission for Local Democracy in the mid-1990s, supported by a number of prominent London politicians who were subsequently to hold office in the new Labour government. For a discussion of this development, see Pimlott and Rao (2002: 55–61).

7 The party's initial candidate was Lord (Jeffrey) Archer, well-known novelist, forced to stand down when found guilty in a case for which he was sent to prison for four years. After initially barring him from the short list, the party then adopted as their second choice Stephen Norris, a former MP with a reputation as a womaniser, but who had considerable experience of London's problems.

8 For a discussion of the campaign and an analysis of the results see *inter alia* Alderman (2000); D'Arcy and Maclean (2000); Rallings and Thrasher (2000).

9 This view is underlined by the mayor's support for London's bid for the 2012 Olympic Games and the financial resources he has also committed to it.

10 As Cole and John (2001) note, the hierarchical and closed structure of the city council worked against it in other areas such as education. Following a highly critical Office of Standards in Education Report in 1999, the city lost control of education to a joint venture company in 2001.

Bibliography

Alderman, K. (2000) 'The Selection of the Conservative and Labour London Mayoral Candidates', *Parliamentary Affairs*, 53: 737–752.

Buck, N., Gordon, I., Hall, P., Harloe, M. and Kleinman, M. (2002) *Working Capital*, London: Routledge.

Cole, A. and John, P. (2001) *Local Governance in England and France*, London: Routledge.

D'Arcy, M. and Maclean, R. (2000) *Nightmare: The Race to Become London's Mayor*, London: Politico's.

Davis, H. (ed.) (1996) *Quangos and Local Government: A Changing World*, London: Frank Cass.

Deas, I. and Hebbert, M. (1999) 'Villes, métropole ou region? Les territoires de la mobilisation à Manchester', in B. Jouve and C. Lefevre (eds), *Villes, métropoles – le nouveaux territoires du politique*, Paris: Anthropos: 163–190.

Flynn, N., Leach, S. and Vielba, C. (1985) *Abolition or Reform? The GLC and the Metropolitan County Councils*, London: Allen and Unwin.

Game, C. (1987) 'Public Attitudes towards the Mets', *Local Government Studies*, 13(5).

GFA Consulting and European Institute of Urban Affairs (1998) *Building Partnerships in the English Regions: A Study Report of Regional and Sub-Regional Partnerships in England*, London: Department of Environment, Transport and the Regions.

Goldsmith, M. and Garrard, J.A. (2000) 'Urban Governance: Some Reflections', in R.J. Morris and R.H. Trainor (eds), *Urban Governance. Britain and Beyond since 1750*, Ashgate: Aldershot: 15–27.

Harding, A. (1997) 'Urban Regimes in a Europe of the Cities?', *European Urban and Regional Studies*, 4: 291–334.

Harding, A., Wilks-Heeg, S. and Hutchins, M. (2000) 'Business, Government and the Business of Urban Governance', *Urban Studies*, 37(5–6): 975–994.

Hebbert, M. and Deas, I. (2000) 'Greater Manchester – "Up and Going"?', *Policy and Politics*, 28(1): 79–92.

John, P. (2001) *Local Governance in Europe*, London: Sage.

Leach, S., Davis, H., Game, C. and Skelcher, C. (1991) *After Abolition*, Birmingham: Institute of Local Government Studies.

Le Galès, P. (2002) *European Cities*, Oxford: OUP.

O'Leary, B. (1987) 'Why was the GLC Abolished?', *International Journal of Urban and Regional Research*, 11(2): 193–217.

Peck, J. (1995) 'Moving and Shaking: Business Elites, State Localism and Urban Privatism', *Progress in Human Geography*, 19: 16–46.

Peck, J. and Tickell, A. (1995) 'Business Goes Local: Dissecting "the Business Agenda" in Manchester', *International Journal of Urban and Regional Research*, 19(3): 251–265.

Pimlott, B. and Rao, N. (2002) *Governing London*, Oxford: OUP.

Quilley, S. (2000) 'Manchester First: From Municipal Socialism to Entrepreneurial City', *International Journal of Urban and Regional Research*, 24(3): 601–615.

Rallings, C. and Thrasher, M. (2000) 'Personality, Politics and Protest Voting', *Parliamentary Affairs*, 53(4): 753–764.

Rhodes, G. (1970) *The Government of Greater London*, London: Allen and Unwin.

Sharpe, L.J. (ed.) (1995a) *The Government of World Cities: The Future of the Metro Model*, London: John Wiley.

——(1995b) 'The Abolition of the Greater London Council: Is there a Case for Resurrection?', in L.J. Sharpe (ed.), *The Government of World Cities*: 11–130.

Smallwood, F. (1965) *Greater London: The Politics of Metropolitan Reform*, New York: Bobbs Merrill.

Stoker, G. (ed.) (1999) *The New Management of British Local Governance*, Basingstoke: Macmillan.

Stone, C. (1989) *Regime Politics*, Kansas: Kansas University Press.

——(1995) 'Political Leadership in Urban Politics', in D. Judge, G. Stoker and H. Wolman (eds), *Theories of Urban Politics*, London: Sage: 96–116.

Taylor, I., Evans, K. and Fraser, P. (1996) *A Tale of Two Cities: Global Change, Local Feeling and Everyday Life in the North of England. A Study in Manchester and Sheffield*, Routledge: London.

Travers, T. (2002) 'Decentralisation London Style: The GLA and London Governance', *Regional Studies*, 36(7): 779–788.

——(2003) *The Politics of London: Governing an Ungovernable City*, Basingstoke: Palgrave.

Travers, T., Jones, G.W., Herbert M. and Burnham, J.J. (1991) *The Government of London*, London: Joseph Rowntree Foundation.

Young, K. (1986) 'Metropolis RIP?', *Political Quarterly*, 57(1).

Young, K. and Garside, P. (1982) *Metropolitan London: Politics and Urban Change, 1837–1981*, London: Edward Arnold.

Young, K. and Kramer, J. (1978) *Strategy and Conflict in Metropolitan Housing: Suburbia versus the Greater London Council*, London: Heinemann.

7 Arrested metropolitanism

Limits and contradictions of municipal governance reform in Los Angeles, Montreal and Toronto

Roger Keil and Julie-Anne Boudreau

Introduction

Towards the end of the 1990s, a perplexing situation occurred in three of the largest North American cities.[1] In Toronto and Los Angeles conservative political forces restructured the system of urban governance. In Montreal, the centre-left provincial government equally undertook metropolitan restructuring projects modelled partly on Toronto, but legitimised by a different ideological discourse. In Toronto an aggressively neo-liberal provincial Ontario government amalgamated six individual municipal governments and one regional administration. Simultaneously, a powerful secessionist movement began to threaten to split the San Fernando Valley, and perhaps other districts, from the City of Los Angeles. In Montreal, the provincial government merged the twenty-eight municipalities on the Island of Montreal into a single city, combined with the creation of a larger metropolitan body. In all three cases, questions of boundaries, efficiency, scale and democracy were central to the efforts to alter the form and substance of urban government (Keil 2000).

The puzzling aspect of this restructuring is, of course, that in Los Angeles and Toronto ideologically driven conservatives took opposing positions – in one case proposing to split large parts of the suburbs from the inner city; in the other case by promoting an amalgamation of smaller municipal governments. In Montreal, social democrats trying to find a 'third way', mixing neo-liberalism with statist social interventions (known as the Quebec model), adopted the same restructuring plan as conservatives in Ontario by promoting municipal mergers.

While questions of institutional size and geographical boundaries are important in discussions of local governance reform, there is another story to be told beyond the predictable issues of efficiency, effectiveness and equity. The classical division (often ideological and hotly contested) between separationists and consolidationists (Keating 1995) is perhaps only of secondary importance compared to the split between those political actors who favour democratisation, social justice and ecological integrity, and those that propose, first and foremost, to protect the market economy (and the privileges and unequal freedoms associated with it) from what they regard as inappropriate efforts to impose social control. While this conflict can be considered typical for capitalist societies, it has received special significance during the current period of neo-liberal restructuring, as market ideologies and practices have gained in significance over other forms and ideas of social organisation and service delivery (Brenner 2002). The ability for this conflict to be resolved by consensus will depend on the incorporation of social movements (both on the left and on the right) into the governance accord. This 'structured coherence' (Harvey 1989) or regional mode of regulation based on a selective co-optation can only work if these social movements have themselves re-territorialised their social claims at that city-regional scale.

All tendencies to create more municipal autonomy and regional integration will have to be seen in the context of more broadly defined (and contested) trends towards a reform of federal relationships among various state levels. Urban-regional integration is clearly dependent on the continued re-articulation of state spaces and scales of political and social action in North American societies (Brenner *et al.* 2003).

After a brief introduction of comparative works on metropolitan governance in North America, we present our arguments in a double chronology. We first report on past metropolitan governance restructuring during the 'long 1990s', the time period roughly between the collapse of international property markets in the late 1980s and the events of 9/11/2001; we then discuss the more recent developments post-9/11/2001. Based on this context, we develop our arguments about (1) globalisation and unequal re-scalings; (2) the re-territorialisation of social movements; and (3) the de-radicalisation and re-articulation of social movement demands in the post-restructuring revision of municipal governance mechanisms such as the debates about municipal charters in Los Angeles and Toronto. We conclude with some reflections on the level of state capacities attained at the city-regional scale in North America, particularly in the sectors of competitiveness, transportation and the environment.

'The myth of the North American City': reflections in a period of 'porous post-Fordism'

A common typology of local government systems would place US and Canadian cities within the *Anglo* group, where local governments enjoy little legal powers, but exert autonomy in practice, particularly in terms of functional service delivery (Goldsmith 1996). Writing from a Canadian perspective, many urban theorists have felt uncomfortable with this categorisation (see, for instance, Goldberg and Mercer 1986). Much of this debate was rooted in a national quest for a collective identity distinct from the United States, while attempting to unite Canadians in a liberal nationalism largely influenced by beloved Prime Minister Trudeau and designed to counter the Quebec nationalist movement. Canadian cities, it was argued, are distinct from US cities.

Variations between the two countries' urban systems were highlighted in terms of their respective legal-institutional frameworks and in terms of national political cultures. Examples of differences in the former category would be (1) that states in the US have written constitutions, which means that they were able to incorporate, at the end of the nineteenth century, home rule provisions; (2) the heavier hand of the Federal government in urban affairs in the US than in Canada, where the most relevant level of government remains the province, which has played a much more aggressive role in municipal affairs than have US states;[2] or (3) the easy incorporation procedures in the US, supported by sympathetic courts.

In terms of national political cultures, Canadian theorists would insist on the central role of private property rights in the US (as enshrined in the Fifth Amendment). Howard Jarvis strikingly embodied this belief as the initiator of the tax revolt initiative called Proposition 13 in California. The Jarvis–Gann property tax limitation initiative was voted in by Californians in June 1978.[3] The central role of property rights in the US political culture has stripped local states of the ability effectively to control growth because of the difficulty in regulating land developers. In Canada, the provincial role in controlling both local governments and land use planning has tempered the pro-growth drive of urban politics. Moreover, property rights are not conceived as central to civil rights as is the case in the US (Garber and Imbroscio 1996: 606).

A second variation between the Canadian and the US political cultures is the meaning assigned to secession. In the US, secession is often understood as a moral and economic individual right: political legitimacy rests on the contractual consent of the people. When this contract is not honoured, secession is considered morally acceptable (Lehning 1998). Dominated by Québécois nationalist claims to sovereignty, discussions on secession in Canada edge more on a debate between communitarian and liberal philosophers and individual and collective rights (Carens 1995; Kymlicka 1998; Tully 1999).

This bilateral focus on national political cultures shaping urban politics was forcefully challenged as the urban political imaginary went through an important rescaling of how urban theorists and activists thought of their role and the role of Canadian cities. While the middle-class progressive regime in place in Toronto clung to its downtown-centred, multicultural, 'typically Canadian' self-image, American and Canadian radical theorists and activists were uncovering the taboos hidden behind these self-congratulating, dichotomising urban myths just as Canadian nationalism and the idea of static national political cultures were challenged by transformations in the North American and international political economy (Croucher 1997). In Montreal, where the desire to distinguish the city from its US counterparts was far less present, the middle-class progressive regime embodied in the Montreal Citizens Movement went through a process of neoliberalisation and suburbanisation to the point of its disappearance after the 2000 municipal mergers, just as Quebec nationalism was facing important political economic, multicultural, generational and linguistic challenges.

In a period of 'porous post-Fordism', where interactions between the US and Canada occur through multiple urban points rather than simply between two coherent national political cultures, North American cities are open to transnational flows and influences of all kinds (Keil and Kipfer 2003). These intersecting influences significantly diminish the importance of categorising North American cities as Canadian versus American. More relevant is to understand how and why city-regions in North America are going through uneven rescaling processes, whereby (1) some city-regions win while others lose in this competitive struggle; (2) the importance of various governmental levels on urban politics varies according to the 'competitive success' of cities and to the policy sector involved; (3) the motives behind new city-regional institutions vary from neo-Keynesianism to neo-liberalism, resulting in opposing territorial reforms such as fragmentation and amalgamation; and (4) social mobilisation beyond existing progressive middle-class regimes has changed its scalar outlooks to various degrees in different city-regions.

Municipal governance restructuring in North America in the long 1990s

During the long 1990s, roughly from the breakdown of global real estate markets in the late 1980s to the events of 9/11/2001, North American urban regions underwent some significant changes in their metropolitan governance, including shifts in responsibilities and policy areas covered by municipal and regional governments. First, the decade saw the advent of a more regionalist view of municipal regulation. This new regionalism entailed a contradictory set of messages but nevertheless constituted a break with much of the downtown-centred urban policy environment of the 1980s and, in sum, resulted in a suburbanisation of metropolitan politics. Regardless of the respective politics of various downtowns (some downtown elites being more neo-Keynesian while others remain neo-conservative), they have all undergone a process of regionalisation through a 'suburbanisation' of policy-making coalitions. This has had significant impacts for leftist regulatory schemes not only at the metropolitan level, but also in provincial/state and national politics as well (Gainsborough 2000; Davis 2002).

Second, urban elites and policy-makers scrambled to adjust their institutions and practices to what they felt were the new rules of a globalised and liberalised intra-urban competition. This has created a 'restructuring-generated crisis' (Soja 2000) that spurred social resistance and various kinds of civil society mobilisation. Much of this resistance continued along the same lines of tension as those outlined by growth-machine theorists: a struggle between use value and exchange value, between the perceived needs of global competitiveness and the needs of local residents (Molotch 1976; Castells 1983; Jonas and Wilson 1999). This new wave of use value mobilisation, however, has been rescaled in two important ways: (1) local urban struggles have been connected nationally through pan-Canadian and even pan-North American urban coalitions, and transnationally, particularly through the anti-globalisation movement and the world social forum; and (2) the political imaginary framing these local urban struggles has jumped scale from being perceived as a local issue to being framed as part of a global struggle pitting neo-communitarianism against neo-liberalism (Boudreau 2003b).

Third, as these elites acted in an environment of internal contestation, all projects of urban-regional government restructuring were also programmes for creating new urban hegemonies. While the structured coherence of 1980s growth politics gave way to a more retrenched set of policies during the first half of the

1990s, municipal governance started to take on more disciplinary roles (Kipfer and Keil 2002). The competitive urban region dovetailed with the carceral city and much of the neo-communitarian discourse developed by urban activists has been reappropriated and instrumentalised by urban elites (Boudreau 2004).

Fourth, Los Angeles, Montreal and Toronto became much more culturally and demographically diverse throughout the 1990s. This development meant that attempts at streamlining governance structures for the sake of global competitiveness had to be weighed against the urban regions' increasing diversity: whether diversity was an asset or a liability in this competition rested mostly on the degree to which the new non-white majorities in Toronto and Los Angeles, and substantive visible minority in Montreal could be made part of the deal.

Fifth, as the real estate crisis gave way to a new boom in the late 1990s, a new politics of growth under some banner of ecological modernisation took hold: new urbanism and smart growth became the buzzwords of an urban revival that drastically changed the fabric of class and space in those parts of the inner cities that had yet been spared previous waves of gentrification. In the suburbs, discourses on smart growth became a powerful mobilising banner for new forms of activism combining middle-class NIMBYism with a discourse on nature preservation in order to stop urban sprawl while resisting densification (Trom 1999; Gilbert and Phillips 2003).

Sixth, metropolitan governance experienced a fundamental re-scaling. While some governance changes could potentially be explained by mere local matters, the new urban North America was deliberately contextualised in a global world of economic and political reconstruction. Moreover, in a context of important state reforms, metropolitan governance has been placed at the centre of intergovernmental reforms, where the struggle for new revenue sources and policy responsibilities at the city-regional level clashed with already existing tensions between the federal and the provincial/state in terms of their respective autonomy.

After neo-liberalism? Metropolitan state re-scaling in the early twenty-first century

In the autumn of 2003, Canadian urban policy was suddenly propelled to the spotlight of the national political stage. Previous election victories of progressive mayors in Winnipeg (1998) and Vancouver (2003) had set the pace for a different kind of metropolitan politics than the retrenchment and suburbanisation of the past decade had entailed (Keil 2002, 2002a). With the decisive victory of social democrat David Miller in November 2003 in Toronto, the front of progressive municipal politicians was strengthened significantly. This progressive urban wave – at least at the level of mayoral politics – has been part and parcel of a broader shift away from the openly revanchist and suburban politics espoused by mayors in the tradition of New York's Rudolph Giuliani, LA's Richard Riordan, Toronto's Mel Lastman and Montreal's Pierre Bourque to a declared urbanist and reformist tendency. We can also count the win of moderate Democrat James Hahn in Los Angeles, after eight years of deep Republicanism under Richard

Riordan, among the instances marking this shift. Clearly the more conservative of the final two Democratic contenders, Hahn, who captured much of the Republican vote, remained the candidate of the African-American population that had been all but marginalised under the previous regime. In all cases, at least lip-service has been paid to the expansion of cities' roles in a federal governance system to a clearly urban (as supposed to the previously suburban) policy agenda, to an internal governance system more representative of the needs of complex urban systems and populations, and – especially in the Canadian case – to the need for more inter-municipal cooperation in the face of federal and provincial constitutional hegemony.

In October 2003, the radically neo-liberal Progressive Conservative (Tory) Ontario provincial government that had first brought amalgamation to Toronto was trounced in an election that lifted a more moderate Liberal majority government into power. While it is too early to tell whether the new government is willing to undo some of the detrimental effects of amalgamation on Toronto and reverse the anti-urban policy direction taken by the former government (something that its Quebec counterpart, the Quebec Liberal Party, has promised to do with respect to Montreal), it is clear that the specific conditions of roll-out neo-liberalism that have determined urban policy in this Canadian province have now come to an end. In fact, solid rejection of conservative candidates in the urban area in favour of Liberal and New Democratic provincial representatives was a clear indication of the widespread disagreement among voters with the specific mix of consolidation and downloading that had governed Toronto for the past eight years. In California, where a recall election swept Arnold Schwarzenegger into gubernatorial office, large cities remained a stronghold of more progressive politics more typical of this state. Continuing tensions between the urban centres and the suburban power base of Schwarzenegger's Republicanism can be expected. The exception to this revival of urban progressive forces is Quebec, where a right-leaning Liberal provincial government was recently elected in large part as a reaction to the left-leaning Parti Québécois's (PQ) forced amalgamation policies of 2000. While the PQ merged all cities on the Island of Montreal (and in every major cities of the province) in order to redistribute suburban growth to strengthen urban centres with an eye on increased global competitiveness, resistance to these mergers came from suburban residents who were successful in electing a suburban-led City Council in the first amalgamated election, as well as a suburban-friendly right-leaning provincial government which has promised to de-merge municipalities.

In addition, both the US and Canadian Federal governments have put forward policy documents aimed at rethinking their role in urban affairs. Paul Martin, new leader of the Canadian Liberal Party and Prime Minister of Canada has put his support behind a 'new deal for cities' allegedly including more revenues at the municipal level, more infrastructure monies, and a localised process of decision making. However, this increasing interest of the Federal level in urban politics does not go without ambiguous resistance in Quebec. The province of Quebec, jealous of its autonomy as a result of French language cultural affirmation politics, resents any Federal incursion into its jurisdiction (municipalities being the responsibility of provinces). However, more transfer monies for immigration settlement programmes, urban infrastructure and economic development are always welcome, so long as Quebec has the final say on how to spend the money. In the US, after strong criticisms on the anti-urban policies of both Republicans and Democrats since Reagan, the current G.W. Bush administration has now issued a new urban policy agenda linked to its redefinition of security in a post-9/11/2001 era. While Reagan had started his anti-urban revolution in the 1980s with a drive for decentralising welfare policies to the states and even municipalities under the guise of a 'new federalism', it is Clinton, who had won the 1992 elections by regaining the votes of the suburban middle-class 'Reagan Democrats',[4] who finished it with his 1996 welfare reform. When Los Angeles was burning during the Justice riots of 1992, the Federal government responded with zero money, nurturing instead a national suburban disgust at urban issues (Davis 2002). During the 2000 presidential electoral campaign, the Democrats under Al Gore reintroduced an urban agenda, while G.W. Bush campaigned on an anti-urban platform, courting Christian fundamentalists' suburban and rural values, and the rural sensibilities of Texan oil tycoons and ranchers. The Federal government has now intervened with a 'war on terrorism', a new economic agenda offering tax breaks to top executives, and a new urban agenda focused on security and neighbourhood watch programmes, school safety, subsidies to corporate downtown redevelopment and to home-ownership (with the American Dream Down Payment Fund) (Bush 2000; Foods 2003).

At all levels of government, from the municipal to the federal, North America is seeing the emergence of an increasingly strong consensus on the need to focus on a new urban agenda after a long decade of suburban neo-liberal politics. A consensus it is, indeed, as both the left and right are cooperating in defining this new urban agenda. The new question is not so much a tension between urban and suburban issues anymore, but rather a conflict on the kind of urban society we want.

Globalisation and uneven re-scaling

Even under the strangely similar but also dissimilar conditions of Canadian and American urban governance, globalisation leads to uneven re-scaling of municipal and regional governments. In Montreal, Toronto and Los Angeles, similar intentions by comparable class factions, populist groups and urban elites led to quite divergent outcomes.

In the three cities, questions of democratisation and legitimacy have been discussed largely in oppositional terms. Secessionist conservatives in the San Fernando Valley spoke the language of local control (articulated potentially with a variety of exclusionary discourses); whereas it was mostly progressives in Toronto who claimed the high road of democratic discourse and local autonomy against an interventionist, authoritarian – and consolidationist – neo-liberal provincial government. The consolidationist option, often associated with interventionist government and compact city ideals, was paradoxically used by neo-conservatives, who are normally suspicious of 'big government', to integrate the regional 'blubber belt' hegemony in southern Ontario. The amalgamation of Toronto in 1997 was a 'suburban ambush' (to paraphrase Toronto ex-mayor John Sewell) on inner-city autonomy. It brought the inner city into the direct political reach of suburban politicians and their agendas. In Toronto, the conservative provincial government used its electoral power base in the exurban ring to perform an imperialist intervention into the governance affairs of the central city. The Toronto case contrasted sharply with the contemporary secession movement in the San Fernando Valley that was, for the most part, supported by suburbanites who wanted to separate their neighbourhoods from the 'ills' of the inner city. In Montreal, opposition to consolidation also came from the suburbs. The inner city was the main concern of the Quebec provincial government, who wanted to create a 'strong', 'big' and 'internationally known' urban core by tapping into suburban growth to redistribute property tax revenues extracted from industrial and commercial development. Suburbanites on the Island of Montreal spoke of stopping the spread of inner-city mismanagement to well-managed suburbs, using the language of local democratic rights and the right to cultural affirmation, as the majority of these suburbs are primarily anglophone as opposed to the francophone majority of the inner-city (Boudreau 2003b).

All three cases offered a sometimes confusing situation in which real and imagined class, 'racial' and ethnic differences were played against notions of home rule, freedom, low taxes, service efficiency, etc. All three positions potentially offered a choice between either reducing urban politics to a narrowly defined administrative exercise or having it live up to its promise of withstanding the enclosure attempts of the state system, and of passing beyond itself and to spill over 'the boundaries that contain it geographically and functionally' (Magnusson 1996: 23). That is, both consolidation and fragmentation can lead to either more closed or more open political processes, to more or less equality and redistributive justice, and to better or worse urban social and natural environments. Particularly the kinds of world city regions represented by Los Angeles, Montreal and Toronto can by no means be confined administratively, socially, ecologically, culturally or economically in a container of territorially bounded government.

In a world of global cities, the ongoing struggle between the institutions of city government and the potentials of insurgent civil society reflects the parameters of the current governance debate. Consolidation and secession are divergent but compatible responses to this challenge. In Toronto, Montreal and Los Angeles, what appear to be limited struggles over local jurisdiction and administration of service delivery are really struggles over the urban dimensions of a globalised world. Through the redrawing of jurisdictional boundaries, urban governance is retooled to deal with new complexities of world city politics. In reality, the current restructuring in Los Angeles, Montreal and Toronto may fall short of achieving this strategic goal as urban contradictions – both internal and external – may be enhanced rather than diminished. Neither consolidation nor fragmentation as a principle of local governance organisation offers clear ideological choices as both are favoured by politicians and theorists across the political spectrum (Keating 1995: 132). The ideological breadth in political alignment with one or the other fundamental position has much to do with the meaning attached to local democracy and with the reach specific actors expect urban politics to have.

Consequently, the real political cleavage remains between those who favour democratisation and those who hope instead to protect the market economy. The latter position may be couched in populist terms to include protecting the privileges of various strata of petit bourgeois segments of the populations, most notably suburban home-owners and their families.

This populist rhetoric is played by local activists and politicians on both sides of the consolidation–fragmentation debate. In Los Angeles, Montreal and Toronto, populism and social mobilisation for local democracy go hand in hand. The way 'local democracy' is discursively presented depends largely on the local political culture, but in the three cases, the populist discourse put forward across the ideological spectrum is very similar. In trying to understand uneven patterns of city-regional state capacities, therefore, it is necessary to go beyond this general discourse on local democracy. Perhaps a more fruitful explanation of this uneven development is that the degree of social mobilisation at the city-regional scale (as opposed to the provincial, local or national levels) influences the effectiveness of city-regional state capacities.[5]

Neo-liberalisation has brought different territorial reform policies (Brenner and Theodore 2002; Brenner *et al.* 2003). This has meant the proliferation of city-regional and supranational institutions, increasing policy responsibilities at these governmental levels, and a number of bilateral and multilateral initiatives coming directly from these levels of government without passing through the national government. A complex set of actors, including policy-makers and elected representatives, are (sometimes explicitly, but many times unintentionally) redefining authority and policy at different territorial scales. The end result of this chaotic process is perhaps some rather important overall changes in the scales at which governance and policy-making now work. The question before us, then, is: How are these new institutional spaces articulated with social struggles at all scales? More generally, to what degree is there not only proliferation of institutions and policy responsibilities at the supranational and subnational levels, but also a rescaling of the *exercise of power*? We argue that the intensification of intergovernmental reforms and urban governance restructuring has created a situation of territorial flux, which has opened opportunities for citizens to develop their own territorial mobilisation strategies, and thus challenges the state's monopoly over territorial policies. Claims for local autonomy (such as resistance to mergers in Montreal and Toronto and secessionism in Los Angeles) could be conceptualised as one manifestation of this strategic territorialisation of civil society movements.

We suggested above that the ability of a city-region effectively to rescale the exercise of power (to build a new 'structured coherence' at the city-regional scale) depends on the incorporation of social movements (both on the left and on the right). This integration or co-optation can work only if social movements have themselves re-territorialised their social claims at that city-regional scale. This re-territorialisation of social movement activities has now become a feature of social movements in general (Kohler and Wissen 2003), and especially in the three urban areas under review here. Activists are struggling to adjust to the changing realities of urban governance organisation that have taken place in these urban areas (Boudreau and Keil 2001). As a consequence, urban movements have created new 'organisational infrastructures' that are better able to deal with the fractured and fragmented realities of re-scaling urban regions (Nicholls 2003). Upon close analysis, mobilising strategies in Toronto seem to be reterritorialising at the city-regional scale (Desfor *et al.* 2004), but not in Montreal and Los Angeles. In the three cities, to be sure, social movements have moved towards territorial and jurisdictional more than sectoral mobilising strategies, but the scale at which they have done so differs. Sectoral strategies of political claims channel efforts in specific policy sectors (housing, health, education, etc.). Jurisdictional and territorial strategies of political claims are attempts by social movements to use one level of government against another, or to create a new level of government altogether by asking for a remapping of political and administrative boundaries (Boudreau 2001, 2003a).

In the cases of Montreal and Toronto, claims for local autonomy are not the ultimate aim, but rather an *instrument* developed for affirming cultural differences in the case of suburban Anglo-Montrealers, or for sustaining a specific vision of urbanity in the case of inner-city Torontonians. In other words, these local autonomy movements are not simply *ad hoc* reactions to municipal mergers: the reason why they were able to mobilise effectively was that they were part of broader struggles specific to each city. The immediate threat of municipal amalgamation was taken as a rallying point, but one has to place this mobilisation in their wider context. Significant here is that seen from the perspective of these wider social movements, resistance to mergers can be interpreted as a territorialised mobilisation strategy. After the immediate struggle against consolidation, various other territorial strategies were developed in Montreal and Toronto, from pressures to put urban affairs back on the federal agenda, partitionism and de-merger to the emergence of a Canadian Charter movement (as we discuss below). In Los Angeles, secessionism (a territorial strategy *par excellence*) has replaced traditional sectoral strategies of mobilisation, such as struggles over land use planning, neighbourhood security and community well-being. Secession gained support largely because activists felt that in the face of the growing complexity of the city, it was useless to attempt to reform it and that gaining political control over their territory would be more efficient. As Hogen-Esch (2002) points out about San Fernando Valley activists, '[d]espite their considerable informal power, the inability to gain an institutional foothold in land use decision making has prompted many Valley homeowner associations – particularly those in the affluent south and west Valley – to support secession'.

The interaction between intergovernmental reforms and the strategic multiplication of the scales at which claims to autonomy are made begin to illustrate that we may be witnessing a rescaling of, not only institutions, but the *exercise of power*. The scale at which social movements focus their claims (the local, the city-regional, the provincial/state or the federal) will affect redistributive policies (a central, yet not always openly articulated element of the struggle in the three cities).

Consequently, depending on places and national contexts, city-regional state capacities vary (e.g. some focus on competitiveness, others on neo-Keynesian compromises). This uneven geography of emerging political spaces challenges existing schemes for both state intervention and activism at multiple scales. In this institutional, territorial and political flux, the main challenge for public policy-making is to stabilise a place for exchanges between institutions at the city-regional, provincial and national levels. The extent to which one can speak of the emergence of a collective actor at the city-regional scale which affects intergovernmental relations, and, more generally, the very role of the state in society and in the economy, depends on the degree of consensus in each city-region. The recent election of left-leaning mayor David Miller in Toronto, combined with a consensus on the need for a 'new deal for cities' in Canada is a perfect example of this consensus. With the continuing drive for 'de-mergers' in Montreal and persistent dissatisfactions by secessionists in Los Angeles, these two city-regions are still grappling with forces of resistance to building city-regional state capacities. Such resistance has virtually disappeared in Toronto, where a new era of reform politics may very well de-radicalise social mobilisation on both the left and the right.

Conclusion

In the three North American cities we have examined, the relationships of metropolitan governance and democracy have been re-regulated during the last decade. In Toronto, Montreal and Los Angeles new, and sometimes surprising, responses to the questions of equity, effectiveness and efficiency in public service provision within metropolitan service provision in metropolitan areas (Kübler and Heinelt in Chapter 2) were found by ideologically widely divergent regional and municipal governments and social movements. The surprising part was the perplexing situation that in Los Angeles conservative secessionists used some of the same efficiency arguments for splitting up the metropolitan government that had been used by their consolidationist counterparts in Toronto; the latter, in turn, paradoxically entertained a predictable anti-statist neo-liberal line of arguments to give birth to the largest, most centrist local state institution in Canada: the amalgamated Toronto mega city; in Quebec, moreover, a left-leaning provincial government was indistinguishable from its neo-conservative counterpart in Ontario in legitimising the consolidation of small governments into one unified urban region. What was less surprising was that the discourses on governance restructuring, and – where they occurred – the real changes in governance arrangements, reflected only a limited range of options. In all cases, governance change was closely linked to a discourse of competitiveness of metropolitan areas on a global scale (Kübler and Heinelt in Chapter 2), yet little attention was paid to internal democracy of metropolitan regions despite persistent claims to local democracy put forward by local autonomy movements. This is the more remarkable as in all three cities, social movement activity loomed large. Both social movements of the right and left entered the fray of the local governance debate with well-articulated claims for local democracy, autonomy and citizenship. Secessionists in Los Angeles, consolidationists in Toronto and anti-consolidationists in Montreal shared a strong penchant for conservative ideas about community, market liberalism and individual freedom. Defenders of Los Angeles' unity, critics of Toronto's amalgamation and some proponents of consolidation in Montreal strongly advocated an agenda of multi-cultural and multi-class urban democracy, state responsibility and collective rights.

In all cases, debates on governance restructuring left larger questions of social, economic and political power untouched, at least in terms of widening citizenship rights and democratic processes in the municipal realm. But as the new governance system congealed in Toronto, and as the secession debate in Los Angeles was at its peak, political actors refocused the metropolitan debate around potential ways in which metropolitan unity could be forged beyond the current state of affairs. In Toronto, in particular, the losers in the fight against amalgamation sought for solutions to issues of missing local democracy and autonomy left unresolved or exacerbated by the combination of amalgamation and downloading. As citizens, politicians, social and business interests woke up to the new reality of a larger but ostensibly less powerful municipality, they entertained a host of ideas for changes to the existing governmental division of labour. Disgruntled opponents to amalgamation regrouped as proponents of more autonomy for that urban region. Among several proposals ranging from provincial status for Toronto to minor changes to the tax system, the proposal of a Toronto charter carried the day. The idea of fixing the demands for more autonomy in a strong consensus document that would force higher-level governments to respect Toronto's special needs was supported by many because it allowed change to happen without entering the murky territory of constitutional alterations which would be almost impossible in a nation stalemated over the question of Quebec sovereignty. Neither the charter nor most other proposals for more autonomy, however, made any concrete and believable proposals for increasing the influence of urban civil society on the institutionalised metropolitan governance process. All proposals concentrated on the functional efficiency and effectiveness of local as opposed to supra-local govern*ments* instead of demanding a broadened bottom-up govern*ance* (Keil and Young 2003). In the California metropolis, an outdated charter document that had been amended to unmanageable proportions since its inception in 1925 was rewritten in a contentious process. The new charter was seen to a large degree to be an attempt to stem the wave of secessions that threatened to break up Los Angeles, but was called by its critics a badly veiled attempt by the mayor to increase his power base. Interestingly, in the end, the charter debate did not lead to the promised extensions of local democracy, although neighbourhood consultation became a big part of the overall strategy. The charter was a state-led restructuring of governing processes that had more to do with the internal workings of a city administration (with strong emphasis on sorting out management–labour relationships) than with the increase of popular democracy in the municipal process (Boudreau and Keil 2001; Keil 2001; Purcell 2002). In Montreal, in a typical Quebec way of privileging the provincial scale, suburban anti-merger activists did not transfer their energies to the city-regional level but instead reinforced the local, while striking alliances with the Liberal provincial government that was elected on the promise of reverting consolidation. The overall strategy for both local activists and the provincial government is to 'occupy' all the political space on urban affairs at the provincial level in order to avoid a federal incursion that would diminish provincial autonomy. Urban activists in Montreal have consequently largely ignored the pan-Canadian and Toronto-led charter movement.

In Toronto, progressive forces have been able to regroup at the metropolitan (and potentially at the regional) level and to use the new scale of metro politics as the terrain of their action. The new political regime under social democratic Mayor David Miller will face demands by continued citizen activism to roll back some of the downloading that came with boundary change during amalgamation. Whether the various social movements which opposed downloading and amalgamation in the late 1990s – many of which supported Miller in the fall 2003 municipal election – can sustain independent pressure on various levels of government or whether they will be co-opted, remains to be seen. Making even more pronounced links beyond the metropolitan boundaries, reaching out to the equally disgruntled citizens of the ex-urban communities, is a still steeper task but not impossible. In Montreal, the newly amalgamated city-region has not led to a unified re-scaled metropolitan progressive movement; rather, the new governance arrangements are challenged by decidedly sub-metropolitan groups based in the old, pre-consolidation municipalities. Moreover, the new borough structure that accompanied municipal mergers has opened the door for novel neighbourhood-based claims in the old city of Montreal, localising even further the pre-merger arrangement. In Southern California, the stunning attempt to re-scale the metropolitan region by splitting more wealthy parts from the City of Los Angeles, coupled with changing the municipal policy environment in favour of more conservative ideas, has so far been unsuccessful and the conservative social movements lined up behind secession have had to regroup and consider other options for future interventions in the metropolitan boundary debate (Boudreau and Keil 2001; Purcell 2001).

For now, the tumultuous years of state-led consolidation in Toronto and Montreal and the failed attempt at secession spearheaded by conservative citizens and small business groups in Los Angeles have left these three metropoles in a state of arrested metropolitan development at the beginning of the twenty-first century. Neither can the boundary issues opened up in the long 1990s be considered laid to rest, nor have the democratic deficits laid open in metropolitan politics been addressed significantly. By 'democratic deficits' we specifically refer to both the lack of democratic process in bringing in governance change, and the equally widening gap between those new claims that have been a product of recent protests against these changes and the readiness or ability of municipal government organisations to deal with them in an era of neo-liberal cutbacks and budget crisis. The charter movements in Toronto as well as the revised charter in LA are weak instances of redressing urban citizenship claims as voiced by those left out of the metropolitan regime. In Montreal, attempts of regaining a pre-amalgamation status quo ante of local municipal government have discouragingly parochial overtones. Over the coming period of time, all three metropolitan areas will have to face serious questions about regional issues that demand attention through an insufficiently prepared mode of regulation. In all three cities, questions of federalism and in particular state/ province–city relations are prominent. Regional elites rally once again around more or less coherent and coordinated programmes and projects of international competitiveness based on kaleidoscopic neo-liberal measures, cultural and 'creative' strategies and overblown mega projects. Alternatives to the growth agenda of the late 1990s are considered as citizens voice their objections to further compromises to living environments, as happened in the recent Toronto mayoral election (which was arguably decided over the staunch opposition of the victorious candidate to a high-profile airport expansion project in the inner city). Overarching social and technical infrastructure issues such as the control of sprawl, the easing of transportation gridlock, and the provision of water and sewerage services stretch the regional imagination and policy-making capacities of politicians, experts, corporations and activists across the urban region. Citizens everywhere cross traditional urban/suburban, ethnic, racial and class divides in fashioning a new urban political ecology that encompasses notions of environmental justice and regional ecological integrity (Pastor *et al.* 2000; Desfor and Keil 2004; Wolch *et al.* 2004). For the purposes of creating a 'structured coherence' of the metropolitan region, various actors will continue to struggle and interact; the systemic, urbanist forces defending the status quo and the continued expansion of the space of accumulation and commerce will not cease to run up against the limits imposed on them by the insurgent practices of everydayness based in the lived urban experiences of urban collectives (Lefebvre 2003).

Notes

1 Research for this paper was partly supported by SSHRC grant 410–2003–1207, Gouvernance métropolitaine et compétitivité internationale: les exemples de Montréal et Toronto.
2 In the Canadian federal system, provinces are equivalent to the states in the United States or to *Länder* in Germany. This provincial strength and municipal weakness in Canada might be explained by a number of factors. First, the Canadian parliamentary system and strict party lines have facilitated the adoption of laws concerning municipalities in provincial legislatures. Second, given the absence of an equivalent to the Voting Rights Act, legislative ridings can be apportioned to advantage rural areas over urban municipalities (although this has been tempered by the Charter of Rights and Freedom included in the 1982 constitution) (Garber and Imbroscio 1996).
3 Proposition 13 was to cut commercial and residential property taxes to 1 per cent of market value. The proposition also called for a return of tax assessments to levels from

1975–1976 and a cap on increases to no more than 2 per cent a year as long as the property did not change owner. A change of ownership permitted a reassessment to market values. As Miller indicates, support for the proposition came overwhelmingly from white, Republican property owners with annual income between $8,000 and $25,000 (in dollars of the time); opposition came from members of public employees' households and from African-Americans (Miller 1981: 2–3).

4 'Reagan Democrats' are Democratic Party members who voted for Reagan as a reaction to what they saw as the absence of middle-class concerns in the Democratic Party platform.

5 For an extensive discussion on these matters that cannot be repeated here for reasons of space constraints, see Boudreau (2003b); Keil (2000, 2000a).

Bibliography

Boudreau, J.-A. (2001) 'Strategic Territorialisation: The Politics of Anglo-Montrealers', *Journal of Economic and Social Geography/Tijdschrift voor economische en sociale geografie*, 92(4): 405–419.

—— (2003a) 'The Politics of Territorialization: Regionalism, Localism and Other Isms ... The Case of Montreal', *Journal of Urban Affairs*, 25(2): 179–199.

—— (2003b) 'Questioning the Use of "Local Democracy" as a Discursive Strategy for Political Mobilization in Los Angeles, Montreal and Toronto', *International Journal of Urban and Regional Research*, 27(4): 793–810.

—— (2004) 'La coalition urbaine réformiste de Toronto et la fusion municipale: une culture participative menacée par la réorganisation territoriale de 1997–1998?', in B. Jouve and P. Booth (eds), *Démocraties metropolita'nes*, Montreal: Presses de l'Université du Québec, pp. 133–154.

Boudreau, J.-A. and Keil, R. (2001) 'Seceding from Responsibility? Secession Movements in Los Angeles', *Urban Studies*, 38(10): 1701–1731.

Brenner, N. (2002) 'Decoding the Newest "Metropolitan Regionalism" in the USA: A Critical Overview', *Cities*, 19: 3–21.

Brenner, N. and Theodore, N. (eds) (2002) *Spaces of Neoliberalism*, Oxford: Blackwell.

Brenner, N., Jessop, B., Jones, M. and MacLeod G. (eds) (2003) *State/Space: A Reader*, Malden: MA.

Bush, G.W. (2000) *An Urban Agenda for the 21st Century*, downloaded from the internet on 17 November, http://www.usmayors.org/seattle2000/bush.htm.

Carens, J.H. (1995) *Is Quebec Nationalism Just? Perspectives from Anglophone Canada*, Montreal and Kingston: McGill-Queen's University Press.

Castells, M. (1983) *The City and the Grass-Roots: A Cross-Cultural Theory of Urban Social Movements*, London: Edward Arnold.

Croucher, S.L. (1997) 'Constructing the Image of Ethnic Harmony in Toronto, Canada: The Politics of Problem Definition and Nondefinition', *Urban Affairs Review*, 32(3): 319–347.

Davis, M. (2002) *Dead Cities: And Other Tales*, New York: The New Press.

Desfor, G. and Keil, R. (2004) *Nature and the City: Making Environmental Policy in Toronto and Los Angeles*, Tucson: University of Arizona Press.

Desfor, G., Keil, R., Kipfer, S. and Wekerle, G. (2004) 'Grenzenloses Wachsen: Zukunftsplanung der Wettbewerbsstadt in Toronto', in D. Schubert and U. Altrock (eds), *Wachsende Stadt*, Opladen: Leske und Budrich.

Foods, R. (2003) *President Calls on Senate to Pass American Dream Downpayment Act*, downloaded from the internet on 17 November, http://www.whitehouse.gov/news/releases/2003/10/20031015–10.html.

Gainsborough, J.F. (2000) *Fenced Off: The Suburbanization of American Politics*, Washington, DC: Georgetown University Press.

Garber, J.A. and Imbroscio, D.L. (1996) ' "The Myth of the North American City" Reconsidered: Local Constitutional Regimes in Canada and the United States', *Urban Affairs Review*, 31(5): 595–624.

Gilbert, L. and Phillips, C. (2003) 'Practices of Urban Environmental Citizenships: Rights to the City and Rights to Nature in Toronto', *Citizenship Studies* 7(3): 313–330.

Goldberg, M.A. and Mercer, J. (1986) *The Myth of the North American City*, Vancouver: University of British Columbia Press.

Goldsmith, M. (1996) 'Normative Theories of Local Government: A European Comparison', in D. King and G. Stoker (eds), *Rethinking Local Democracy*, London: Macmillan.

Harvey, D. (1989) *The Urban Experience*, Oxford: Blackwell.

Hogen-Esch, T. (2002) *The Coalition Dynamics of Secession in Los Angeles, Reform, L.A. Style: The Theory and Practice of Urban Governance at Century's Turn*, University of Southern California, School of Policy, Planning and Development, John Randolph Haynes and Dora Haynes Foundation Conference.

Jonas, A.E.G. and Wilson, D. (1999) *The Urban Growth Machine: Critical Perspectives Two Decades Later*, Albany: State University of New York Press.

Keating, M. (1995) 'Size, Efficiency and Democracy: Consolidation, Fragmentation and Public Choice', in D. Judge, G. Stoker and H. Wolman (eds), *Theories of Urban Politics*, London: Thousand Oaks and New Delhi: Sage Publications.

Keil, R. (2000) 'Governance Restructuring in Los Angeles and Toronto: Amalgamation or Secession?', *International Journal of Urban and Regional Research*, 24(4), December: 758–781.

——(2001) 'Consolidation and Secession in Los Angeles: The Dialectics of Urban Governance Reform at the End of the 20th Century', *European Journal of American Culture*, 20(1): 22–35.

——(2002) ' "Common Sense" Neoliberalism: Progressive Conservative Urbanism in Toronto, Canada', *Antipode*, 34(3): 578–601.

——(2002a) 'Urban Governance Restructuring: A Template for New Progressive Politics or the Endrun of Neoliberal Urbanism?', in O. Schmidtke (ed.), *The Third Way Transformation of Social Democracy: Normative Claims and Policy Initiatives in the 21st Century*, Aldershot: Ashgate: 201–220.

Keil, R. and Kipfer, S. (2003) 'The Urban Experience and Globalization', in W. Clement and L.F. Vosko (eds), *Changing Canada: Political Economy as Transformation*, Montreal and Kingston: McGill-Queen's University Press: 335–362.

Keil, R. and Young, D. (2003) 'A Charter for the People? A Research Note on the Debate about Municipal Autonomy in Toronto', *Urban Affairs Review*, 39(1): 87–102.

Kipfer, S. and Keil, R. (2002) 'Toronto Inc.? Planning the Competitive City in the New Toronto', *Antipode*, 34(2): 227–264.

Kohler, B. and Wissen, M. (2003) 'Globalizing Protest: Urban Conflicts and the Global Social Movements', *International Journal of Urban and Regional Research*, 27(4): 942–951.

Kymlicka, W. (1998) 'Is Federalism a Viable Alternative to Secession?', in P.B. Lehning (ed.), *Theories of Secession*, London: Routledge.

Lefebvre, H. (2003) *The Urban Revolution*, Minneapolis: Minnesota University Press.

Lehning, P.B. (ed.) (1998) *Theories of Secession*, London: Routledge.

Magnusson, W. (1996) *The Search for Political Space*, Toronto: University of Toronto Press.

Miller, G.J. (1981) *Cities by Contract: The Politics of Municipal Incorporation*, Cambridge, MA: The MIT Press.

Molotch, H.L. (1976) 'The City as a Growth Machine: Towards a Political Economy of Place', *American Journal of Sociology*, 82: 309–330.

Nicholls, W.J. (2003) 'Forging a "New" Organizational Infrastructure for Los Angeles' Progressive Community', *International Journal of Urban and Regional Research*, 27(4): 881–897.

Pastor, M., Dreier, P., Grigsby III, J.E. and Lopez-Garza, M. (2000) *Regions that Work: How Cities and Suburbs Can Grow Together*, Minneapolis: University of Minnesota Press.

Purcell, M. (2001) 'Metropolitan Political Reorganization and the Political Economy of Urban Growth: The Case of San Fernando Valley Secession', *Political Geography* 20(5): 101–121.

——(2002) 'Politics in Global Cities: Los Angeles Charter Reform and the New Social Movements', *Environment and Planning* A, 34(1): 23–42.

Soja, E. (2000) *Postmetropolis*, Oxford: Blackwell.

Trom, D. (1999) 'De la réfutation de l'effet NIMBY considérée comme une pratique militante: Notes pour une approche pragmatique de l'activité revendicatrice', *Revue française de science politique*, 49(1): 31–50.

Tully, J. (1999) 'Liberté et dévoilement dans les sociétés multinationales', *Globe*, 2(2): 13–36.

Wolch, J., Pastor Jr, M. and Dreier, P. (eds) (2004) *Up Against the Sprawl: Public Policy and the (Re)Making of Southern California*, Minneapolis: University of Minnesota Press.

8 The coming of age of metropolitan governance in Helsinki?

Anne Haila and Patrick Le Galès

Finland is a northern European centralised country where robust municipalities have enjoyed resources and autonomy. However, the crisis of the early 1990s led to a profound restructuring of the state which put pressure on municipalities. This forms the context in which the issue of metropolitan governance arose.

Finland was created out of two established European state systems, those of Sweden and Russia (Alapuro 1997: 18–19). The inherited Russian powerful bureaucracy is mixed with a Nordic corporatism and a large welfare state: hence there is a very powerful and centralised state. Finland is characterised by its extensive welfare state and robust autonomous municipalities. Although Finland was a latecomer to the Nordic welfare state model, its achievement has been spectacular (Kautto *et al.* 1999; Lehto 2000). As a small centralised country, Finland has adopted the Scandinavian welfare state model with a very high level of homogeneity and integration. In comparison with other European cities, the standards of collective goods and the well-being of the inhabitants are very high in Helsinki, Turku and Tampere. Municipalities, the basic level of local government, have played a key part as the main providers of social services, thus controlling an important share of public expenditure.

Between 1989 and 1994, Finland and Helsinki had to face a series of new developments which cannot be detailed in this chapter: (1) the collapse of the Soviet Union leading to the closure of the special political and trade link; (2) a major recession in the early 1990s; (3) Finland's decision to join the EU in a proactive way; (4) the arrival of first waves of immigrants from Russia, Estonia, Yugoslavia and Africa; and (5) the remarkable economic recovery after the mid-1990s which made Finland the fastest growing country in the EU. All this led to the restructuring of the state in Finland, which defines the parameters under which the issue of metropolitan governance emerged.

In this chapter we suggest that the rise of metropolitan governance is the result of the interaction, and conflicts, between state strategies and groups within cities that are trying to gain more resources and autonomy. The emerging level of metropolitan governance is organised around policy networks and a level of governmental coordination imposed by the government.

Autonomous municipalities in the Helsinki metropolitan area and the metropolitan governance question within a European context

As mentioned in the Introduction to this book, Finnish municipalities, as part of the Northern European model of local government, are seen as pillars of the democracy characterised by important powers and a high level of legitimacy within a universalist highly integrated welfare state. The recession Finland faced at the beginning of the 1990s was deep: the unemployment rate rose as high as 20 per cent in some regions. In Helsinki, the unemployment rate varied between 10 and 39 per cent in different neighbourhoods (Lankinen 2001). The recession, together with joining the EU, was the profoundly disturbing exogenous event which set in motion the process of state restructuring, including the choice to limit public expenditure, and raised the issue of metropolitan governance. One method with which the state began saving was to shift the burden of providing social services to municipalities. The welfare state began turning into welfare cities.

In Finland, the autonomy of municipalities is stated in the Constitution. One aspect of this autonomy is a right to collect taxes (§121). The Local Government Act (1995) states that municipalities can decide the amount of local income tax (called municipal tax) and that of real estate tax (§66). Local income taxes form the main source of local revenue. Real estate taxes are less than 5 per cent of local public revenues. Corporate taxes are collected and redistributed by the state. The tax rate is decided by the government and companies pay the same amount of taxes (29 per cent) despite their locations. Thus location, in terms of taxes, is a matter of indifference for companies setting up in Finland.

Financial reforms that were introduced during the 1990s decreased state subsidies and increased municipalities' share of corporate taxes. Thus the reforms gave municipalities more autonomy (in how to arrange their social services), but also increased competition between them. State grants given to Helsinki decreased from 831 Euros per inhabitant (in 1993) to 96 (in 1998). At the beginning of the 2000s state grants for Helsinki became negative: Helsinki was now compelled to subsidise other municipalities. Helsinki's share of the nationally collected corporate tax increased from 123 Euros per inhabitant (in 1994) to 1070 (in 1998). Seen from the point of view of Helsinki, the change in type of revenue was dramatic: the proportion of corporate tax in relation to total revenue increased from 5.2 per cent in 1994 to 31.9 per cent in 1998 (Haila 2001). Since 2000, the state has gradually decreased municipalities' share of corporate tax. Cities that have been successful in attracting companies have protested. The issue of corporate taxes has been debated between the state and cities, and tests the limits of municipal autonomy.

The economic crisis of the 1990s posed a challenge to the established practices of urban governments, and precipitated local government management reforms. Increased autonomy and new financial incentives made municipalities more entrepreneurial, outside-looking and involved in business developments, without, however, giving up their traditional key tasks in providing social services. Decentralisation of power, autonomy and flexibility led to differentiated practices in organising and running urban governments in Finland (Sandberg 1998). Despite resistance, political leaders, as well as the part of the state bureaucracy inside the ministry responsible for cities and regions, have begun implementing public policies that allow differentiation between cities, although this violates the pre-existing principles of universalism (equal social services for various groups in all municipalities).

The economic growth that followed recovery from the recession benefited different regions unevenly. Helsinki was one of those regions that began booming and this growth spilled over into surrounding municipalities. Overall, the Helsinki metropolitan area accounted for 20.8 per cent of the Finnish population in 1990, 23 per cent in 2000. The population of Helsinki, which had been relatively stable for a long time, even faced a small decline, grew from 490,691 inhabitants in 1990 to 555,474 inhabitants in 2001. Helsinki and Espoo, the two main municipalities of the Helsinki metropolitan area, were the two fastest growing municipalities in Finland.

The concentration of economic growth and population in the Helsinki metropolitan region created a tension between Helsinki and the rest of Finland. Under these new circumstances, maintaining the welfare state, providing equal quality of life in different regions of the country, maintaining integration and modernising the management of public services was a challenge for the state. State policies, in the universal welfare state model, aimed at regional equality. In a large, sparsely populated country, which contains the remote Lapland and less developed eastern regions, that meant rigorous redistribution mechanisms rooted in the welfare state.

Joining the EU had a major impact on Helsinki. Once a tiny and sleepy capital of a small social democratic country on the fringes of Europe, it suddenly found itself on the focal point of the Baltic Sea, between the current EU, the soon to join Baltic states, the oriental border of Europe and St. Petersburg, in a prosperous and booming economic region thanks to the remarkable success of the firm Nokia (Steinbock 2001). Joining the EU was therefore a considerable change of scale for Helsinki urban actors with immediate political challenges. Well prepared to join the EU, Finnish elites have rapidly seized the initiative. In Helsinki, politicians who ran the city council of Helsinki and its related organisations immediately embraced Europe. Before long they were ready to expand the airport, to build a new harbour in Vuosaari, to compete with Stockholm and to ally with the neighbouring Estonian capital Tallinn. The city of Helsinki and its Lord Mayor Eva-Riitta Siitonen became very active in different transnational networks such as Eurocities and the EU capitals of Europe (she chaired both at once), the Union of Baltic cities, and the network of Nordic cities. In the words of the mayor, Helsinki is a 'pocket-sized metropolis', but very active on the international scene with a wide range of responsibilities.

Simultaneously, the world success of Nokia marked the rapid insertion of the Helsinki economy in the world economy. Soon, Finnish CEOs, including

Nokia's, argued to decrease the income tax for expatriate IT workers in order to attract the best from India or Silicon Valley – a complete breach of the Finnish political landscape. The prosperous new IT bourgeoisie operated on a different scale and questioned the basis of social policies. At the same time Baltic and Somali migrants, mostly in Helsinki, contributed to the diversity of the population. Suddenly, urban elites had to think about the political management of those new populations and some were arguing for a multicultural Helsinki, much to the surprise of other parts of Finland. The concept of the quiet fellow traveller of Helsinki within the homogeneous Finnish state was severely under question. Helsinki elites were looking beyond the nation-state, a partial exit strategy (Le Galès 2002).

These two dynamics demonstrate that changes of scale brought in new problems that emerged on the political agenda: economic development, competition with other cities, differentiated housing needs, multiculturalism, the fight for corporate taxes, provision of services, transportation and environmental issues. It gradually became apparent that these problems could not be dealt with easily by individual municipalities, hence the salience of the metropolitan governance issue. These developments had a major impact. Urban elites in Helsinki were led to articulate a different common interest from the rest of the country which derived either from *ad hoc* cooperation due to increasing interdependence, or from the newly conceptualised view of the interests of the metropolitan area, for example in the case of economic development.

Four municipalities

In most metropolitan area, and Helsinki is no exception, one can find a legacy of past battles, annexation and political rivalries which constrains contemporary debate. The Helsinki metropolitan area consists of four cities with different histories and policies:

- Helsinki, the capital of Finland, with 555,474 inhabitants (in 2000); Helsinki was founded by a Swedish king (in 1550) and made capital of the country by a Russian czar (in 1812).
- Espoo, 213,271 inhabitants, was founded in 1458 and became a city in 1972.
- Vantaa, 178,471 inhabitants, was founded in 1351 and became a city in 1974.
- Kauniainen, which is located inside Espoo and has 8,550 inhabitants, was founded in 1906 and became a city in 1972.

The history of drawing borders between these four municipalities has some enduring legacies. In 1928, the Ministry of the Interior nominated an administrator to study the incorporation of the suburbs into Helsinki. In 1944, the government announced the annexation, which was implemented in 1946, and the metropolis of Helsinki was born (Brunila 1962). The city of Helsinki had been able to influence the development of these annexed suburban villa settlements even before the annexation of 1946. Helsinki, by far the dominant municipality, took a strong stance when the organisation of its suburban municipalities was at stake (Saukkonen 1962: 424). The last annexation took place in 1966, when Vuosaari was annexed to Helsinki. As neighbouring municipalities were starting to grow, they organised themselves to make sure that no more annexation would be possible. They feared they would 'fall like ripe fruit into the arms of Helsinki', as suggested by the former chairman of the city council of Helsinki, Teuvo Aura (Kolbe 2002: 200).

The metropolitan governance debate is shaped by the unequal nature of the four cities and especially by the conflict between the dominant municipality Helsinki and the new town Espoo. The current lord mayor of Helsinki is conservative. For a long time Helsinki was run by conservatives and social democrats, but now the Green Party has become the second largest party. Social democrats hold classic views about metropolitan government: build more housing, control the land, improve the management of public services. By contrast, the conservatives defend the idea of social and spatial differentiation. Espoo is more conservative than Helsinki and differs from the classic social democrat model. The conservative council is closer to business interests, tries to avoid bureaucracy and is keen to promote 'new public management' ideas. Used to manage fast growth, the council prides itself on developing innovative solutions to organising services. It has become keen to develop a different culture from that of Helsinki. Vantaa (the former name, the Rural Commune of Helsinki) was for a long time a rural area which grew as a suburb to Helsinki. The international airport of the Helsinki region is located in Vantaa. The development of the airport gave Vantaa a new stimulus and it began to grow as an edge city to Helsinki. Social democrats have power and Vantaa is more working class than Helsinki, Espoo and Kauniainen. The council is run as a classic labour city with a powerful local administration. Kauniainen has its origin in the founding of a real estate company that sold building sites. One guiding principle which still persists today in Kauniainen policy is to preserve its villa settlement nature. This means zoning large lots and less high-rise. Forty per cent of inhabitants are Swedish speaking (in Finland overall 5.6 per cent) and the Swedish National Party is the largest party followed by conservatives. Such differences between cities in the metropolitan area, reinforced by the tradition of strong municipal autonomy, explain the suspicion with which the question of metropolitan governance was met.

Social services and housing: interdependence and professional networks

Social services are the main distinctive feature that differentiates Nordic municipalities from the rest of Europe. In Finland, social services represent 30 per cent of the budget of large municipalities (in the municipality of Helsinki expenditures in social and health services make up 50 per cent and in education, 25 per cent of the overall budget). Such a high level of welfare spending has improved the health of the population and produced remarkable results in the fight against poverty. In the 1990s, however, the provision of social services became a difficult issue. The concentration and diversification of the population in the metropolitan areas put a stress on the provision of public services such as schools, hospitals and day care. The decrease in state subsidies worsened the situation. New problems led municipalities to work out new *ad hoc* forms of cooperation. Helsinki and Vantaa have an agreement concerning social services for homeless people. There are HIV housing centres organised for the metropolitan area. Such cooperation is based upon the tradition of the universal values of the welfare state and norms entrenched within social professions. Professional networks are the driving force for this type of cooperation.

Housing is one of the most difficult issue in the Helsinki metropolitan area. The problem in Helsinki is the shortage of land and the high price of housing coupled with the rapid rise in the population. The housing question calls for cooperation, not only between the four cities but also with municipalities further away from Helsinki. The small residential settlements along the railways line from Helsinki show signs of increasing urban sprawl. They house some of the population increase of the Helsinki region and have even developed faster than some regional cities such as Rovaniemi, Kuopio and Seinäjoki. The latter are towns, proper urban governments, with resources to accommodate people and provide public services; the former are settlements without history and civil servants, unprepared to handle fast growth.

The four municipalities in the Helsinki area have different resources and policies for solving the housing problem. Helsinki has created many small flats, social housing and housing for ethnically mixed immigrants. Espoo has created more semi-detached owner-occupied housing and less housing for immigrants. Espoo does not want to espouse the urban model of Helsinki and build dense residential neighbourhoods, but instead to build houses and defend its suburban way of life. Kauniainen wants to preserve its villa settlement nature.

The population growth and the different responses to this challenge by the four municipalities have created new phenomena in Finland: emerging social differentiation and segregation, and competition between municipalities. The city of Helsinki is therefore under pressure to give up its stress on social housing policy. Indeed, Helsinki is losing its corporate taxes and state subsidies while Espoo is attracting good taxpayers with a housing policy that offers accommodation to the wealthy upper and middle classes. In Helsinki there is pressure to build up-market houses for rich taxpayers rather than accommodation for immigrants and social welfare recipients. Politicians in Helsinki are debating whether Helsinki should change its housing policy to bring in more tax revenue. The Finnish system of local income tax as the main source of local revenue forces cities to compete for residents and affects their housing policy choices. This dynamic runs against any attempt to organise metropolitan cooperation.

Utilities

The organisation YTV manages several utilities. It is concrete evidence of long-term cooperation between the four municipalities of the Helsinki metropolitan area. YTV is a municipal organisation with 260 employees and a budget of

133.4 million Euros. Its statutory duty includes waste management, public transport planning and air pollution control. It buys services mainly from the private sector. Over the years, through the opening up of competition, it has tried to lower the cost of services, for example in local transport or by organising a large district heating system which is more efficient in terms of energy consumption. Waste management was privatised fifteen years ago (a joint venture between a Finnish and a French company), then buses. Water by contrast is run by a municipal company, Helsinki water. The members of YTV's executive board come from the four municipalities: seven from Helsinki, three from Espoo, three from Vantaa and one from Kauniainen. YTV runs services for the four municipalities, some, such as transportation, for the whole region.

YTV is an interesting organisation in terms of metropolitan governance. It seems efficient and runs smoothly in a highly technocratic style. Although politicians sit on the board, the organisation is run with as little politics as possible. This has negative consequences. YTV integrates the management of different services for the four municipalities. It should be emphasised that transport, energy and water are not small services. However, there is no link, or only a very limited one, between the planning exercise of each municipality and YTV strategy. YTV runs services according to its own logic without any integration of the strategies or policies of the municipalities in which it operates. A second negative aspect of YTV management comes from the absence of public debate and the transparency of choices. No consumer groups are represented on the board or consulted for different decision processes. Examples elsewhere have suggested that politicians (part-time amateurs in this technical area) are likely to be 'captured', so to speak, by the agency. A regulatory agency usually gives a formal say to consumer organisations. Here major choices are being made in the name of the four municipalities without much public debate, without consumers' representatives and without clearly identified political representation, as council representatives are not easily identified in terms of accountability.

From a democratic metropolitan governance point of view, utilities are too essential a subject to be left in the hands of an organisation such as YTV without more debate and more control. Utilities and transport include more and more technologies and structure the development of urban areas. They also raise questions of surveillance, public space and sustainable development.

Economic development: cooperation and competition

As far as firms are concerned, borders between municipalities are irrelevant and can even be harmful. In the Helsinki metropolitan area, economic development has been a major factor providing incentives for cooperation. Gradually, in their relation with large firms and other European cities, urban political elites from all the municipalities have become convinced they have to elaborate a strategic vision, an 'appropriate' vision for the economic development for common good for the Helsinki metropolitan area within the global economy. This has both marketing and political logics as it is used to negotiate with the state.

In the economic development domain, cooperation has flourished among the municipalities in relation to the demands of economic actors and business interests. The Helsinki Development Corporation, for instance, is a joint body which organises the marketing of the Helsinki region for global investors. It has offices in Moscow and Stockholm. The two science parks in the region, Innopoli and Viikki, are joint organisations between municipalities, universities, government organisations and firms. Culminatum is another joint organisation comprising municipalities, chambers of commerce, industries and universities. Its task is to foster the economic development of the Helsinki region. Vantaa and Helsinki work together in the area of logistics because of the international airport and links with the new Vuosaari harbour. They have developed a strategy for the Helsinki region to become a logistics centre for the Baltic Sea, including the airport and the port.

There is a commitment among urban elites to increase 'the competitiveness of the area', and to raise its profile. The government, business leaders and municipalities have enthusiastically espoused a vision of a 'knowledge society', and promote Helsinki as the 'learning city'. They have created a complex web of links connecting research, universities, capital, firms and municipalities. Municipalities and the economic elite have found a common interest in trying to attract highly educated information technology workers to the Helsinki region. The wish to raise the international competitiveness of the region has temporarily pushed aside competition between cities and makes the elite work for the international profile of the city.

Increased opening of and participation in European horizontal networks have further fostered the cooperation between municipalities. The joint venture Culminatum has participated in drawing an urban policy for the Helsinki metropolitan region together with the mayors of the four cities. The role of Culminatum has been to develop the know-how and expertise base of the region. It aims at developing the Helsinki metropolitan region as one of the leading innovation centre in the world. In order to achieve this it has proposed the establishment of a new international university and the creation of a twin city of science of Tallinn and Helsinki.

The lord mayor of Helsinki has organised an informal committee called Helsinki Klubi (Helsinki Club), comprised of the mayors of Helsinki, Espoo and Vantaa as well as representatives from the business community, public administration, science, the media and the cultural community. This informal group is a good example of a Finnish model of partnership which relies upon networks to structure a particular mode of governance. The club is based upon a coalition that is trying to elaborate and to impose a legitimate view of the common good for Helsinki. The club does not use only the resources of the main organisations (municipalities, chamber of commerce), but in particular it also uses the joint bodies which have recently flourished within the urban area, that is, the Helsinki Metropolitan Development Corporation, the City of Culture Foundation, Culminatum. All these are multi-partner bodies. The club has worked out a strategy to develop the Helsinki region and drawn a 'vision' representing the

Helsinki area as 'a Baltic Rim business and logistical centre which draws its strength from science and the arts' (Helsinki Klubi 1997). Its view of the future is to develop the Helsinki region as (1) a creative centre of technology, learning and culture, (2) a centre for business and logistics in Northern Europe, and (3) a safe, pleasant and attractive living environment. Different projects are planned under this programme. The implicit political message in the document is that the Helsinki region should be given the resources and the autonomy to grow, to be competitive on the global scene.

Networks of metropolitan governance

At the level of the metropolitan area, the governance of the Helsinki metropolitan area seems to be a mix of robust governments, that is the four municipalities and dynamic metropolitan networks. The Municipalities, that is the world of government, are very well organised and established. They run services, sometimes in innovative ways. They are still very active in their traditional domains of intervention such as social services, planning, housing, transport and education. But they have become more involved in marketing, internationalisation, culture and economic development. The new tax system has provided incentives to cities to become more responsive to market logics and to attract firms. Although they remain powerful bureaucracies, they are in closer contact with firms, which are, to a limited extent, integrated to manage different services. In the world of government, politicians and parties still play an important role. Conservatives, social democrats and the Green Party (a typical urban party opposed to rural interests from the north and the east) run the councils by seeking consensus. However, political conflicts between parties and between municipalities, together with the relations with central government, still structure the governance of the area.

In different policy areas the four municipalities have increased their cooperation. Mechanisms as well as pressure to cooperate developed because of the new scale of social and economic problems which increase the interdependence of the municipalities. Beyond the world of government, the governance of the area is organised by formal and informal networks which are dependent on old divisions between the conservatives, the Helsinki University of Technology and the business community on the one hand, and the left, environmental groups and cultural associations on the other. The club, the informal group organised by the lord mayor of Helsinki mentioned above, is just one example. Beyond the club, there are other examples of informal networks and multi-partner bodies. Both in the business world of clusters, research and development, and in the world of culture, environment and the third sector such networks seem to be very dynamic, providing integration mechanisms at the level of the metropolitan area.

It is too early to assess the performance of this mode of governance but if all projects under suggestions become implemented, this would indicate a clear move towards a more informal governance structure at the metropolitan level – a more flexible, responsive, oligarchic and non-accountable structure. It remains to be seen whether the club will deliver and whether interests which are excluded from this rather conservative group will give up, resist or jump on to the bandwagon. It also remains to be seen whether the club and other new networks will become more than an umbrella organisation or whether city councils will hold on to their resources, expertise and stability.

State-led pressure for metropolitan governance: controlling Helsinki's growth and the break away from the universalist welfare state

The economic and demographic boom of the Helsinki metropolitan area has created two distinct but related spatial problems for state elites: (1) how to control economic growth in Helsinki to maintain the basis of strong social and economic equality within the country, and prevent social polarisation and political conflicts between the main city and the northern and eastern rural parts of the country; and (2) how to foster the competitiveness of the Helsinki metropolitan area, so central to the Finnish economy, and manage the growth by developing infrastructures, housing and the environment. The result has been new territorial strategies organised by state elites to cope with conflicting pressures and goals. The dynamics of metropolitan governance building, still in their primary stage, emerged as an answer to these contradictory goals and interests.

The concentration of economic development and wealth in the Helsinki metropolitan area makes it impossible for state elites, and in particular the representatives of the Ministry of the Interior responsible for the regional development of the country, to ignore the issues of such unbalanced economic dynamism. The ministry, however, has a difficult position and limited potential to act for the Helsinki region because of the strong pressure of rural interests. In general, state elites fear the marginalisation of Finland as the north-east corner of Europe. Furthermore, the competitiveness of Finland depends upon the competitiveness of the Helsinki region, the core region of Finland. Size is seen as an issue because the Helsinki metropolitan region is not very large in comparison with St Petersburg, for instance. Although size is not the only, and perhaps not even the most crucial, factor for economic success, the ministry refers to the policies of neighbouring Scandinavian countries that have created a district with 3.2 million people, Öresund, by building a new bridge connecting Copenhagen and Malmö. This reference implies the idea that a metropolitan area can solve its problems of size. It can also be seen as a way of legitimising the ministry's efforts in the Helsinki region, which is subject to criticism from the rest of Finland. Framing the metropolitan issue in terms of international competitiveness and the size of the area is also a trick to put pressure on municipalities. It is their task to develop cooperation and key projects. International economic competition between urban regions is used as a legitimising device by the ministry to facilitate the cooperation between municipalities.

The Ministry of the Interior is also concerned with the internal problems of the Helsinki region. Urban sprawl, with its negative impacts on land use and increasing demands for public infrastructure investment, is not in accordance with national guidelines for sustainable development. The scenario of the metropolitan catastrophe, that is anarchic urban sprawl fuelled by economic growth, internal migration and the globalisation processes, is seen as a problem which has to be tackled in order to promote social integration, economic competitiveness and sustainable development. The ministry is convinced that such a catastrophe can be averted through the effective management of the Helsinki metropolitan area's growth.

Despite these worries and wishes, and obviously because of the pressure of rural interests, the Ministry of the Interior does not have any ambitious plans for mergers of municipalities in the Helsinki region. It has developed an incentive programme for municipality mergers (supposedly to reduce the cost of bureaucracy) and has introduced a new way for municipalities to form larger entities. Traditionally, the statistical units of municipalities were administrative units. Helsinki collected and published statistics about Helsinki, Turku about Turku and Tampere about Tampere. During the 1990s steps were taken to further municipalities forming what are called *functional urban regions* (FURs). In 1993, new regional development legislation introduced the concept of a district, new regional governance level between the municipality and county levels. Districts were defined according to travel to work. In 1995, the Ministry of the Environment published a report introducing a method for describing the urban network in Finland (Vartiainen 1995). This study was the basis for the Urban Network Study (Vartiainen and Antikainen 1998) by the Ministry of the Interior, which described the nodes and networks covering the whole of Finland.

State reforms in the 1990s have reduced the potential for direct intervention on the part of the ministries, which have lost control of some policy instruments. The new planning and construction law, for instance, reduced ministry control and cancelled the *a priori* approval of municipalities' plans. Instead of any concrete merger plans the ministry fosters cooperation, but also competition. Officials and ministers alike are keen to play the 'divide and rule' strategy between Helsinki and the other municipalities. They are therefore trying to enforce cooperation between municipalities in the Helsinki metropolitan area in order for them to improve their effectiveness but without providing extra resources.

Uneven economic development and Helsinki's demographic growth challenge the principle of universalism. The Ministry of the Interior is at the forefront of the territorial restructuring of the Finnish state and has been particularly active since the late 1990s. National urban policy advocates differentiation among cities that are now rewarded for developing strategies that differentiate them from other cities. The irony of this national urban policy which began at the end of the 1990s was that the Helsinki metropolitan region was excluded from it. A new regional policy has been initiated to respond to EU incentives. Despite rural interests, and without explicitly mentioning it, the new policy gives more importance (and potentially resources) to the fast-growing Helsinki region without giving up support for the countryside. The new and controversial aspect of the new regional policy – the centre of expertise programme – implemented over the past years is that it accepts different economic development and different policies between regions – thus recognising that there is not much that the state can do to enforce regional equalities. Municipalities are encouraged to develop their strength and specialisation to gain resources from the centre. This new policy is strongly opposed by those who represent the north of the country or those attached to the Finnish egalitarian welfare state.

The new legislative framework which has strengthened the autonomy of municipalities and increased the competitive pressure hinders the cooperation between municipalities. At the same time the ministry itself has less capacity to impose cooperation. The ministry fears that political and cultural opposition between rural and urban municipalities will develop when municipalities compete to attract inhabitants, economic activities and shopping centres.

Paradoxically, this new type of state intervention provokes reactions and creates unity to face increasing state pressures. When they demand more resources for the need of their disadvantaged populations and infrastructure investments, urban elites are told to find new ways to finance themselves without tax increases. For example, the social democratic (before 2003) prime minister suggested that Helsinki should sell its landed properties to raise revenues; this contradicts traditional social democratic policies of land ownership and planning.

New types of oppositions and cleavages are therefore emerging. The six largest cities, Helsinki, Espoo, Vantaa, Tampere, Turku and Oulu (which represent 55 per cent of job increases and 76 per cent in IT job increases) have agreed to begin a joint urban policy, to act collectively on certain issues and demand the ability to negotiate directly with the state. The impetus for the forming of this coalition was the decision to leave Helsinki outside the national urban policy and the redistribution of corporate taxes in such a way that these successful cities are to lose their share of the corporate taxes. The former mayor of Vantaa, Erkki Rantala, calls this initiative a defence struggle because these cities are national, even international, first-class actors, the economic dynamism of the country. He considers that their development capacities are taken away. For him, the cut in the share of corporate tax revealed the attitude of the state. The mayor of Helsinki, Eva-Riitta Siitonen, defends the initiative by appealing to democracy. This initiative of the six cities makes their voice heard more loudly in the government and counteracts the pressures of powerful rural interests. It also shows mixing of scales. Three cities in the Helsinki metropolitan region are joined by cities of Tampere, Turku and Oulu in the middle, west coast and north Finland.

In this context, conflicts between municipalities and the state, and between Helsinki and the state in particular, have created an incentive for municipalities in the Helsinki metropolitan area to organise themselves to defend their interest against the state and the rest of the country. This is therefore a key point: gentle agreement within the social democrat consensus leading to the ever-increasing welfare state has been replaced by tensions and conflicts. In that process, the interests of the Helsinki metropolitan area, under attack from the rest of the country, and under attack from the centre, started to emerge. The cleavage between the interests of Helsinki and those of the rest of the country has become a major issue to manage for central government. Fiscal policy, provision of public services, public investment, economic development, employment policy and immigration have created open political conflicts with a territorial dimension. The territorial organisation of the state, the regions and the munici-palities is under restructuring with fierce political debate. The Helsinki metropolitan governance question takes place in this context of the transformation of the Finnish state.

In the Helsinki metropolitan area, cooperation between municipalities and the emergence of metropolitan governance did not emerge to solve practical problems only. The driving force behind the collective action of these municipal-ities has been the urge to defend themselves against (1) small town and rural interests and (2) the state. The restructuring of the Finnish state started the process and provided the impetus which led Helsinki municipalities to reorganise themselves.

What does it mean for metropolitan democracy?

The slow making of metropolitan governance in Helsinki has been pushed mainly by state interest and a coalition of actors interested in economic develop-ment. Finland is becoming a more diverse and differentiated democracy imbued with EU polity in the making. The Finnish central and local state responded to the demands for citizen participation by passing a new planning and construction law at the end of the 1990s. The new law extends the potential of citizens to participate in the planning process. All those affected by planning are granted a say, not just landowners, and the period of consultation has been increased. Citizens have a right to be informed about plans at the beginning of the planning process.

The new law has increased the amount of complaints. In Helsinki the target of these complaints has been a new master plan, which aims to increase the density of Helsinki. Helsinki needs more housing and taxpayers, and to answer this demand planners have zoned new residential land. Citizens have organised them-selves to oppose this densification plan. In one residential neighbourhood, Lauttasaari, residents' association have mobilized inhabitants to oppose the Helsinki planning office's plans. They have arranged meetings, written to public forums and published a pamphlet to protect their neighbourhood. To call such protests 'participation' can be misleading. They are also expressions of self-interest. People criticising the densification defend their neighbourhood and ignore the collective interest of the whole city of Helsinki.

The forces and interests opposing the making of metropolitan governance can be divided into three groups. First, rural political interests oppose any strengthening and allocation of resources to urban areas, especially to Helsinki. Antipathy against Helsinki in Parliament and the ministries is a popular issue in the political debates in Helsinki, as in most centralised countries. Second, citizen groups oppose metropolitan governance by arguing that it is not democratic. The influential Helsinki Club is not an open forum: it symbolises the drive towards oligarchic rather than democratic metropolitan governance. Third, opposition comes from the municipalities themselves. Any suggestion of merger is fiercely rejected within the residential area of Kauniainen and Espoo, far less so in Vantaa and Helsinki. The mayor of Espoo regards the talk about a joint metropolitan government as 'idle talk' (according to *Länsiväylä*). It is commonly argued that different political traditions and cultures will prevent the formation of any kind of metropolitan governance in the Helsinki region. Cities are competing with each other and in the Helsinki metropolitan region one city in particular, Espoo, the middle class municipality in the making, is rising and could develop isolationist rather than integrating tendencies. Vantaa and Espoo are rather dispersed suburbs of Helsinki. The recent growth of the metropolitan region has transformed Espoo and Vantaa into secondary urban centres competing with Helsinki. Their political elites are keen to encourage the development of a polycentric urban system with shopping centres and office parks beyond the borders of Helsinki. This development reinforces the differentiation tendency of these two municipalities from Helsinki.

However, all in all, the issue of democracy has not been at the forefront of the metropolitan governance question. In Helsinki the traditional view prevails, that is, that the metropolitan level of governance is not a democratic level and should not be so. To a large extent, democratic life is deeply embedded within the communes and each city proudly defends its own local democratic organisations either in terms of representative democracy or in terms of procedural and deliberative democracy. There is therefore an increasing gap between the 'club', technocratic networks to organise metropolitan governance and the issue of democracy that remains embedded at the communal level. Exceptions to the rule might include some section of the Green Party and a few associations opposed to development projects. This situation, although awkward in the longer term, is built upon robust local democratic arrangements. According to the lord mayor of Helsinki, however, some sort of metropolitan government may emerge in the future.

Conclusion

The four municipalities of the Helsinki metropolitan area have contributed to the making of metropolitan governance in two ways: through professional network cooperation in the social services in particular, and by joining a coalition of actors aiming at developing the competitiveness of Helsinki and raising its international profile. However, despite pressures from the centre, they have resisted any attempt to institutionalise metropolitan governance further.

Despite cooperation in providing day-to-day services, joint strategies and visions to develop the region as an international hub, cities in the Helsinki region are competing with each other. They try to attract inhabitants (the main source of local revenue, through housing policy) and companies (by providing industrial sites).

What is also interesting in the Helsinki case is the fact that although one can see a sort of growth in coalitions in the making at the level of the metropolitan area, the municipalities within the Helsinki area have not abandoned their commitment to maintaining a high level of social services. There is, on the contrary, a driving force to oppose state demands, as well as limits as to what business interests may argue for. Although the municipality of Espoo might be willing to go a little further, the new importance given to economic development issues has not yet led to social services restructuring or to housing policies changes. This trend has proved more remarkable, although to a limited extent, at the central level.

The experience of developing metropolitan governance in Helsinki show that cooperation between cities in the metropolitan area is carried out in different compositions at different levels concerning different issues: with one network for promoting international economic competition, another for providing day-to-day social services. In this sense, we are talking not so much about metropolitan governance but about various networks carrying out various tasks that are not really coordinated, except that at a macro level they are controlled by the state. The most accurate way to describe metropolitan governance in the Helsinki region is as cities uniting and acting collectively against the state to oppose measures imposed by the state to worsen the conditions of cities.

Bibliography

Alapuro, R. (1997) *Suomen synty paikallisena ilmiönä 1890–1933*, Helsinki: Hanki ja Jää.

Brunila, B. (1962) 'Asemakaavoitus 1918–1945', in *Helsingin kaupungin historia. V osa. Ensimmäinen nide*, Helsinki: Suomalaisen kirjallisuuden kirjapaino.

Haila, A. (2001) 'How to Manage Globalization: The Case of Helsinki', *Quarterly Helsinki*, 3, City of Helsinki Urban Facts.

Helsinki Klubi (1997) *Helsingin seudun menestysstrategiat ja kumppanuushankkeet*, 15 December, Helsinki: Helsinki Klubi.

Kautto, M., Heikkilä, M. and Hvinden, B. (1999) *Nordic Social Policy: Changing Welfare States*, London: Routledge.

Kolbe, L. (2002) 'Helsinki kasvaa suurkaupungiksi', in *Helsingin historia vuodesta 1945*, Edita: Helsinki.

Lankinen, M. (2001) *Alueellisen eriytymisen suunta Helsingissä ja pääkaupunkiseudulla 1990-luvulla*, Helsinki: Helsingin kaupungin tietokeskus, tutkimuksia 6.

Le Galès, P. (2002) *European Cities, Social Conflicts and Governance*, Oxford: Oxford University Press.

Lehto, J. (2000) 'Different Cities in Different Welfare States', in A. Bagnasco and P. Le Galès (eds), *Cities in Contemporary Europe*, Cambridge: Cambridge University Press: 112–130.

Sandberg, S. (1998) 'The Strong CEOs of Finland', in K.K. Klausen and A. Magnier (eds), *The Anonymous Leader, Appointed CEOs in Western Local Government*, Odense: Odense University Press.

Saukkonen, J. (1962) 'Helsingin kunnalliselämä vv 1918–1945', in *Helsingin kaupungin historia. V osa. Ensimmäinen nide*, Helsinki: Suomalaisen kirjallisuuden kirjapaino.

Steinbock, D. (2001) *The Nokia Revolution*, New York: AMACOM.

Vartiainen, P. (1995) *Kaupunkiverkko. Kuvausjärjestelmän kehittäminen kansallisiin ja kansainvälisiin tarpeisiin*, Helsinki: Ympäristöministeriö, Alueidenkäytön osasto.

Vartiainen, P. and Antikainen, J. (1998) *Kaupunkiverkkotutkimus 1998, Kaupunkipolitiikan yhteistyöryhmän* julkaisu, Helsinki: Sisäasiainministeriö.

9 Reform and democracy in the Rotterdam region

An evaluation of the attempt to create a regional government

Linze Schaap

Introduction

The city of Rotterdam, with over 600,000 inhabitants, is the second largest in the Netherlands. It has quite a reputation to keep in Dutch public administration of being a frontrunner in the renewal of government and governance. At an earlier stage than the Dutch capital Amsterdam, it divided itself into sub-municipalities, decentralising policy-making responsibilities to directly elected area councils called 'deelgemeenten'. Rotterdam was the first municipality to discover the advantages of citizen involvement in the regeneration of deprived areas when it invented the so-called 'social renewal'.[1] It has frequently had an ambitious political elite, whose performance has led to grand projects of city regeneration, transforming it into a small Manhattan, for example, after the destruction of the city centre during the bombardment of World War II.

However, the city of Rotterdam has another reputation, one to be less proud of. As the present mayor has often said, Rotterdam is number one on the wrong lists: unemployment, poverty and public insecurity. Hence, there are social problems that demand governmental attention.

These problems were important reasons to start thinking about government reform in the 1990s, that is, the creation of a regional government layer in the Netherlands. Rotterdam, again, was number one in that reform process. Observers still doubt whether the list on which Rotterdam holds its first position is a positive or a negative one. It all depends on the perspective one takes. Analysts who start their analysis in the metropolitan reform tradition will support the strategy of creating a regional tier of government, public choice researchers will at least doubt it, and the picture changes again with the network approach inherent in new regionalism (see Chapter 2 and also Kickert *et al.* 1997; Schaap 2003).

Whatever one's theoretical background, reforming is easier said than done. This is a general statement and when applied to the Netherlands it becomes more relevant than ever. The obstacles to reform are particularly hard to overcome when aiming at the creation of a regional layer of government in the Netherlands, as history shows. The Dutch meso-level is quite complex (Toonen 1993). Several attempts were made during the twentieth century and all of them failed. The last attempt was made in the 1990s, aimed at creating so-called 'city-provinces' directly elected by the citizens. The city of Rotterdam and the surrounding municipalities were the first to advocate the idea of becoming a city-province. They were dissatisfied with the number of policy actors that governed the metropolitan area of Rotterdam, among them eighteen municipalities, a province, water boards and national departments. However, the reform project failed, and resulted in the creation of a formalised inter-municipal cooperation; it is multi-functional, but the number of functions is limited.

Reforming is not a technical issue and not an issue to be dealt with without public debate. Reform has several consequences: not least it affects the relations between citizens and government. To put it differently, reforms influence democracy, that is the way democracy functions, not just its structure. This has been a hard lesson to learn in the Rotterdam region. Whereas politicians and mayors considered the creation of city-provinces to be of no interest to the residents, the citizens themselves were of a different opinion. The first indicator was the result of a referendum in which a vast majority of the Rotterdam voters said no to the city-province. An even stronger indicator of voter dissatisfaction was the local election on 6 March 2002, during which a new political party, or more correctly put, a new political leader frightened all the vested interests.[2] His name was Pim Fortuyn (he was murdered two months after the elections). In Rotterdam he gained about 35 per cent of the vote, an enormous number in the Dutch context. His party became the biggest party in the council, bigger even than the social democrats, for decades by far the most dominant party in Rotterdam. Fortuyn campaigned with slogans on the limitation of immigration, harsh policies towards integration and adaptation of immigrants,[3] more effectiveness in public administration, more public safety, hence law and order and the destruction of the closed nature of politics. Above all, he promised to 'listen to the people' and do what they wanted. Many citizens strongly distrusted 'old politics' and therefore voted Fortuyn.

So, reform is not a technical issue and neither does it take place in a vacuum situation. Various developments in government and society influence reform processes. Both issues are dealt with in this chapter. It contains an evaluation of the Rotterdam reform attempts from a democratic point of view. Democracy, however, is a concept with various meanings. In this chapter I apply the distinction between representative and participatory democracy, the first being the main example of input legitimacy, the latter being linked to output legitimacy.

The reform process as such and the resulting formalised cooperation are evaluated. To understand this evaluation fully, some knowledge about Dutch sub-national government is necessary; the next section therefore contains a short overview of its characteristics. In the following sections two basic democracy models are discussed. They are attached to two more general public administration approaches. An overview of problems at the Dutch regional level is presented, followed by a discussion of the reform attempt in the 1990s in the Netherlands, especially in Rotterdam. After that, the reform attempt, the present situation and the proposed city-province are analysed from a democratic point of view.

Dutch sub-national government

At first sight, sub-national government in the Netherlands has a rather clear structure. It has a three-layer system all over the country: local government consisting of municipalities (*gemeenten*), provincial government (*provincies*) and central government. Matters are a bit more complicated though. Beside these three all-purpose layers there are water boards (*waterschappen*), responsible for water management and water quality. Moreover, the European Union must increasingly be considered as another level of government. And to add to the complication, at the regional level many inter-municipal cooperations exist, which often have important service delivery tasks or function as inter-municipal deliberation and negotiating forums.

Despite quite a number of complicating features in Dutch sub-national government, uniformity is the key word. Municipalities to a large extent have similar tasks and similar political structures. The relations between the layers are cooperative and organic. This system was created in the middle of the nineteenth century. Its founder was the statesman Thorbecke, who was inspired by the German Historic Law School when designing the Dutch system (Toonen 1990: 283). It proved to be able to cope with the immense growth in public tasks, though it was developed and formalised in the era of a somewhat 'minimal state'. Nevertheless, the system has been kept until today in spite of the growth in complexity of the modern state due to the welfare system and due to the continuously increasing number of public tasks imposed by internationalisation, differentiation and crisis periods.

From an international comparative point of view it can be said that Dutch sub-national government has 'Germanic' traditions, as Loughlin and Peters state (1997: 48ff.). In this volume the Germanic state tradition is part of the 'North and Middle European' tradition (see Chapter 2). Loughlin and Peters found some influences of the Napoleonic state tradition on the Netherlands and not without reason. Especially when looking at the position of the mayor at the municipal level and the Queen's Commissioner at the provincial level, some resemblances to the Napoleonic tradition are obvious. Nevertheless, the Netherlands mainly belong to the Germanic tradition. As said previously, the German Historic Law School was a very important inspiration for the designer and founder of the Dutch system.

The nature of intergovernmental relations in the Netherlands is a so-called 'decentralised unitary state' (Toonen 1990). The characteristics of this system are the following:

- Interdependent relations between the layers: the relations between the layers of government are not necessarily hierarchical, or based on a clear separation of powers between the layers. They are mainly relations between interdependent entities.

- The autonomous position of the municipalities. They have a general competence: no *ultra vires* principle. The 'open household' of municipalities and provinces is constitutionally protected.
- Provinces exercise supervisory powers over municipalities, whereas central government does the same over provinces. Supervision does not mean 'commanding', but approval of local initiatives, or at least non-resistance.
- The unitary nature of the state is not the same as centralisation. The 'unitary' character shows itself in the large uniformity of public services of the welfare state: the level of income compensation, for example, does not depend on the city one lives in, or on the political colour of the local council. Local government is bound to central policy guidelines. In particular, local income and social security policies are prohibited.
- 'Co-governance' is the instrument most frequently used. Central government legislates after due consultation with local governments and in particular their representative associations. Local authorities implement these central policies (and, to a minor degree, so do provincial authorities). This implementation, however, is not mechanistic in character (Derksen and Schaap 2004: 104ff.). Three different types of co-governance can be distinguished: mechanistic co-governance (municipalities hardly having any possibilities to adapt national policies), administrative co-governance (adaptation is possible; there is some discretionary right, but within more or less strict limits) and political co-governance (in which municipalities are obliged to create certain policies but are left with the freedom to determine their contents).
- Decentralisation: municipalities are autonomous to a certain extent; and even in policy areas where their tasks largely consist in implementing central policies, they often have a large degree of policy freedom (based on discretionary competencies, local presence, knowledge and information). Policy freedom is left to local authorities, enabling them to cope with local situations and to realise political goals.

Inter-governmental relations between the three layers are flexible. The 'co-governance system' is particularly important (Toonen 1990). Due to co-governance the Dutch governmental system has been able to cope with the enormous growth in its tasks and responsibilities without structural changes (except amalgamations) and without cutting down on policy discretion of municipalities. The real amount of sub-national government freedom depends on discretionary competencies as well as the strategies of sub-national authorities. The centralisation resulting from the growth of the welfare state has, therefore, not destroyed sub-national governments' importance. Although their autonomy has decreased enormously, their policy freedom is still intact. Centralisation cannot withstand a vivid local (or provincial) democracy.

Problems at the regional level

In Dutch sub-national government, several problems exist, not least at the regional level, that is the level between municipalities and provinces. One of the problems is lack of clarity at the regional level. There are twelve provinces, but their tasks are limited to environmental issues, spatial planning, traffic, mobility, wildlife preservation and reserves (John 2001: 131). Central government is present at the regional level as well: it has regional agencies for housing, environmental issues, physical planning and health. Third regional actors are the water boards, responsible for water control. They are ambitiously expanding their responsibilities. Last but certainly not least, municipalities play regional roles as well, since they have established all kinds of inter-municipal cooperation – some based on a special law on inter-municipal cooperation, others without any legal foundation. Some are no more than informal agreements, others are binding contracts. Sometimes there are shared companies or organisations, sometimes municipalities have a partly shared civil service.

The main problems are the overlap of tasks, non-transparent responsibilities and the absence of democratic control. As a directly elected body at the regional level does not exist, municipal councils find it hard to know what is going on in inter-municipal arenas, let alone control it. Provincial councillors face similar difficulties. The lack of democracy is evident.

The difficulties with regional governance are felt in metropolitan areas in particular. At the end of the 1980s the initiative was again taken to establish a regional government layer – 'again' because since World War II quite a number of attempts have been made. All of them failed. In 1989, a new round of policy discussion on the structure of sub-national government began in the Netherlands (Koppenjan 1993). Central government, and especially the Ministry of the Interior (1990, 1991, 1993), was the great stimulator. Official policy was aimed at establishing a new governmental layer in metropolitan areas, as an intermediate structure between the present municipalities and provinces, or even as a replacement of the latter. Seven metropolitan areas were defined, among them Amsterdam, Rotterdam and The Hague, each area containing the city and the surrounding municipalities. Other less urbanised regions were expected to be governed as usual. The choice of creating such a layer in only a few areas in the country was rather revolutionary; this was quite a turning point in Dutch administrative history. The uniformity model introduced by Thorbecke, one of the pillars of the system, had not been challenged this obviously before.

Rotterdam reform attempts

In this section, the focus is on one of the metropolitan areas in the Netherlands in which reform attempts have been made. The Rotterdam region, as stated in the introduction, was a frontrunner in the reform debate. In this region the policy initiative was well understood and received. In some policy-makers' opinions, the Rotterdam region, consisting of eighteen municipalities, lacked a uniting governmental body, for which reason consolidation was necessary. At the same time, the need for regional policies was felt in all municipalities. Various problems – unemployment, an imperfectly working labour market, housing problems, environmental issues – called for area-wide governance in a situation where there was no regional government to be held responsible for policy-making.[4]

Towards the creation of a city-province?

Since 1991, attempts have been made to alter the situation. The mayors in particular saw opportunities which the elected local politicians did not yet see (Cachet and Koppenjan 1996: 94).[5] They quickly started to negotiate and in March 1991 they produced a document entitled *Strategic Vision* (OOR 1991a). This *Strategic Vision* was a list of shared regional policy problems and, to some extent, a basis for their solutions. These problems were related to several policy areas: housing, spatial planning, mobility, environment, culture, public health and tourism.

In the policy debate there was no doubt about the necessity of a new regional governmental body as part of the solution. Instead, there was to be a regional layer instead of the traditional provincial government. In the policy document two models were discussed; they were rejected because they were expected to be ineffective (OOR 1991a: 62–63). A stronger structure was to be found. All participating municipalities agreed to this: they supported the strategic vision and the necessity of developing a clear regional structure. A foundation for the forthcoming reform process was achieved based on consensus.

The following years were spent discussing the formation of the proposed regional government. Aspects such as the structures and the responsibilities of the forthcoming government layer were discussed at length. It looked like a genuinely innovative process: there was enthusiasm, many actors involved believed in the process they were part of, they believed in its success, and they thought of many new, almost revolutionary aspects for the new regional body. Central government was initially prepared to let the local and regional actors decide so centralism, uniformity and blueprint planning were definitely to become features of the past. Previous attempts at creating a regional government had been initiated, stimulated and supported by central government alone, whereas in the 1990s the reform process was a collaboration of central and local government.

After a few years, however, the discussion and the preparations became more complex and time consuming. Some central policy-makers became impatient and civil servants of the Ministry of the Interior, acting as guardians of the constitution, discovered that all the innovative elements in the plans, formulated by the cooperating municipalities, were definitely not in accordance with the constitution. The final law proposals contained very few of the innovations originally suggested: the proposed regional government was called a city-province, and its structure and powers resembled more and more that of an ordinary province (Derksen and Schaap 2004: 243). Ironically, the enthusiasm many municipal actors had started with was based on the belief that they were building a new structure *without* the province; now legislative proposals contained the idea that they were establishing one.

Time pressure on local and regional actors was intensified, enthusiasm began to dwindle, differences in opinion began to become irritating and sometimes the grounds for an inter-municipal battle. Support from interest groups started to fade away, civic opposition became manifest. Many became aware of the fact that the reform process was a game played by only a few participants, that is, the mayors, some politicians and civil servants. Getting popular support was never a rule of the game. Municipalities had hardly done more than paying lip-service to the necessity of telling people what was going on: that is, information was thought important, not consultation, let alone participation. And even the information aspect was handled very poorly. No wonder, one might argue, that when a referendum was held in Rotterdam in 1995, over 85 per cent of the voters cast their vote against the establishment of the city-province (the referendum was not conducted in the other participating seventeen municipalities). Although the verdict on the part of the voters was very convincing, the reasons for this advice to the city council were less clear (the referendum had only an 'advisory' character). Several reasons played a role: a general though vague mistrust towards politicians and the feeling that they were playing games that were irrelevant to the people; the conviction that the creation of the city-province would mean the end of Rotterdam (though the mayor tried to suggest that Rotterdam would not become smaller but larger, an argument not very much favoured by the surrounding municipalities); the supposition that tax levels would rise; and, last but certainly not least, the serious lack of information on pros and cons.

The municipal Council of Rotterdam respected the outcome of the referendum and opposed the creation of a new city-province. The reform process was in shambles. Some municipalities wished to stop it, others demanded central government to continue and to force Rotterdam into cooperation. A special committee was established in the summer of 1995 with the task of finding a solution. Its report contained some solutions, but all of them were unacceptable to the majority of the municipalities. It simply overlooked the differences of opinion, and the depth and the nature of these differences (Schaap 1998). Augmenting time pressure generated opposite effects from those expected: with hindsight one can state that because of the constructed lack of time many decisions that were made resulted in unexpected situations. The same holds for the wish for certainty. Characteristic features of the whole process were attempts to grasp the policy problems and to decide in great detail which governmental layer should get which tasks.

At present, the region is still governed by the same actors who were in charge before the reform started, with one exception: the formal cooperative body of the City-Region, a compulsory cooperation between the eighteen municipalities, has been forced upon them by law.

Evaluation: democratic character

How can we evaluate the Dutch attempts in the 1990s to create a city-province as a regional tier of government? In the remainder of this chapter, the focus is not on the effectiveness of the reform attempts, or on their failure, but on the democratic character of the process as such and of the present situation.

Democracy has more than one face: representation vs participation

Democracy and democratisation, or, less abstractly formulated, the relations between citizens and government, have been on the agenda for decades. In the 1960s, 1970s and early 1980s, the issue of government–citizen relations attracted much attention, from academics as well as politicians and the general public. In those decades, the central topic of discussion was the position of individual citizens: their capabilities, their interests and their attitudes. From the citizens' point of view, governments were large and bureaucratic, and barriers to public participation. Such barriers were creating legitimacy problems, which could be solved only by bridging the gap between citizen and government through democratisation, enhanced responsiveness and more openness.

In the 1980s and 1990s, priorities changed: emphasis on legitimacy decreased, and issues of effectiveness were assigned a higher place on the agenda, heavily influenced by the New Public Management ideology. Measures such as privatisation, new management styles and 'contracting out' were taken. In short, attention shifted from democracy and participation to efficiency and management. However, in recent years, participation and democracy have become political and scientific issues again, not in place of effectiveness, but in addition to it.

Concepts of democracy can be divided into more general approaches with respect to public decision making and administration: the *government* approach and the *governance* approach (cf. Kickert *et al.* 1997; Rhodes 1997; John 2001).[6] The distinction between representative and participatory democracy can be applied one-to-one to that between government and governance (though some tensions between this one-to-one coupling can be formulated, see John 2001: 154ff.), and to consolidation and new regionalism (Chapter 2 of this volume).

Government and representative democracy

The *government* approach considers public administration as one entity to be governed as a bureaucracy. The government system is perceived as one system basically founded on Weberian thought. It therefore emphasises the necessity of clear distinctions between the levels of government in a hierarchical and consolidated structure, combined with direct central government control. These distinctions should be preferably constitutional or at least legally based. Next to this, a clear division of tasks between governmental levels is regarded as being essential. Capacities and authorities should be as exclusive as possible, divisions should be fixed, networks closed and policies routinised.

In this view, problems of sub-national government are mainly due to overlapping authorities, unclear distinction of responsibilities, too much centralisation and lack of autonomy for local government. The solutions are seen to be in disentangling responsibilities, decentralisation and, last but certainly not least, increasing the problem-solving capacity of local government by facilitating the amalgamation of local authorities. Inter-municipal cooperation is a rejected solution, since it is supposed to obscure the separate responsibilities of each autonomous municipality. If the geographic scale of a local authority is too small compared to the scale of the societal problems at stake, amalgamation or even the creation of a new layer of government is preferred.

The democracy type attached to the government approach is representation. Starting point of the paradigm of representative democracy is the impossibility of government by the people itself (as was the case in the ancient Greek city-states). Citizens are too numerous, they are considered as being unwilling to act as self-governors, and large-scale participation is supposed to have negative effects on the stability of the government system (see Almond and Verba 1963; Luhmann 1981; Daemen 1983). Representation is thus perceived to be the most suitable form of citizen participation. Policies aimed at enhancing participation are therefore targeted at strengthening representation in order to improve the representative system (Tops and Depla 1993). This strategy aims at improving the effectiveness of government and the functioning of democracy within the existing system of representative democracy, in which citizens appear as subjects, voters and clients. During the last decade, Dutch central government has taken some measures to improve the representative system. A reformulation of the respective roles of the municipal councils and the Board of Mayor and Aldermen (the executive) is the most important one.

Governance and participatory democracy

The *governance* approach focuses on cooperation between government actors and between government and non-governmental actors. This approach is derived from insights from studies on policy networks (Kickert *et al.* 1997) and governance (Rhodes 1997). In this approach, the focus is no longer on creating a new layer of government, but on making things work. It emphasises the relevance of checks and balances as necessary features of a pluralistic society. Decisions are thought to be made in a context of interdependencies in extensive networks (empirical statement). Many actors are involved, governmental as well as non-governmental ones. Government responsibilities may be specific ones, but government agencies do not escape from interdependencies: they often need the cooperation of non-governmental actors. To put it differently, governmental actors are not in control by simply being in government. Policy processes are characterised by trial and error; experimenting is common. Structures are decentralised and fragmented, and are to ensure flexibility and innovation of government performance; control is also decentralised.

The governance approach recognises that problems are centred on the difficulty of municipalities cooperating with each other, the possible inflexibility of the present division of tasks and the existence of the power of veto for some actors, as well as somewhat closed frames of reference (cf. Schaap and Van Twist 1997). The solution is the facilitation of cooperation by creating overlapping authorities and increasing efficiency. In this approach, it becomes clear that an efficient structure (at face value) often becomes penny wise and pound foolish.

Inter-municipal cooperation is perceived as essential for all governmental entities, since it may prevent power concentration. Autonomy is not only impossible but unwise as well.

The democracy type linked to governance is not only representative, but experimental and participatory. It starts from a different angle. Citizens not only act as clients or voters, they also participate in 'the processes of formulation, passage and implementation of public policies' (Parry *et al.* 1992: 16, quoted in Lowndes, 1995: 165). This applies to individual citizens as well as to organisational actors. In a nutshell, civil society is important in the governance of a country. Improving citizen participation in this model means enhancing the participatory dimension of democracy. Its main characteristic is a fundamental change in the role of the citizen. In this strategy, citizens are considered as creative contributors to the policy-making process. They are seen to act as 'policy co-producers'. The result is that the whole configuration of policy-makers and their roles has to be reconsidered; government is no longer the key actor in the policy-making process, but rather the facilitator of self-governing, self-steering citizens and associations of citizens. Key concepts in this participatory strategy are social capital, self-steering and self-government, decentralisation of responsibilities, and interdependencies between societal actors and civil society. In the Netherlands, several strategies have been thought of, several experiments with 'interactive policy-making' have been conducted. The results, however, have not always been convincing (Edelenbos and Monnikhof 2001).

Discussion

Both democracy models are applied in many liberal democracies. This can easily be observed when analysing democratic renewal. In the Netherlands, for instance, two strategies of democratic reform can be observed: perfecting representative government and enhancing participatory democracy. These strategies are not mutually exclusive: instruments from the perfecting strategy can be combined with techniques of stimulating participatory democracy. This can be formulated in even stronger terms: the two strategies can be seen as complementary.

The pure form of representative democracy will always show deficiencies when applied in practice: deficiencies such as a lack of responsiveness to minorities, small groups or individual interests. It is common knowledge that because of this the representative system needs some form of addition to facilitate the direct influence of citizens and organisations on the policy process. The same applies to the ideal of direct or participatory democracy: direct democracy is generally seen as a strategy that does not work in the practice of big government systems such as states and (most) cities.

As a result, we usually find elements of both strategies in projects of democratic reform. Nevertheless, it is often possible to characterise projects as being predominantly influenced by one of these two strategies. In the Netherlands, a substantial number of local communities and local authorities have recently been experimenting along the lines of participatory democracy. Without concluding that this is a dominant trend, it can be observed that these experiments colour the Dutch debate on democratic reform. Discussing democratic reform in the Netherlands, therefore, usually involves discussions on the relevance and possibilities of techniques of direct democracy, such as the referendum, or the prospects of using information and communication technology (ICT) in collective decision making, or the possibility of a transfer of some power to self-governing neighbourhoods or associations (Daemen and Schaap 2000).

The question is, does this apply to the reform attempts in the Rotterdam region? To answer that question, two sets of evaluation criteria have been formulated (see Table 9.1). Using these criteria, in the following section a twofold evaluation is made of the democratic level of the reform process itself and the democratic level of the present situation.

Table 9.1 Democracy evaluation criteria

Representative democracy	*Participatory democracy*
Sound voting system, therefore: • Clarity on political goals • Openness on political choices • Citizens know what they choose • Councillors and members of Parliament know and support what the executive is doing • Citizens have the possibility to evaluate main proposals during elections, before the point of no return	Involvement of citizens and interest groups in policy-making, aimed at consensus and popular support of decisions, therefore: • Open policy processes • Real involvement of citizen, initiated by themselves or stimulated • Popular influence • Public accountability of the executive and councillors

How democratic was the reform attempt? And how democratic is the present situation? Both questions are answered by using the criteria from both the representative democracy and participatory democracy approaches. It should be stressed, however, that this is an analysis from the outside. That is, the criteria are developed for analysis only and not necessarily elements of the actual debate in the Rotterdam region.

How democratic was the reform process?

Rotterdam has a tradition of pragmatism and trust between elites (John 2001: 56); the other municipalities in the region share much of this tradition. That might be an explanation as to why the reform process had a fast start. Many issues were handled, many decisions were taken, and consensus and mutual understanding seemed to be the trademarks of the mayors and aldermen who were in the forefront of the reform process.

Regarding the criteria of the representative democracy, one may conclude that none of these criteria were met. In the 1990 local elections, the regionalisation of government was not an issue. In the first years of the reform process, councillors hardly knew what was going on. Nevertheless, they seemed to support it. No earlier than in the 1994 local elections, at least in the main city Rotterdam, the establishment of a city-province became a hot issue. After the elections, a referendum was held. Over 85 per cent of the voters voted against it. The voters in the referendum had clearly punished the almost confidential and hidden character of the reform process (the same happened in Amsterdam). Then the city council of Rotterdam opposed the creation of the city-province as well. One might conclude that representative democracy, at least in Rotterdam and at least at this point, had learnt what the voters really wanted. It complied.

Regarding the criteria of participatory democracy, the picture is not entirely different. Although some 75 per cent of the inhabitants were aware of the fact that a city-province might be created, few of them supported it (Schaap 1997: 177ff.). None of them was really involved in the process, not even interest groups. Even regional business people (in Rotterdam this means the chairmen of multinational companies) complained now and then, when they might have benefited most from the creation of the city-province. It was a reform process almost entirely prepared by a small group of municipal civil servants, some mayors and aldermen, a few councillors and some central government civil servants and their minister.

How democratic is the present situation?

What is the present situation in the Rotterdam region? First of all, there is no regional government. The eighteen municipalities still exist, as do the water boards and the province South Holland. The municipalities still cooperate in the so-called *Stadsregio Rotterdam* (City-Region Rotterdam).[7] This City-Region is a formal and compulsory cooperation of the autonomous municipalities in the Rotterdam area. It is based on a special 'Framework Act'. The cooperation of the municipalities within the Rotterdam City-Region and between the City-Region and the provincial government has its difficulties, but it functions. It is interesting, however, that no actor involved in the present arrangement is satisfied. Some municipalities desperately want to leave the formal cooperation they are forced to participate in due to central legislation, other municipalities enforce the cooperation, others are still striving to establish a city-province.

The government actors involved are looking for good attitude and position. The province of South Holland hesitantly cooperates with the City-Region, though the latter might be seen as a policy competitor, even now. They share some responsibilities and capacities, but this situation of overlapping authorities functions. The province acknowledges the advantages of the City-Region. Central government, however, does not know what to do, for all kinds of political and historical reasons. There is no majority in the national Parliament for any proposal, leading to a standstill in the reform process. The legislative has decided to support the proposal of the Ministry of the Interior to extend the period of compulsory cooperation of the municipalities within the Rotterdam City-Region. At the same time, Parliament is not fulfilling the request (or even demand) of a large majority of the municipalities involved for direct regional council elections. The Minister of the Interior strongly opposes such direct elections for a City-Region council and so does a majority in Parliament.

Let us apply the democracy criteria again. From the point of view of representative democracy, the present situation is far from ideal. A number of important decisions are hardly under the control of elected politicians. Meetings and discussions of councillors belonging to the same political party, which were usual at the time most councillors believed that the creation of the city-province was only a matter of time, have ceased. In the regional council (no direct elections, it consists of a representation of the eighteen municipal councils in the Rotterdam area) they no longer organise themselves along party lines, but only along municipality lines. The councillors identify themselves with the interests of their municipality, not with regional interests. For citizens, it is very hard to gain insight into what councillors want: the election process, therefore, is imperfect. Direct elections for the City-Region council might enhance the representative nature of the council, but will not necessarily do so. Many policy actors supporting such direct regional elections fail to see that they might be a bit confusing to the voters. What to elect? There would be no real regional government, since the City-Region is formally a cooperation between autonomous municipalities (the executive of the City-Region consists of a couple of mayors and aldermen of some of the participating municipalities). Despite this, there would be a council, directly elected by the voters. Some might call this confusing, or the creation of a city-province after all and at last. If so, the result of the Rotterdam referendum would have been ignored after all.

Again, when evaluating the democratic level by using the participatory criteria, the picture is no better. Policy processes are rather closed and definitely not transparent. Citizen involvement is hard to find. The small number of civil servants and mayors and aldermen mainly focus on each other and on other policy actors such as the province and central departments.

In Table 9.2 an attempt is made to present and summarise the current situation. It should be kept in mind that the focus is on the City-Region, not on the involved municipalities and provinces. They are only mentioned when the way they function could compensate for possible failures of the City-Region.

Conclusion

When we apply both evaluation criteria (representation and participation), the conclusions are rather negative both in relation to the reform process and the present situation.

An explanation might very well be that in the Netherlands debates on the organisation of government obviously lack the value of democratic legitimacy. As far as it is taken into account, many of the involved politicians and civil

Table 9.2 Evaluation of present democracy in the Rotterdam City-Region

Representative democracy criteria	Participatory democracy criteria
Clarity on political goals The board of the City-Region succeeds in setting rather clear goals, despite the fact that the executive board of the City-Region has to negotiate, since it consists of mayors and aldermen of municipalities with very different interests.	*Open policy processes* The policy processes are processes of mayors, aldermen, civil servants and a number of City-Region councillors. In some cases, societal actors are invited to get involved.
Openness on political choices Openness is not so well reached. The board and council do issue press releases and try to publish the decisions. One of the problems, however, is that the political debate behind the decisions cannot be traced, if there is any. The council is organised along municipality lines, not in political parties.	*Real involvement of citizens, initiated or stimulated by them* Possibilities are very limited, due to the closed nature of the policy processes.
Citizens know what they choose Citizens do not choose; the council is an indirect representation. It represents the eighteen municipal councils, not the electorate. During municipal elections, decisions of the City-Region council hardly play any role. This is partly because the political parties do not know what is going on.	*Popular influence* Very limited, if any.
Councillors and members of parliament know and support what the executive is doing Those municipal councillors who are members of the City-Region council too to some extent know what the executive is doing. Others have an information problem. In some cases, especially when a (municipal) alderman is a member of the executive board of the City-Region, he or she has to defend the regional decisions. Municipal accountability for regional decisions.	*Public accountability of the executive and councillors* Not very well developed. Members of the board do, however, increasingly defend their decisions in the mass media.
Citizens have the possibility to evaluate main proposals during elections, before the point of no return They do not.	

servants only seem to recognise representative democracy. They clearly overlook the facts that:

- Representation is not the only way to gain legitimacy, sometimes not even the best way. Legitimacy does not necessarily mean decision making by elected politicians, but can be reached by the participation of those whose interests are involved.
- Political parties are still the only channels for recruitment of representatives, whereas at the same time the functions of political parties are being eroded and their importance is decreasing.
- It is very hard for representatives to monitor all the changes in a reform process such as that analysed in this chapter. In general: representation needs maintenance, whereas the political elite in the Netherlands is very reluctant to acknowledge that there might be some problems with representation. Investments, not least intellectual ones, in other ways of gaining democratic legitimacy are necessary. The network society needs other, additional, roads to democracy.

The possibilities are there. The City-Region clearly lacks a democratic structure. As far as it is possible to foresee future decisions, is it not likely that the legislative will decide to create a fully-fledged regional layer of government. Therefore, the need to find alternative ways of enhancing the democratic character of regional policy-making is increasing. It is too early to be optimistic. It is hard to find a sense of urgency. Especially in the city of Rotterdam the political culture is changing in a different direction. Instead of emphasising the possibilities and advantages of participatory democracy, the political elite seems to focus mainly on representation and on 'doing what we promised to do'. Reinventing democracy is not very high on the agenda.

Now, what does the case of Rotterdam tell us about the three central issues relating to democratic metropolitan governance, identified in this volume (see Chapter 2)?

First of all, we need to wonder to what extent the reform attempts and the present situation affect the openness and closeness of policy networks. This is not easy to say, not least because of the complexity of these concepts (cf. Schaap and van Twist 1997). Two dimensions are important. The first, social, dimension deals with the accessibility of the network, that is the possibilities for new actors to become involved in policy-making. This is an easy question: the present City-Region is a closed unit, created by law. Participating municipalities are not allowed to leave, whereas other municipalities cannot become members. The same holds for the province of South Holland and the water boards in the area.

Network openness has, as stated, another dimension – a cognitive one. Networks tend to have frames of reference of their own and seem to develop standard values, standard behaviour and standard solutions to problems. During the reform attempts, the network was definitely closed in a cognitive sense (Schaap 1997). New ideas, alternative solutions to the governmental problems were neglected and ignored. At present, the City-Region seems still to fight the battle of creating a city-province and is suspected of still being cognitively closed.

Second, a relevant question is whether the type of legitimation has changed. One might say that both kinds of legitimation, input and output legitimation, are important. Input legitimation means a strong say for elected politicians. As has been argued in this chapter, elected politicians, that is the councillors of the municipalities in the Rotterdam region, hardly knew what was going on during the reform attempts and still lack adequate knowledge on the policies formulated by the City-Region. So one might conclude input legitimacy is rather weak.

Output legitimation, on the other hand, seems to be stronger. The City-Region is first of all a service provider. It is, for instance, responsible for public transport and traffic policies. The City-Region is a functional governmental body and does deliver services. One might wonder, however, if the mere delivery of services is a sufficient basis for legitimacy, that is for societal support.

The last topic is the consequence for the civil society–state relations. One can only guess what these consequences are – no studies in this respect have been conducted in Rotterdam. On the one hand, it is easy to see that the creation of the City-Region has led to both centralisation and decentralisation. Some municipal tasks as well as some provincial tasks have become the responsibility of the City-Region. This will not necessarily have resulted in a change in the relations between state and civil society. On the other hand, it has become clear that whereas directly elected councils used to be responsible, at present the responsibilities lie with a functional, indirectly elected body. So the possibilities for societal involvement have decreased. That is, as long as only the formal democratic accessibility of government is taken into account. The City-Region has the ability to use instruments of participative democracy. These do not depend on the existence of a formal representative body. So far, however, it has not succeeded in applying them.

The picture presented here of the Rotterdam region is a somewhat negative one. The reform attempts were of a very closed nature and a rather small number of actors was involved. Changing democracy was not perceived as an issue that would bother the citizenry. But it did. The political-administrative elite could have learned from that mistake. They could have concluded that openness of policy-making processes, citizen participation and involvement of civil society actors were important factors to be taken into account. They could have but they did not. In that respect, Rotterdam resembles the Anglo type of government more than the Middle and Northern European one.

Notes

1 Social Renewal is a way of stimulating citizens to become active in the regeneration process: citizens themselves help their neighbours and together try to improve the living conditions in their streets, supported by civil servants.
2 The technocratic way of dealing with the reform attempts was certainly not the only cause of voter dissatisfaction, but it was important.

3 Without becoming racist, though he did address feelings of alienation and dissatisfaction with 'multi-cultural society'.
4 An elaborate evaluation can be found in Schaap (1997) and Schaap (2003).
5 Note that Dutch mayors are appointed officials, not elected politicians. The Crown (in fact, the Ministry of the Interior) appoints them. This will probably change in 2006. The present Dutch government (January 2004) is preparing a proposal for changing the law and having directly elected mayors starting 2006.
6 When applied to issues of metropolitan government, the government approach compares to the metropolitan reform tradition. The governance approach shows similarities with Bogason's 'Institutional Network Analysis Bottom-up' (Bogason 2000: 109ff.).
7 This City-Region is not to be mistaken for the city-province that never got beyond its *statu nascendi*.

Bibliography

Almond, G. and Verba, S. (1963) *The Civic Culture: Political Attitudes and Democracy in Five Nations*, Princeton: Princeton University Press.
Bogason, P. (2000) *Public Policy and Local Governance, Institutions in Postmodern Society*, Cheltenham: Edgar Elgar.
Cachet, A. and Koppenjan, J.F.M. (1996) 'De vorming van de stadsprovincie Rotterdam: een onmogelijke opgave?', in M. van Dam, J. Berveling, G. Neelen and A. Wille (eds), *Het Onzichtbare Bestuur. Over provincies, stadsprovincies en regionale vraagstukken*, Delft: Eburon: 91–116.
Daemen, H.H.F.M. (1983) *Burgerzin en politieke gematigdheid: een toetsing van de theorie van de burgercultuur*, PhD thesis, University of Enschede.
Daemen, H.H.F.M. and Schaap, L. (eds) (2000) *Citizen and City, Developments in Fifteen Local Democracies in Europe*, Delft: Eburon.
Derksen, W. and Schaap (2004) *Lokaal Bestuur*, Den Haag: Elsevier.
Edelenbos, J. and Monnikhof, R. (eds) (2001) *Lokale interactieve beleidsvorming, een vergelijkend onderzoek naar de consequenties van interactieve beleidsvorming voor het functioneren van de lokale democratie*, Utrecht: Lemma.
John, P. (2001) *Local Governance in Western Europe*, London: Sage.
Kickert, W.J.M., Klijn, E.H. and Koppenjan, J.F.M. (eds) (1997) *Managing Complex Networks*, London: Sage.
Koppenjan, J.F.M. (1993) *Management van de beleidsvorming*, Den Haag: VUGA.
Loughlin, J. and Peters, B.G. (1997) 'State Traditions, Administrative Reform and Regionalization', in M. Keating and R.J. Loughlin (eds), *The Political Economy of Regionalism*, London: Cass: 41–62.
Lowndes, V. (1995) 'Citizenship and Urban Politics', in D. Judge, G. Stoker and H. Wolman (eds), *Theories of Urban Politics*, London: Sage: 160–181.
Luhmann, N. (1981) *Politische Theorie im Wohlfahrtsstaat*, Munich: Olzog.
Ministery of the Interior (1990) *Bestuur en stedelijke gebieden. Bestuur op niveau* (BON 1), Den Haag: Ministerie van Binnenlandse Zaken, Tweede Kamer 1990–1991, 21062, no. 3.
——(1991) *Bestuur op niveau, deel 2. Bestuur en stedelijke gebieden* (BON 2), Den Haag: Ministerie van Binnenlandse Zaken, Tweede Kamer 1990–1991, 21062, no. 7.
——(1993) *Bestuur op nivo, deel 3. Vernieuwing bestuurlijke organisatie* (BON 3), Den Haag: Ministerie van Binnenlandse Zaken, Tweede Kamer 1992–1993, 21062, no. 21.
Overlegorgaan Rijnmondgemeenten (OOR) (1991a), *De regio als nieuw perspectief*, Rotterdam: OOR.

Parry, G., Moyser, G. and Day, N. (1992) *Political Participation and Democracy in Britain*, Cambridge: Cambridge University Press.

Rhodes, R.A.W. (1997) *Understanding Governance*, Buckingham: Open University Press.

Schaap, L. (1997) *Op zoek naar prikkelnde overheidssturing, Over autopoiese, zelfsturing en stadsprovincie* (The Search for Inciting Governance, on Autopoiesis, Selfgovernance and City Province), Delft: Eburon.

——(1998) 'Leren van de Rotterdamse stadsprovincievorming' (Learning from the Rotterdam City Province Formation), *Openbaar Bestuur*, (1): 8–11.

——(2003) 'Government or Governance in the Rotterdam Region', in J. Magone (ed.), *Regional Institutions and Governance in the European Union*, Westport, CT: Praeger:153–173.

Schaap, L. and van Twist, M.J.W. (1997) 'The Dynamics of Closedness in Networks', in W.J.M. Kickert, E.H. Klijn and J.F.M. Koppenjan (eds), *Network Management in the Public Sector*, London: Sage: 62–77.

Toonen, Th.A.J. (1990) 'The Unitary State as a System of Co-Governance: The Case of the Netherlands', *Public Administration*, 68(3): 281–296.

——(1993) 'Dutch Provinces and the Struggle for the Meso', in L. Sharpe (ed.), *The Rise of Meso Government in Europe*, London: Sage.

Tops, P.W. and Depla, P. (1993) 'Vernieuwing van de lokale democratie: een ordening van de discussie', *Acta Politica*, 28(3): 327–361.

10 Metropolitan governance in Germany

Dietrich Fürst

Introduction

To what extent there really are *metropoles* in Germany could well be debated (Blotevogel 2000). There exists, however, a resolution of the German Conference of Planning Ministers[1] (*Ministerkonferenz für Raumordnung*) of 1997 (MKRO 1997) according to which there are seven *metropolitan regions* to be developed which constitute the backbone of Germany's regional structure: Berlin/Brandenburg, Hamburg, Munich, Rhein-Main (Frankfurt), Rhein-Ruhr (Ruhr Valley), Stuttgart and Halle/Leipzig/Dresden/Chemnitz (Saxonian Triangle). But that definition is a political one intended to draw political attention to those regions with the aim of thus boosting their development within a global competitive context. The term 'metropolitan regions' as used in the present context refers to major urban areas, which would include Hanover and Bremen as well. It does not imply the 'global city' concept nor does it refer to any particular problems which are exclusively bound to large conurbations.

Three of the 'metropolitan regions' (Berlin, Bremen and Hamburg) are in a particular situation since the 'central city' is a *Land* (a federal state) and 'regional governance' would require inter-state agreements. Hence they constitute special cases which in the following will be excluded.

Metropolitan governance is a very recent topic in Germany. What we have in abundance, instead, is a discussion on the best organisational structures for metropolitan regions. That has been debated among territorial reformers and scholars of public administration since at least the 1970s (cf. Fürst *et al.* 1990; Akademie für Raumforschung und Landesplanung 1998). Hence, the empirical and theoretical basis for the following is small. In what follows, I address three questions

1   When confronting the definition of 'metropolitan governance' used in this book (see Chapter 2 by Kübler and Heinelt) with the empirical facts one would find discrepancies. Hence my first research question refers to the empirical substance of German metropolitan regions.
2   When comparing the German cases with others (e.g. with US metropolitan regions; cf. Norris 2001a) we observe that more German local governments are about to go regional. What accounts for the difference?

3   The *Hanover Region* and the *Stuttgart Region* are today the most advanced
      models of metropolitan governance in Germany. Could one of them – or
      both – become a best practice model for German metropolitan regions?

German metropolitan governance: basic characteristics

When describing and comparing patterns of governance the approach adopted by
DiGaetano and Strom (2003) seems to be helpful. The authors differentiate
between structural, cultural and agency levels of governance. 'Structural' refers to
the institutional and economic as well as technical context; 'cultural' means
'political culture' and traditions – 'culture is linked to governance by ideological
constructions through which participants in the political process interpret
local events' (DiGaetano and Strom 2003: 360); 'agency' encompasses political
actors, differentiated as to their embeddedness in traditional patterns of flexibility
to react to changing framework conditions.

The structural dimension plays a strong role in Germany: The country has a
long tradition in metropolitan governance with respect to *regional land use*.
That tradition goes back to challenges of the industrialisation process which led
to the institutionalisation of spatial planning (Fürst and Ritter 1993: 5). Already
in the 1920s in many of the larger urban areas within the Prussian provinces
associations of local governments for regional planning existed. The regional
planning tradition became influential for *metropolitan governance*: Regional
planning is a mode of inter-institutional, inter-sectoral and supra-communal
governance. Although restricted to regional land uses it is strongly related to
regional governance, because plan-making involves all regional actors
concerned. By establishing regional planning organisation a regional *organisational
nucleus* was introduced in all metropolitan areas capable of producing binding
regional decisions. For the regional plan has statutory power and is binding to
public agencies. With metropolitan regions being challenged by global economic
and technical changes, the *organisational nuclei* could support the development
of new forms of governance, at least in principle (however, with slow progress:
Wiechmann 1998: 224f., 271f.). The German situation thus differs from others –
such as the American, where, according to Norris (2001a: 533), 'in the absence
of institutions of metropolitan government, metropolitan governance would not
occur in these conurbations'. Consequently, there is also a fairly clear understanding amongst the regional actors of how the region is defined, and the
regional planning associations have become supportive of regional discourses
and interactions between major regional actors which may even have fostered
social capital for intra-regional cooperation (cases at hand are Hanover, Munich,
Stuttgart; cf. Fürst *et al.* 1990; Kujath *et al.* 2001).

Under the pressures of sub-urbanisation with fiscal disparities, social segregation and environmental problems, the processes of economic restructuring and EU
integration (*competition of regions*), the rapid technological developments in
important infrastructures (such as public transport, waste disposal, energy) and
large private investments (e.g. urban entertainment centres, urban shopping malls),

things changed dramatically in the 1990s. The solutions developed in the 1990s were getting more complex leading to a broad range of region-specific *governance patterns*. But despite differences in socio-economic structures, institutions, specific regional collective problems and path-defining traditions which accounted for the differences between *metropolitan governances*,[2] the metropolitan regions portray a number of common features:

- Economically and politically they are the most important regions of their respective *Länder*, and mostly state capital regions at that. They therefore receive special attention and support on the part of their *Land* governments.
- The problem structures are very similar – and similar to the problems of most other metropolitan regions: suburbanisation with intensified regional division of labour, scarcity of land and fiscal resources within the central city, growing fiscal disparities between core city and suburban cities, shrinking local capacities to act *vis-à-vis* large private investors, growing competition from other urban areas, etc.
- The pressure to reorganise the regional government structures stems mainly from within the region, resulting from the stronger competition between regions and *lesson drawing* (Rose 1991). Fewer are cases where one of the stimuli for regional reorganisation is the need to become better organised when competing for government subsidies.

Different patterns of governance

Characteristics of the patterns of governance

In order to specify more clearly what those *patterns of governance* look like, it may be important to differentiate whether metropolitan regions are mono-centrically or poly-centrically structured. But in the German case that distinction does not help much since the majority of metropolitan regions have become 'poly-centric' even though they started with strong mono-centricity (cf. Frankfurt, Hanover, Munich, Stuttgart). More important for differences within the landscape of German metropolitan regions are

- the number of autonomous local governments comprising a region (compare Stuttgart with 179 local communities to Hanover with only twenty), and
- the size structure of local governments: Regions with 'primate cities' (which is the 'normal situation') display different patterns of cooperation than regions with 'oligopolistic structures', where two or more cities of similar size dominate (which is the case in the Ruhr Valley).

Furthermore, it has to be emphasised that metropolitan governance in Germany is dominated by local governments. They coordinate their activities regionally to a growing extent, and the prevailing tendency is to do it *issue-wise*, where tasks overtax the single community (such as energy and water provision, public transport, cultural amenities, etc.) or where cooperation yields cost savings. The organisational model chosen for that purpose is the *special joint authority* (*Zweckverband*), which gives full control of the results to the local governments involved. The propensity of local governments to organise regional cooperation issue-wise results in a multitude of uncoordinated regional organisations. Local governments prefer organisational disorder – instead of a regional unitary administration – because they wish to prevent a 'new regional level', that is, a new regional decision-making body which is independent of their influence.[3]

This leads to a pattern of metropolitan governance with not only issue-wise limited but also closed policy networks dominated by local governments.

In cases where existing local *government* structures are overlaid by different issue-oriented regional networks with other actors taking the lead, their predominantly *functional* concern has the effects that their membership is not bound to a specific region nor do all the relevant actors within a given region participate, and that the different sectoral *governances* very often act in isolation from each other (Wiechmann 1998: 232f.).[4] In addition, the different 'logics of action' of the actors tend to produce transaction costs for cross-over arrangements. Even recent endeavours of the *Land* governments to stimulate innovative processes for the regional economy had difficulties in overcoming that divide. Although state incentives led to network-based public–private partnerships on a regional scale the cooperation between the business sector and local politicians (and administrators) tended to be strained. In a similar vein, the third-sector activists organise their own system of regional governance around issues such as *agenda 21 processes* with a particular subset of local politicians and administrators involved (cf. Schubert *et al.* 2001). In many metropolitan regions, therefore, one could discern at least three different circles of regional cooperation: business-centred, political and third-sector governance. They may fuse with respect to issues (as in regional conferences to establish *regional development concepts* or in *agenda 21 processes*), but only if induced to do so by special incentives.[5]

When analysing German metropolitan governance one should take into consideration that it is traditionally dominated by local politicians and in particular by local administrations. Parties do not play a strong role nor do we find interest groups much involved. Only very recently actors from the business sector have tried to gain influence, and in such cases the local *chamber of commerces* have been their main 'representatives'. In general, German business corporations are remarkably reluctant to participate in political processes to define regional development paths[6] (in contrast with the USA: Levine 2001: 197f.; DiGaetano and Strom 2003: 384f.). But influenced by globalisation, the fiscal crisis of cities and the pressure of the *Land* governments' public–private partnerships as well as corporatist modes of governance have strongly increased in the 1990s (cf. also DiGaetano and Strom 2003: 370).

Due to the dominant role of local governments we observe patterns of metropolitan governance which are strongly institutionalised. Reasons for this seem to be to make the collective cooperation more effective and to insure against risks that other participants may not keep to collective rules and may not contribute accordingly (political culture of distrust).

A further facet is the role played by planning associations. Some of the regional planning associations are only a forum collectively to define the paths of regional development, others are more active and contribute to developing new patterns of *metropolitan governance*. But there can be no doubt that regional planning associations play a role by using their *power to define regional issues* because they are *born regional actors* legitimately representing regional interests. In addition, regional planning associations in metropolitan regions are generally better equipped with personnel and financial resources than planning associations in rural areas (cf. Wiechmann 1998: 235f.).

From those characteristics it follows that government structures dominate the patterns of *governance*. That holds both for the actors involved in regional cooperation and for the issues discussed regionally. The tendency towards institutionalisation is enforced by the German administrative law which requires political decision making to be transparent, controllable and legally restricted – deviations from which may invoke the spectre of *corrupt administration* (cf. Bossong 2001). But it may also be due to the strong local autonomy guaranteed in the Constitution (Art. 28) and defended by local politicians as a good of the highest order. If representatives of the business sector are included then it is primarily on the basis of formalised public–private partnerships.

Some organisational characteristics

Organisationally metropolitan government in Germany is generally based on a tow-tier system, that is, of municipalities and of *associations* formed exclusively by local governments. The private sector is – if at all – only included via advisory boards. Regarding the associations, four basic models can be distinguished (Fürst *et al.* 1990):

1 *A multi-tiered (federal) solution*: at present this exists only in Hanover (if one does not take into account the *Stadtverband Saarbrücken*, because the latter does not encompass the whole metropolitan region). The model consists of a county level which covers the whole region and disposes of a wide range of tasks and corresponding revenues and has a directly elected regional parliament.

2 *An inter-municipal solution of a type of regional development agency with directly elected regional parliament*: there is only one region – Stuttgart – that has developed this type of solution, but others may be about to follow (e.g. Frankfurt). The association has only limited competencies, hardly any executive functions but may initiate projects.

3 *Pure planning districts (Zweckverbände)*: this is the most common type (Hanover until 2000, Frankfurt since 2000, Munich and the Ruhr Valley). A couple of well-defined tasks are assigned to the association, the assembly consists of representatives of the local governments which are nominated by the local councils.

4   *Inter-municipal coordinating devices*: these come in different forms: special
    districts, inter-municipal agreements, coordinating networks. The political
    bodies are the 'councils' consisting of delegates who are not free to vote but
    need the consent of their 'parent' organisation.

The array of functions transferred to a regional association in general contains:
planning functions, regional marketing, and infrastructural tasks (transportation,
waste disposal, sewage system). In the 1990s an additional task became fashionable on the regional level: the elaboration of regional development concepts. But
very often this was performed by an additional body, the 'regional conference',
instead of shifting the task to the existing regional bodies.

The associations are financed by contributions of the members (local governments). The different models act differently due to differences in the *basis of
legitimacy* (directly elected assemblies vs delegates), *different degrees of governing
power* (array of competences) and *different degrees of autonomy* (organisational
core vs networks). Differences in that sense refer to how independently the region
may act *vis-à-vis* local egoisms (more independently where the representatives are
directly elected) or how strongly the region may act (stronger the more functions
and the more fiscal resources the association may control).

In general, the institutionalisation of directly elected regional councils meets
strong opposition from local governments fearing for their autonomy. Hence,
such models had to be imposed by the state, as was the case in Frankfurt (until
2000)[7] or in Stuttgart (from 1994). In recent times, however, a remarkable
change has taken place. In the case of Hanover the directly elected regional
council was initiated by local governments and then put into state law. Whether
that is an exceptional case due to particularly favourable political opportunity
structures are discussed below.

The more softly the association is organised the more it is dependent on the
chief executive officer (CEO). It is primarily this person who shapes the image
and standing of the association within the region. Associations which are well
accepted within the region have more latitude and tend to adopt the role of
regional development agencies even though they are not formally institutionalised as such (Hanover prior to 2000, presently Munich, Stuttgart).

Why do local communities cooperate on a regional level in Germany?

Cooperation is precarious and flourishes only under special conditions. Indeed, it
is burdened with high transaction costs. The most important adverse factors
which Norris (2001b: 562f.) identified and which – to a certain extent – are also
relevant for German metropolitan regions are local government ideology, the
residential bias of the people, constitutional status of local governments, territory (i.e. sovereignty over the territory), state political tradition (i.e. in favour of
local governments), electoral structure and state-elected officials (i.e. with
strong ties to local politics), the strength of pro-sprawl and pro-fragmentation
forces, and local government financing and tax structure.

Although German regions suffer from more or less the same impediments to regional cooperation, we nonetheless observe a growing propensity to 'go regional'. This holds although the factors mentioned by Norris (2001a) are also true for most of the German metropolitan regions. In addition, paradigmatically local politicians and administrators think – as emphasised before – in terms of *government structures* when talking about the regional capacity to act: Networks are considered unreliable because they do not lead to binding decisions, and changes of political leadership within the local governments could break agreements reached within networks.

But that poses a dilemma for local governments: their propensity for regional institutionalisation faces 'institutional dynamics of its own', with the new regional bodies tending to centralise power. In the past this dilemma has impaired the readiness of local governments to join regional collective actions easily.

Factors facilitating regional governance

What, then, could facilitate regional governance? The discussion in the literature and the empirical evidence seem to suggest the following.

In particular, two kinds of *structural framework conditions* seem to be important. For one, in the German context, with a strong statist tradition and heavy reliance on institutions to solve societal problems, regional cooperation faces higher transaction costs. However, in the wake of the increasingly competitive nature of the global economy (DiGaetano and Strom 2003: 374), the fiscal crisis of the public sector and the need to rely more strongly on regional self-governance for economic restructuring, awareness rose and paradigm shifts came about resulting in local governments joining their efforts to address problems of common concern. Second, the state strongly induced regions to collaborate with the *Land* governments regionalising regional restructuring policy and enticing collaboration through fiscal incentives. This was spurred by globalisation and the increased inter-regional competition raising the need for *local collective competitive goods* (Le Galès and Voelzkow 2000: 2f.). Those were issues which required the collaboration of the regional business sector, and more often than not led to public–private partnerships (Heinz 1998).

The need to cooperate politically on a regional basis requires *regional promoters* or at least promoters who stimulate regional thinking. Regional leadership is rare, however, unless there is a 'born leader', an actor who is institutionally legitimised to take the lead. Where metropolitan regions have such promoters institutionalised (e.g. the regional planning associations) the process may develop more quickly (Hanover, Stuttgart, Frankfurt). Such regions apparently have lower transaction costs than those in which the regional promoter must first gain recognition and needs political legitimisation.

The *central city plays an important* role in developing patterns of governance (Lefèvre 1998: 21). Even if the city is not the promoter, it depends on its support as to how quickly and in what direction the *patterns* are developed (cf. Kujath *et al.* 2001: 143f.). Traditionally, central cities are in conflict with their surrounding communities or suburbs (fiscal drain, battle against losing better-off inhabitants to the suburbs, etc.). Yet German central cities have apparently undergone a paradigm change recently, realising their dependency on the suburbs which has made them shift to a more cooperative policy style.

There can be no doubt that *paradigm changes* played a major role in the renaissance of the discussion on metropolitan governance in the 1990s, and not least the neo-liberal paradigm stressing the idea of competition between regions (cf. Lefèvre 1998: 22; Brenner 2000: 320f.). Furthermore, the need and the direction of reform have been embedded in the general discourse on state changes towards an *enabling state* and the discussion on *new public management*. For the present phase of reorganising metropolitan regions it seems decisive that regional cooperation became the buzz-word of the time (Baumheier *et al.* 1998).

Regional cooperation was also intensified by the fact that in the 1990s *new patterns of cooperation with reduced transaction costs* came up. Until then it was a common practice for local governments in German regions to resort to regional cooperation only when issues were to be resolved which were regional in nature or could no longer be dealt with locally. Those were the tasks which required legal constructions with binding decision-making power. Networks could facilitate the decisions but were not considered relevant institutions. It was only in the 1990s that networks became accepted modes of governance (such as 'round tables', regional conferences), at a time when new topics were arising (regional development concepts, regionalisation of regional structure policy) and 'round tables' were used and accepted as modes of political problem solving (Messner 1995). This required a considerable learning process, considering the German legalistic political culture. Earlier, 'round tables' etc. had been judged problematic or at least as not in accordance with the constitutional structures of local government (Berkemeier 1972; Bossong 2001).

Weighing up the different factors, *paradigm shift* seems to have played the most prominent role in boosting regional cooperation and raising the attractiveness of the regional level as political arena (cf. Swanstrom 1996). The paradigm change has been reinforced by EU Structure Funds and the discussions on EU-integration as well as on globalisation, and has been closely linked to *changes in the state*: in response, the state endeavours to foster regional self-help potential (*regionalisation*), and the *Länder* are engaged in making their metropolitan regions more competitive by empowering them (even encouraging them to install lobbying capacities in Brussels).

The influence of the state differs, of course. Differences may be due to whether the central city is governed by the same party as the *Land*.[8] But party differences are clearly of minor importance when it comes to strategy: The general thrust is the same in almost all the *Länder*. That includes organisational support (reorganisation of the region), but only to the extent that it does not spark off general territorial reform. This means that the impulse for regional reorganisation must come from within the region (as in Hanover, see p. 160).

In addition, the reorientation is reinforced by inter-regional *lesson drawing* (Rose 1991; Dolwitz and Marsh 1996). The regions take notice of what others do, if this is considered successful, adopt programmes or institutional devices accordingly.

Significant differences

But still there are considerable differences between the regions. If looking for explanations (following approaches like those of Scharpf 2000: 73f. and DiGaetano and Strom 2003) one would find traces (1) in the incentives and forces to act; (2) in the constellation of actors supporting or impeding regional cooperation; (3) in the dominant political orientation of the actors; (4) in the models of action most familiar to actors; and (5) in the political opportunity structures.

Incentives and needs for cooperation differ considerably depending on the graveness of economic restructuring, on the equivalent devices to cope with regional problems and the 'felt incidence' of the problems. Highly institutionalised regions such as the Ruhr Valley contain many equivalent devices to absorb problems, thus rendering local governments less willing to join forces regionally unless obliged to do so by state government. Institutions endowed with larger corporations developing *corporate citizenship* and relying on the regions' potential to attract qualified 'talents' will find the business sector more supportive of regional cooperation than other regions. Thus a new interest for regions has come from larger corporations eager to improve regional *quality of life* when *competing for talents* (Florida 2001). In the Ruhr Valley in the 1980s this motive led private corporations to initiate '*Pro Ruhrgebiet*'[9] but also resulted in new project-bound networks between business and politicians in Hanover (EXPO 2000), Frankfurt (organisation 'Metropolitana')[10] and Hamburg (application for the Olympic Games of 2012). Hence, not all metropolitan areas are bound to the same incentives and needs for action.

Although in polycentric urban areas there are 'born' leaders (central cities), their acceptance by the suburban cities is generally low, with the effect that without supporting *political opportunity structures* (which in general means state support) they can change very little. That is particularly the case for those metropolitan regions cross-cutting *Land* borders – that holds for many of the German *metropolitan regions* (of the ten major metropolitan regions five crosscut *Land* borders). Without formal state agreements, they are reduced to 'soft' forms of cooperation (in general, loosely organised networks).

With respect to actor's orientations the most relevant aspects relate to (1) the relationship between local governments and the region; (2) the competitive or cooperative orientation of the dominant actors; and (3) the openness or closedness of the political arena *vis-à-vis* economic actors. As to the relation between *local governments* and the *region*, the direct election of mayors is not very conducive to regional cooperation because it strengthens the local orientation of local actors. As to the *competitive* or *cooperative mode* of interaction, regions with different party dominance between the central city (very often social democratic) and the suburban communities (very often conservative) show a more competitive relationship. As to the *openness* or *closedness* towards the business sector some of the regions are more weakly, others more strongly attuned towards *meso-corporatist* modes of action (Voelzkow 2000). The reasons for this are unclear – it may be due to tradition, could be the result of a deep economic crisis in the region (Ruhr Area), but could also be the result of a corporatist political culture which developed on the basis of party affiliations (probably Stuttgart).

Which concepts of governance are preferred depends not least on *how familiar they are to the dominant actors*. In regions with a tradition of local engagements of the business sector (e.g. Stuttgart) neo-corporatist structures develop more easily between politicians and business, while in regions without such traditions, where parties and local politicians govern the process (Frankfurt, Hanover, Hamburg, Munich), the special district or planning association may be the more appropriate model. Where the state administration defines the 'appropriate' organisational model (as in Bavaria, Baden-Württemberg, North Rhine-Westfalia, cf. Frenzel 1998: 171f; Kujath *et al.* 2001: 149f.), regional cooperation tends to be organised more 'strongly', that is, government models of the type of inter-communal associations prevail.

Changes in the patterns of governance imply high political costs (transaction costs). They are easier to realise where *changed framework conditions* or opportunity structures reduce transaction costs. In Stuttgart, as well as in Hanover, such conditions were present (cf. Frenzel 1998; Fürst and Rudolph 2002). One of the most important changes refers to a *paradigm shift*. For instance, in Stuttgart a general paradigm change of the relevant actors in favour of a new organisational structure supported the reorganisation: The local business sector was impressed by gloomy forecasts on the future of the region (which strongly depends on the automobile industry), the politicians feared the competition of the regions, and the *Land* government was interested in strengthening its metropolitan region in relation to European competition. In addition, the *Land* governments launched *regionalisation processes*, entailing new patterns of governance, in relation to which the state gives incentives for regional cooperation. But *situational changes* are also important. Thus, in the case of Hanover, it was primarily the coincidence of the expiry of office of the CEOs of the City of Hanover, the County of Hanover and the Planning Association (*Kommunalverband Großraum Hanover*) combined with the advent of 'EXPO 2000' which spurred considerations to improve the organisational structure of the region.

Hanover and Stuttgart as best-practice models for Germany?

Stuttgart and Hanover are presently the only two regions with directly elected regional councils, if one excludes the particular situation of Saarbrücken.[11]

The Hanover model has been in place since November 2001. It is a first for German standards because the formation of such a strong regional organisation had been vetoed by local governments in the past on the grounds of Art. 28 of the Basic Law (*guarantee of local autonomy*). It follows the well-established concept of *county* and thus the German *government* tradition. Its features are the following: The whole region which formerly consisted of the county-free city of Hanover, the surrounding county of Hanover and the planning association (*Kommunalverband Großraum Hanover*) merged into one county (*Region Hanover*) with the planning association being abolished and the city of Hanover becoming a (formally) county-dependent municipality. There is now a directly elected regional parliament with a directly elected president who is the CEO, and who is also presiding over parliament and representing the metropolitan region politically. Between the different levels of local governments a division of labour has been established which basically leaves all functions closely related to private households at the local level, while most of the functions related to economic development, environmental policy, large-scale infrastructure and social assistance funding are raised at the regional level.

The reorganisation took place in a remarkably short time-span (first initiative 1996, implementation 2001). The following conditions apparently facilitated the reform (cf. Fürst and Rudolph 2002; Priebs 2002).

Apart from the fact that the CEOs of the city, the county and the planning association were about to leave office and the EXPO 2000 offered opportunity structures for organisational change, an important factor was that the redistributional effects of the reorganisation were comparatively small: Prior to the change there were four kinds of local government in the region – the aforementioned city of Hanover, county of Hanover and planning association[12] as well as twenty suburban communities dependent on the county. Now only three are left because the planning association was integrated into the *Region Hanover*, that is, the greater regional county. Thus the planning association was the only 'loser'. Ironically, it was that body which did most to push forward the reform, being the 'lead agency' to carry through the process (the chief regional planner was the promoter of the process).[13]

The losses to be incurred by the organisational reform were only minor. With the exception of the planning association, all the other bodies did not suffer much change in relation to their former situation. An exception may be the city of Hanover, which lost its former status as a county-free community. But even there the practical losses were minor: Some less important functions were transferred to the region, but in exchange the city gained financial relief because social assistance (to be paid by the local governments) was assigned to the region. This entails implicit inter-municipal fiscal equalisation since via the contributions to the county (*Umlage*)[14] the other local governments contribute to financing social assistance. In fact, the city of Hanover had a strong defining power in the organisational reform and nothing was changed against its will. In addition to getting fiscal relief, the city got better access to local planning of its neighbouring communities by integrating them into a common organisation.

A major factor in facilitating the reform was the general *paradigm change* adopted by most of the local governments, namely thinking in categories of regional competition and seeing the development of local governments as closely connected and even dependent on the well-being and development of the region.

The new regional organisation will, however, change the patterns of governance dramatically. This is particularly the case since regional reorganisation was combined with the introduction of an internal administrative reform modelled after the principles of *new public management*. The strong *government* component limits the potential for network-based patterns of *governance*, since they would bypass the powers of the regional parliament. Should such bypassing the parliament take place, it would follow rather subtle forms such as outsourcing functions on privately organised actors.

Hanover, therefore, is about to take a different path of development than Stuttgart. In the case of Stuttgart, regional reform was put on the political agenda in 1991 by the city of Stuttgart and the business sector, with the aim of improving the economic competitiveness of the region which suffered major economic restructuring at the beginning of the 1990s. The new *Region Stuttgart*, enacted in 1994, was developed by enriching the former regional planning association (*Regionalverband*) with additional functions such as public transport, regional waste disposal and regional marketing, and endowing it with a directly elected regional parliament. The new association may also initiate projects if they are deemed important for regional development. In addition, the director of the association has considerable latitude in decision-making, not requiring the prior approval of the parliament. That holds especially for matters of economic development, with the director using his influence extensively for building project-centred networks and instigating new initiatives. The project-centred approach opens up a development path bringing the regional association closer to a regional development agency (cf. Steinacher 1999), and translating the relationship between the regional parliament and the director into one of *principal–agent interaction* (Benz 2003).[15] In a way very similar to that of a development agency, the present director of the association identifies issues of strategic importance, shapes them for political decision-making and organises the adequate means and structures to implement the solutions (Steinacher 1999).

Probably the Stuttgart model is best suited to the situation of German metropolitan regions and more future-fit. The regional parliament provides the regional association with sufficient leeway *vis-à-vis* the restrictive local interests, at the same time offering the necessary capacity to resolve regional conflicts via its party organisation and majority decision rule. The *Region Stuttgart* corresponds well to the requirements defined by van den Berg and Braun (1999) for building the *organising capacity* of metropolitan regions: an *administrative organisation*, the *capacity for strategic networking* (given by the association and its director), *leadership* (embodied in the director), *vision and strategy* to enable regional collective actions, and the capacity to mobilise political and societal support.

In comparison to the *Region Stuttgart*, the Hanover approach may be too traditional face the challenges of metropolitan regions within the context of globalisation. Structural tensions built into the Hanover model may be

1   *Between region and central city*: the regional president directly rivals the mayor of the central city since both are elected directly by the people, both represent Hanover and both play a strong role in their respective parties.

2   *In the limited capacity of the region to integrate the business sector*: not only the 'traditional' government-oriented model (and the tradition of the German public law) rejects closer relations between the business sector and the public sector. The Hanover business sector is also particularly reluctant to join forces with local politicians since its interests are already satisfied without that move, and in addition most of the major corporations in the Hanover region are branch offices (cf. Schubert *et al.* 2001: 180f.).

3   *In difficulties of the region to become a regional entrepreneur*: first, the region does not dispose of functions which are very attractive for the mass media or could raise the regional identity of the public. Second, any claim for leadership would be challenged by the local governments since it raises fears of centralising powers in the region to the detriment of local governments. Third, the local governments are still competing for private investments and not ready to leave the regional distribution of private investors to the 'superior wisdom' of the region. Fourth, it seems that local governments are more capable than the region of developing entrepreneurship, because the region is a 'federation' and hence – due to more complicated decision-making structures – more clumsy in initiating actions.

Conclusion

In the German case, cooperation in metropolitan regions has to surmount higher transaction costs due to the dominance of territorially acting local governments, the strong statist tradition (moving problems upwards to be handled by the state) and a compartmentalised structure enforced by public law to strongly separate the public and the private spheres. Metropolitan governance therefore became more dynamic once the transaction costs had been lowered, with state incentives to cooperate regionally, with large enterprises developing *corporate citizenship* and with local communities undergoing a *paradigm change* making them aware of their regional interdependence and the importance of regionalisation processes.

Within that framework, German metropolitan governance seems to follow a road between a *'federation' of local governments* (cf. Hanover) and a *regional development agency* (cf. Stuttgart). Both options, however, outline different paths since they are *best suited* to different tasks and hence emphasise different priorities: The Hanover option stresses the reduction of fiscal disparities, improving regional infrastructure provision, effectively dealing with environmental issues and strongly representing regional interests internally and externally. The Stuttgart option, in contrast, predominantly aims at improving the economic position of the region. Both, however, rely on a directly elected political body, which seems to be the emerging pattern of more advanced metropolitan governance. Such 'parliaments' strengthen the institutional basis of metropolitan governance by providing an institutionalised way of defining a regional common interest – by political representation and territorial interest intermediation. The 'common interest' is subsequently intensified by party competition (cf. Benz 2000: 102f.). The effect of such arrangements is threefold:

1   *Functional* patterns of governance are integrated by *territorial* underpinning.
2   The implicit tendencies of patterns of governance to become corporatist devices are contained by a controlling governmental body (parliament).
3   The conflict resolving capacity of governance is enhanced by decision modes which incorporate the shadow of hierarchy (majority decisions, formal hierarchies).

Institutionalised regional interest and the possibility of resolving conflicts by majority vote expand the self-governance capacity of the region in principle. In contrast, councils of delegates have only a weak capacity to resolve conflicts because in general they are governed by a factual unanimity rule. The reason for that is that such a regime gives each local government veto power. Without actual veto power local governments would refrain from joining regional associations.

Nonetheless, regional parliaments constitute a potential for creating a *regional interest* but do not necessarily guarantee that a regional interest materialises. Rather, the regional interest may be reduced to insignificance in a situation in which the regional parliament controls only minor functions and where a deep distrust divides regional/metropolitan and local governments, with local governments having countervailing powers since they are the major players implementing regional programmes (see the case of the Frankfurt region until 2000, Fürst *et al.* 1990: 33f.).

The regional capacity for self-government will be enhanced if the business sector is actively involved in shaping the regional future. That could be achieved more easily with regional development agencies than with a *'federation' of local governments*. For the former can organise networks of actors cutting across the public and private spheres.[16] The wider array of integrated actors could improve the proficiency of regional collective actions by expanding the options to act. In addition, networks could contribute more freely to the formation of *social capital*, thus supporting regional cooperation (cf. Offe and Fuchs 2001) without forfeiting the parliament's conflict-resolving capacity.

In contrast, *federations* are more strongly fixated on local governments. The latter are *territorial* actors who tend to consider regional issues from a parochial vantage point. Although regional parliaments will mitigate the parochial effects, there is a tendency for regional councils or parliaments, with the majority of the members having strong local ties, to define regional issues in terms of inter-municipal distributional problems. The politicians tend to be stimulated to present themselves *vis-à-vis* their electorate as little heroes who fight successfully for local voters or for the local government. Politicians are incited to establish their political profile at the expense of raising conflict or denying quick consent. In addition a *'federation' of local governments* has more difficulties integrating the private sector than development agencies. For federations are more strongly controlled by political actors and tend to intensify the linkages between administration and politicians rather then between administration and the private sector. Close links to the private sector may be considered as bypassing the parliament or unclogging the channels for uncontrolled influences (Bossong 2001).

However, under pressure to improve regional competitiveness, the differences between the Stuttgart model and the Hanover model may diminish, at least in the area of restructuring the region economically. For by emulating successful examples of other regions even the Hanover Region has become capable of developing new modes of collaboration between the public and private sectors. Spurred on by the looming danger of economically falling behind, the city of Hanover and the Hanover Region, together with major local enterprises and regionally based international corporations (such as TUI, VW, CONTINENTAL, Interbrew), have established the *Hannover Implus*, a public–private partnership in the legal form of a company (see Egner *et al.* 2004: 45–60). To represent the interests of the city and the region of Hanover, the lord mayor of Hanover and the president of the region are members of the supervisory board, together with two representatives from the business sector. In addition, a commission consisting of members of the city council and the regional assembly plays an advisory role.

But there remains a difference from the Stuttgart region. While in the latter case the regional body could become a lead partner in new kinds of regional governance, the Hanover Region could barely go beyond public–private partnerships when integrating the private sector in public policics.

Notes

1 In reaction to the European process of the *European Spatial Development Perspective* (ESDP).
2 These differences are to do with whether there is a strong regional control centre or many sectoral control centres, how informal networks are related to formal government structures, to what extent economic actors are involved, whether and how strongly the regional *meso-corporatism* has been organised, whether there are competing government structures which could perform functions of *regional governance* (regional planning associations, large counties, prefect-structures: *Bezirksregierung*).
3 But regional organisational fragmentation is also the result of endeavours of regional associations to *outsource* new tasks on operational units in order to reduce the influence of politicians (*de-politicisation*). For by outsourcing, the association could broaden and intensify its regional governance potential without being subject to stronger political control.
4 This is enforced by the *sectoral* incentive programmes installed by the different state ministries to foster regional cooperation. The number of uncoordinated issue-centred networks is increased by such programmes although some of them may be no more than *symbolic use of politics*.
5 *Agenda 21 processes* are sponsored by local governments, counties and state governments; the *regional conferences* are predominantly based on government subsidies;

the *third sector* is presently receiving much political attention under the reorientation of the state towards the *enabling/activating state*.

6 The fact that business elites organise regional associations to foster the image and attractiveness of the region, as is done by *Pro Ruhrgebiet e.V.* (Ruhr Valley), *MAI e.V.* (Munich-region) or *Metropolitana e.V.* (Frankfurt), should not be regarded as *regional governance*.

7 Under the pressure of local governments the directly elected regional parliament was abolished in 2000 by state law.

8 Thus we observe that the state is more reluctant when the metropolitan region belongs to the opposition party (Munich).

9 'Pro Ruhrgebiet' was founded in 1981. Today the members consist of 270 enterprises and seventy private individuals.

10 'Metropolitana' is a project to improve the attractiveness of the region initiated by the business sector. According to one of its founders, the former chairman of the Deutsche Bank (Breuer 2001), the reason for initiating that project was that larger companies had difficulties in attracting qualified members to Frankfurt from abroad .

11 Until 2000 the region of Frankfurt also had a directly elected regional parliament (*Umlandverband Frankfurt*), which in 2001 was abolished and substituted by a new regional associational structure.

12 Responsible for regional planning, the coordination of regional public transport, regional recreation sites and regional marketing.

13 In fact, the regional planner took to the strategy of aggressive defence: If the association was to be dissolved, the best strategy was to sit in the driver's seat and have defining power for what will be the future substitute. Accordingly, all the staff members of the association had a fair chance to be taken over by the new county even in their former function.

14 The German county organisation is legally an 'association of local governments' based on the principle of subsidiarity. Therefore local governments finance the county by transferring parts of their own fiscal resources to the county (*Umlagen* = contributions).

15 According to principal–agent theory, the agent (here the director) pursues his own goals within the latitude provided by the prinicipal's intentions (here parliament) and his powers to enforce them. The principal lacks the information intensity which the agent possesses. Thus the agent has room for manoeuvre which he or she uses in his or her interest (cf. Moe 1984).

16 However, as is shown later in the case of *Hanover Region*, a *'federation' of local governments* is able to involve the business sector actively in shaping the regional future.

Bibliography

Akademie für Raumforschung u. Landesplanung (1998) *Regionale Verwaltungs- und Planungsstrukturen in Großstadtregionen*, Forschungs- und Sitzungsberichte Bd 204, Hannover.

Baumheier, R., Fürst, D., Jung, H.-U., Kegel, U., Kummerer, K., Thormählen, L., von Rohr, G. and Zeck, H. (1998) *Interkommunale und regionale Kooperation. Variablen ihrer Funktionsfähigkeit*, Akademie für Raumforschung und Landesplanung-Materialien no. 244, Hannover.

Benz, A. (2000) 'Politische Steuerung in lose gekoppelten Mehrebenensystemen', in R. Werle, U. Schimank (eds), *Gesellschaftliche Komplexität und kollektive Handlungsfähigkeit*, Frankfurt-am-Main: Campus: 97–124.

——(2003) 'Regional Governance mit organisatorischem Kern – das Beispiel der Region Stuttgart', *Informationen zur Raumentwicklung*, 8/9: 505–513.

Berkemeier, K.H. (1972) 'Das kommunale Schein-Parlament: Ausgeschaltet aus dem Planungsprozeß', *Zeitschrift für Parlamentsfragen*, 3: 202–208.

Blotevogel, H.H. (2000) 'Gibt es in Deutschland Metropolen? Die Entwicklung des deutschen Städtesystems und des Raumordnungskonzepts der "Europäischen Metropolregionen" ', in D. Matejovski (ed.), *Metropolen. Laboratorien der Moderne*, Schriften d. Wissenschaftszentrums Nordrhein Westfalen, Bd 5, Frankfurt-am-Main: 2000, 139–167.

Bossong, H. (2001) 'Der Sozialstaat am Runden Tisch. Entrechtlichung durch Verfahren', *Die Verwaltung*, 34: 145–160.

Brenner, N. (2000) 'Building Euro-Regions – locational Politics and the Political Geography of Neoliberalism in Post-Unification Germany', *European Urban and Regional Studies*, 7: 319–345.

Breuer, R.-E. (2001) 'Es geht hier um eine Optimierungsinitiative', in J. Schultheis (ed.), *Die Zukunft der Regionen: Die Metropolitana FrankfurtRheinMain*, Frankfurt-am-Main.

DiGaetano, A. and Strom, E. (2003) 'Comparative Urban Governance. An Integrated Approach', *Urban Affairs Review*, 38: 356–395.

Dolwitz, D. and Marsh, D. (1996) 'Who Learns What From Whom: A Review of the Policy Transfer Literature', *Political Studies*, 44: 343–357.

Egner, B., Haus, M., Heinelt, H. and König, Ch. (2004) *Participation Leadership and Urban Sustainability*. Country Report Germany, Darmstadt: Darmstadt University of Technology.

Frenzel, A. (1998) *Stadtregionale Entwicklungssteuerung im Standortwettbewerb*, PhD thesis, University of Halle-Wittenberg.

Fürst, D. and Ritter, E.-H. (1993) *Landesentwicklungsplanung und Regionalplanung. Ein verwaltungswissenschaftlicher Grundriß*, Düsseldorf: Werner-Verlag (2nd edition).

Fürst, D. and Rudolph, A. (2002) 'Structures of Regional Governance – the Hanover Metropolitan Region', in W. Salet, A. Thornley and A. Kreukels (eds), *Metropolitan Governance in Spatial Planning. Comparative Case Studies of European City-Regions*, London/New York: Spon.

Fürst, D., Klinger, W., Mönnecke, M. and Zeck, H. (1990) Regionalverbände im Vergleich: Entwicklungssteuerung in Verdichtungsräumen, Baden-Baden: Nomos.

Heinz, W. (1998) 'Public Private Partnerships', in: H. Wollmann and R. Roth (eds), *Kommunalpolitik. Politisches Handeln in den Gemeinden*, Bonn: Bundeszentrale für Politische Bildung: 552–570.

Kujath, H.J., Dybe, G. and Fichter, H. (2001) *Europäische Verflechtungen deutscher Regionen und ihre Auswirkungen auf die Raumstruktur des Bundesgebietes*, Erkner: Institut für Regionalentwicklung und Strukturplanung.

Le Galès, P. and Voelzkow, H. (2000) 'Introduction: The Governance of Local Economies', in P. Le Galès and H. Voelzkow (eds), *Local Production Systems in Europe: Rise or Demise?*, Oxford: Oxford University Press: 1–24.

Lefèvre, Chr. (1998) 'Metropolitan Government and Governance in Western Countries: A Critical Review', International Journal of Urban and Regional Research, 22: 9–25.

Levine, J. N. (2001) 'The Role of Economic Theory in Regional Advocacy', *Journal of Planning Literature*, 16: 183–201.

Messner, D. (1995) *Die Netzwerkgesellschaft: wirtschaftliche Entwicklung und internationale Wettbewerbsfähigkeit als Probleme gesellschaftlicher Steuerung*, Cologne: Schriften des Deutschen Instituts für Entwicklungspolitik.

MKRO/Ministerkonferenz für Raumordnung (1997) 'Bedeutung der großen Metropolregionen Deutschlands für die Raumentwicklung in Deutschland und Europa.

Beschluß vom 3. Juni 1997', in Bundesministerium f. Raumordnung, Bauwesen und Städtebau (ed.), *Entschließungen der Ministerkonferenz für Raumordnung 1993–1997*, Bonn, 51.

Moe, T.M. (1984) 'The New Economics of Organization', *American Journal of Political Science*, 28: 739–777.

Norris, D.F. (2001a) 'Whither Metropolitan Governance?', *Urban Affairs Review*, 36: 532–550.

—— (2001b) 'Prospects for Regional Governance under the New Regionalism: Economic Imperatives versus Political Impediments', *Journal of Urban Affairs*, 23: 557–71.

Offe, C. and Fuchs, S. (2001) 'Schwund des Sozialkapitals? Der Fall Deutschland', in R.D. Putnam (ed.), *Gesellschaft und Gemeinsinn. Sozialkapital im internationalen Vergleich*, Gütersloh: Bertelsmann: 417–514.

Priebs, A. (2002) 'Die Bildung der Region Hannover und ihre Bedeutung für die Zukunft stadtregionaler Organisationsstrukturen', *Die öffentliche Verwaltung*, 55: 144–151.

Rose, R. (1991) 'What is Lesson Drawing', *Journal of Public Policy*, 11: 3–30.

Scharpf, F.W. (2000) *Interaktionsformen. Akteurszentrierter Institutionalismus in der Politikforschung*, Opladen: Leske & Budrich. American edition: Scharpf, F.W. (1997) *Games Real Actors Play: Actor-Centered Institutionalism in Policy Research*, Boulder: Westview Press.

Schubert, H., Fürst, D., Rudolph, A. and Spieckermann, H. (2001) *Regionale Akteursnetzwerke. Analysen zur Bedeutung der Vernetzung am Beispiel der Region Hanover*, Opladen: Leske & Budrich.

Steinacher, B. (1999) 'Regionales Management für regionale Probleme', in *Auf dem Weg zu einer neuen regionalen Organisation?*, Rhein-Mainische Forschungen H. 116, Frankfurt-am-Main: 35–63.

Swanstrom, T. (1996) 'Ideas Matter: Reflections on the New Regionalism', Cityscape, 2: 5–21.

Van den Berg, L. and Braun, E. (1999) 'Urban Competitiveness, Marketing and the Need for Organising Capacity', *Urban Studies*, 36: 987–999.

Voelzkow, H. (2000) 'Regieren im Europa der Regionen. Vom Wohlfahrtsstaat zum Wettbewerbsstaat, vom Makro-Korporatismus zum Meso-Korporatismus', *Informationen zur Raumentwicklung*, 9/10: 507–516.

Wiechmann, Th. (1998) *Vom Plan zum Diskurs? Anforderungsprofil, Aufgabenspektrum und Organisation regionaler Planung in Deutschland*, Baden-Baden: Nomos.

11 Governing without government

Metropolitan governance in Switzerland

Daniel Kübler, Fritz Sager and Brigitte Schwab

Introduction

During the twentieth century Switzerland's socio-economic and territorial structure was profoundly transformed by urbanisation.[1] Very much in contrast to the widely publicised cliché of the home of Heidi, the Matterhorn, cheese and chocolate, Switzerland at the beginning of the twenty-first century is a service-based economy and a highly urbanised country. According to the 2000 population census, 73.3 per cent of the population nowadays lives in cities or communes within metropolitan areas. However, pressures and problems resulting from this urbanisation process have been ignored for a long time. It was only in the late 1990s that the federal government started to show serious concerns for problems faced by cities and metropolitan areas. In 2001 the *Federal Agglomeration Policy* was finally launched. Among other objectives, it includes important efforts to increase the governance capacity of urban areas, hampered by extensive institutional fragmentation within Swiss federalism.

In this chapter, we discuss the problems and prospects for area-wide governance in Swiss metropolitan areas. In the first part, after briefly recalling the structural territorial and geographic conditions of urbanisation in Switzerland, we review the ways in which local governments have responded to the necessity of governing institutionally fragmented metropolitan areas. We show that intergovernmental cooperation has been the main route towards achieving area-wide governance in Switzerland so far, with conflict-avoiding behaviour being the main factor of success. In the second part, we retrace the articulation of democratic government institutions to metropolitan governance. We argue that in spite of accountability problems, legitimacy of local government structures is still high in Swiss metropolitan areas, not least because of direct democracy. Citizen participation is extensive, sometimes to the point of making area-wide governance difficult. In the conclusion, we discuss the Swiss case in the light of the three dimensions of the 'cube of democratic metropolitan governance' (see Chapter 2). Although metropolitan governance in Switzerland does not seem to be overly problematic with respect to the cube, the absence of a metropolitan public sphere is a serious drawback.

Metropolitan areas and governance in Switzerland

Metropolitanisation and local government structures

As in most other OECD countries, urban growth related to industrialisation made cities in Switzerland grow beyond traditional communal boundaries in the early twentieth century and gave rise to *metropolitan areas*.[2] Extension of urban space continued during sub-urbanisation after the World War II, when separation between housing and labour intensified thanks to the 'democratisation' of the private car: new housing was constructed mainly outside the core cities. During the 1960s and 1970s, tertiarisation of the economy made soil prices in central locations soar and increased the demand for individual housing, thereby exacerbating urban sprawl to places situated far outside core cities and even outside suburbia (peri-urbanisation). The result was further urban sprawl and, due to the exodus of wealthy families, demographic stagnation and even loss of population in core cities. However, in the mid-1980s, living in the city became chic again and core cities stopped losing population. The inflow of wealthy new urbanites led to redevelopment and gentrification of central city neighbourhoods. At the same time, peri-urban sprawl continued, while spatial mobility increased thanks to the construction of powerful mass transportation systems. In the process, some regional centres and small metropolitan areas were absorbed by larger ones, leading to the emergence of five large urban regions: Zurich, Basle, Geneva-Lausanne, Bern-Fribourg and the 'Ticino urbano' around Lugano. These large urban regions are usually structured around one central metropolitan area which entertains intense socio-economic relationships with smaller metropolitan areas and regional centres.

In spite of increasing territorial interconnectedness, the institutional structure of Switzerland has remained virtually unchanged since the beginning of the twentieth century. As far as the communal level is concerned, annexation of suburban communes by major cities occurred between 1893 and 1934. The most significant of these annexations took place in Zurich (1893: eleven suburbs; 1934: eight suburbs), Winterthur (1922: five suburbs), St Gallen (1918: two suburbs) and Geneva (1931: three suburbs). Back then, suburban communes with feeble resources agreed to amalgamate with prosperous cities that lacked space for further development. After 1934, such amalgamations were very rare or were not significant in terms of population or surface area. Indeed, most suburban communes were able to consolidate their economic basis, whereas core cities ran into financial difficulties due to the loss of wealthy taxpayers during the phases of sub- and peri-urbanisation. Since communes have to agree to amalgamation and cannot simply be obliged to do so by higher state levels,[3] this configuration is an obstacle to territorial reform in most urban areas: rich suburban communes ferociously oppose any step towards annexation by financially distressed core cities (Geser 1999: 426). Only the extraordinarily wealthy city of Lugano managed, in 2004, to annex eight suburbs, thereby almost doubling its population. Similarly, the territory of cantons – the intermediate

Table 11.1 The ten largest metropolitan areas in Switzerland

Metropolitan area	Population	Number of communes	Cantons concerned
Zurich	1,084,027	133	Zürich, Aargau, Schwyz, Baden-Württemberg (D)
Basle	691,606	118	Basel-Stadt, Basel-Land, Solothurn, Baden-Württemberg (D), Alsace (F)
Geneva	636,937	127	Genève, Vaud, Ain (F), Haute Savoie (F)
Bern	349,096	43	Bern, Fribourg
Lausanne	311,441	70	Vaud
Como-Chiasso	246,736	57	Ticino, Como (I)
Lucerne	196,550	17	Luzern, Nidwalden, Schwyz
St Gallen	146,385	11	St Gallen, Appenzell I. Rh., Appenzell A. Rh.
Lugano	136,032	77	Ticino, Varese (I), Como (I)
Winterthur	123,416	12	Zürich, Thurgau

Source: Swiss Statistical Office, population census 2000.

territorial level between communes and the Swiss Confederation – has not witnessed major change since the mid-nineteenth century. Cantons, as the federate states, are the constitutive entities of Swiss federalism, and the formal hurdles to changing cantonal boundaries are so high that they are almost impossible to implement (Germann 1999: 397). Finally, the creation of regional institutions (i.e. situated between the communes and the cantonal level) during the 1970s has been limited to peripheral mountainous regions in order to improve infrastructure for economic development.

Hence, unlike most other Western European Nations, Switzerland has seen no significant reform of its institutional territories during the twentieth century, and the likeliness of such a reform coming about in the near future is very small. As a consequence, institutional fragmentation of urban areas is high in Switzerland, and it is very likely to remain high in the years to come (Table 11.1).

There is thus a manifest lack of congruence between functional urban spaces and territorially bound decision-making structures. Regarding the actor constellation for metropolitan governance, the stability of the institutional territories means that *cantons* and especially *communes* currently are and will continue to be central players for problem management in metropolitan areas.

Metropolitan cleavages, centrality problems and intergovernmental conflicts

Swiss metropolitan areas not only show a high degree of institutional fragmentation, the urbanisation process has also led to social segregation, resulting in new political cleavages separating the core cities, the suburban and the peri-urban zone. In the core cities, the exodus of wealthy families starting with sub-urbanisation and intensified with peri-urbanisation has left behind above average proportions of economically disadvantaged segments of the population. Accordingly, the electorate and the political elites of the core cities tend to show a higher sensitivity for social policy issues, and their political affinities are with the left. This leftist orientation of core cities has not significantly changed with the recent inflow of new urbanites: the urban lifestyle with the cultural amenities they are seeking is also mainly based on state expenditures. The strengths of both the traditional union-based left and the intellectual 'new' left therefore jointly contribute to a dominance of social democratic and green parties in the core cities. In the suburban zone, industry and newly located service-activities such as retail and shopping malls attracted low qualified workers and employees. Because of low wages, the proportion of immigrants among them is high. In terms of urbanism, the suburban picture is often a disaster: some minuscule reminiscences of a past rural village are surrounded by high-rise apartment houses, industrial buildings and shopping malls with hectares of parking lots. Inter-ethnic conflicts, feelings of insecurity and nostalgia for the rural past pave the way for national-conservative parties and populist groups who are on the rise in these places. In the peri-urban communes, the situation is completely different. Residents are mostly wealthy families who can afford individual housing. Economically successful, and mostly bound to a traditional male breadwinner family model, their political affinities lie with economic liberalism. This results in majorities of liberal-conservative parties at communal elections.

Thus, preference structures in Swiss metropolitan areas are characterised by a threefold spatial–political cleavage: core cities are oriented to the left, suburban communes to national-conservatism, peri-urban communes to economic liberalism (Kübler 2004b). The political landscape is shaped accordingly: red-green core cities are surrounded by national-conservative and liberal-conservative communes. At the same time, this also means that political majorities in core cities more and more differ from those found in 'their' canton, usually dominated by the conservative hinterland.

In addition to political cleavages, relationships between core cities and surrounding communes have become tense because of economic disparities. Due to the significant financial autonomy of Swiss communes,[4] institutional fragmentation has induced *spillovers* into the distribution of costs and benefits within metropolitan areas: surrounding communes free-ride on centrality infrastructures provided by the core cities. A report commissioned by the federal government estimates that centrality charges are particularly important in the areas of culture, education, health, transport and policing, where per-capita expenditures of core cities exceed those of surrounding communes (Schweizerischer Bundesrat 1999). There are thus uncompensated centrality charges for core cities, and substantial fringe benefits for sub- and peri-urban communes. In the past decades, the problem of uncompensated centrality charges has become an important reason for conflict between core cities and surrounding communes, whereby conflicts not only exist between communal authorities, but also between other political and economic actors based either in the core city or in the suburbs.

Finally, the process of metropolitansation has also had an effect on the involvement of cantons as important players in urban issues. Switzerland as a whole has become increasingly urbanised, and especially so in some cantons. In addition to the traditionally urban cantons of Basel-Stadt (population share living in urban areas: 100 per cent) and Geneva (99.2 per cent), other cantons such as Zug (95.5 per cent), Zurich (95 per cent) and even Ticino (86.3 per cent) can now be considered as highly urbanised.[5] In the extent to which they want to be responsive to citizens' demands, the authorities of these cantons are increasingly compelled to formulate policies responding to urban problems. As cantonal regulation density has increased, cities' financial and legal room for manoeuvre has been reduced. This has led to significant conflicts over the control of urban policy issues between cities and 'their' cantons, often further fuelled by diverging policy preferences resulting from different political majorities in the cantonal and city governments. These conflicts most often concern policy fields where both the communal and the cantonal levels have significant competencies (such as land use planning, urban and regional public transport, environmental policy, drug policy or, more recently, police policy), but sometimes also extend to fields in which communal prerogatives are important (such as urban redevelopment, economic promotion, cultural policies, etc.).

Achieving area-wide governance in a fragmented setting

Political cleavages, economic disparities and intergovernmental conflicts as a result of territorial fragmentation have also shown the interdependence between the actors involved in metropolitan issues. Unlike in most other European countries, in Switzerland there is however no institution whereby cooperation could be enforced: metropolitan areas are the 'lost dimension in Swiss federalism' (Linder 1994: 77). Reforms of territorial institutions in metropolitan areas are highly unpopular (Kübler *et al.* 2001), and in the absence of such reforms, voluntarism is the only path through which area-wide governance can be achieved in Swiss metropolitan areas.

Indeed, surveys on local government activities have shown that the importance given to policy-oriented cooperation among local authorities in metropolitan areas increased during the 1990s (Ladner *et al.* 2000), as a response to increasing urban sprawl. Focusing on horizontal cooperation between communes, a survey conducted in sixteen large and mid-sized metropolitan areas found 444 mechanisms of purpose-oriented inter-communal cooperation, that is, more than two dozen for each metropolitan area (Arn and Friederich 1994). In terms of policy fields, these cooperational structures are most important in land use planning, transport and environmental protection, but also in energy and water supply, waste disposal, cultural institutions, social welfare, etc. There is a wide variety of legal forms: legal entities, associations established under private law, cooperatives, joint-stock companies, inter-communal associations under public law, as well as public and private law foundations. Not only horizontal cooperation between communes, but also *vertical* intergovernmental cooperation have become more and more important for metropolitan policy-making (Schenkel and Güller 2000). Cantons and in some cases even the Confederation are also often associated with purpose-oriented cooperational arrangements, especially so in the fields of land use planning, transportation and environmental protection. Here too, there is a great variety of forms, ranging from discussion platforms or consultative commissions to formal organisations charged with implementing a particular service. In any case, public–private partnerships are very common in Swiss metropolitan governance: since non-governmental agencies are not bound to any particular territory they can execute area-wide public tasks more flexibly. In addition, through project-based financial contracts, governmental partners can easily get involved with a non-governmental agency – thereby offering an easy way to achieve single-level or even multi-level intergovernmental coopera-tion. There is even evidence that non-governmental agencies have become the main vectors for the emergence of a truly regional scope in some areas of metropolitan policy-making (Kübler and Wälti 2001). Besides intergovernmental cooperation in metropolitan areas, cantons with urban centres started, in the early 1980s, to reform their mechanisms of inter-communal fiscal equalisation. Earlier, these mechanisms had mainly aimed at redistributing fiscal resources from rich to poor communes. Now, they also explicitly aim at compensating centrality charges within metropolitan areas. The most significant reform in this realm was implemented by the canton of Zurich in 1999, where the canton now compels surrounding communes to pay a significant amount to the city of Zurich in compensation for centrality charges in the fields of culture, policing and social welfare.

Thus, metropolitan governance in Switzerland basically results from hori-zontal, as well as vertical cooperation between existing institutional entities, sometimes with the significant involvement of non-governmental actors. The general picture of Swiss metropolitan governance thereby conforms quite nicely to the precepts of *new regionalism* (see Chapter 2), where relationships between existing institutions are reharnessed through purpose-oriented policy networks. Concerning the actual achievement of area-wide governance in the Swiss setting, two main explanatory factors come to the fore.

First, area-wide governance capacity very much depends on the behaviour of actors within the various cooperation schemes. Due to the strong veto-positions of the local authorities involved in these schemes, a major point in this context is the behaviour and the attitude of the core-city *vis-à-vis* the other communes. This is particularly important given the deepening political cleavages between the core-city and the rest of the metropolitan area. In order for the core-city to be acceptable as a partner for cooperation to its surrounding communes, coopera-tion schemes are usually set up in a way that the core-city cannot dominate decision-making procedures, thereby explicitly putting it at a disadvantage in terms of power and influence. This must be seen as an organisational safeguard fostering trust necessary for cooperation. Beyond such formal aspects, there are also informal rules which aim to ensure trustworthiness, for example, such as the 'common law'-rule that the core-city has to yield the chair of coordination schemes to other communes, in spite of it ensuring most of the necessary administrative resources.

Second, higher state levels are also very important in shaping incentive structures for horizontal and vertical cooperation in metropolitan areas. On the one hand, cantons have become more actively involved in policy fields relevant to the development of metropolitan areas, such as transport, planning, social policy etc. In these cases, cantonal regulations often cast the 'shadow of hierarchy', thereby fostering cooperation among communes. On the other hand, the Confederation recently began to get involved in policies addressing urban and metropolitan issues, on the basis of a new article added to the federal constitution in 1999 (Art. 50). In this context, the *tripartite agglomeration conference* (*Tripartite Agglomerationskonferenz*) was created in 2001, involving representatives of all three state levels, in order to work towards coherence of policies and strategies relevant to metropolitan problem solving. More significantly, however, the federal government defined, in 2000, a so-called 'agglomeration policy' (*Agglomerationspolitik des Bundes*), according to which it offers financial support for urban policy projects in specific metropolitan areas, under the condition that these projects involve area-wide cooperation among the centre city and surrounding communes as well as the canton (Schweizerischer Bundesrat 2001). Projects supported by the Confederation in this context concern the strengthening of structures for area-wide policy-making (Lucerne, Fribourg, Bern, Lausanne) or the upgrading and conversion of urban areas into a set of broader urban functions (Neuchâtel, Zurich, Delémont, St Gallen) (Tobler 2002). Although the federal government's financial engagement is rather modest to date, it has reserved substantial amounts to finance improvement of public transport infrastructure. Thus, whereas area-wide governance capacity in Swiss metropolitan areas used to reside in conflict-avoiding behaviour within intergovernmental arrangements, incentives set by higher government levels will probably become a second important element in the near future. Of course, it is too early to assess the effects of this 'agglomeration policy', but it is very likely that the important volume of funding involved will act as a facilitator for cooperation within metropolitan areas.

However, *political leadership* as a driving force for achieving area-wide governance capacity does not appear to be significant in Switzerland. Being a 'consensus democracy' (Linder 1994: 168), the major preoccupation of politicians is negotiation and seeking for compromises between various viewpoints. Visible political leadership is traditionally scarce. In addition, the emergence of strong leaders is limited by direct democracy (see p. 177), resulting in regular defeat of visionary politicians at the ballot box.

Metropolitan governance and the practice of democracy

Representative accountability

With respect to its impacts on democratic procedures and processes, the existing *new regionalist* governance of Swiss metropolitan areas has repeatedly been described as problematic. Focusing on the formal legal procedures of metropolitan cooperation schemes, Arn and Friederich (1994) pinpoint their deficiencies in terms of democratic control and participation as well as the integration of minorities. Indeed, actors involved in metropolitan cooperation schemes are not elected to their functions, but are usually delegates chosen by the governments of the participating jurisdictions. At best, when these delegates are members of the government, there is a certain indirect accountability – direct election of communal and cantonal governments being the rule in Switzerland. At worst, when they are civil servants, or experts chosen from non-governmental agencies, lines of accountability are unclear.

If we shift the focus from formal legal procedures to the actual functioning of metropolitan governance, some of the reservations against *new regionalism* have to be reassessed. Examining the field of illegal drugs policy in Swiss metropolitan areas, Kübler and Wälti (2001) found no evidence that purpose-oriented networks of area-wide governance precluded public debate or reduced the influence of elected bodies. On the contrary, they argue that such cooperation schemes allowed for new platforms of political debate to emerge above the local level, thereby fostering the formation of a specific metropolitan scope in the political debate on drug issues.

In their assessment of the question of democratic accountability and representation with respect to metropolitan governance in Switzerland, Kübler and Schwab (2006) compared twenty-one schemes of area-wide governance in the fields of urban public transport, water provision, services for drug users and cultural policy. Drawing on a typology proposed by Savitch and Vogel (2000), they classified these coordination schemes according to whether they corresponded to the metropolitan reform tradition's precepts of area-wide governance achieved through consolidated institutions, or rather to the new regionalist ideas of area-wide multi-level network governance. Their results concerning the impact of new regionalism on democratic accountability are ambivalent. In some cases of new regionalism, decisions on policy options were made autonomously within the area-wide cooperation scheme, without involving governments or councils of participating jurisdictions. But there were also cases of new regionalism where area-wide cooperation schemes merely served to *prepare* decisions on policy options, which were then approved in a cascade of local decisions made by the single jurisdictions according to democratic rules and procedures, that is, involving governments, councils and citizens. Thus, there is evidence that new regionalism can pose problems of accountability – but need not necessarily do so. Beyond such traditional accountability mechanisms that correspond to the 'overhead model of democracy', Kübler and Schwab found clear evidence that involvement of civil society actors was more substantial in new regionalist-type mechanisms of area-wide governance. Citizens' associations – such as user groups, single-issue associations, etc. – were not only involved for consultation on policy formulation, but sometimes also genuinely associated with the decision-making process within area-wide policy networks. New regionalism in the Swiss case seems to foster the recruitment of the energies of citizens' organisations into public governance, and can therefore be seen as a context favourable to 'associative democracy' (Hirst 1994; Cohen and Roger 1995).

Direct democracy

Political participation in Switzerland is not confined to voting. Direct democracy is very elaborate, particularly at the local level, but also at the cantonal and the national levels. Direct democracy in Switzerland is based on three legal instruments. The *mandatory referendum* submits important parliamentary decisions automatically to a popular vote. What is considered an important decision is defined in the federal constitution (for the national level) in cantonal constitutions (for the cantons) and in communal regulations (for the communes). Through the *optional referendum* parliament bills can be challenged by a popular vote if a quota of citizens sign up. With the *popular initiative*, a quota of citizens signing up in a certain period can propose a new bill to be submitted to a popular vote. The extent of direct democracy at the cantonal and local level varies considerably across cantons. In some cantons and some communes, there is an additional possibility for referenda and initiatives to be launched by qualified minorities within the cantonal or communal parliaments. Variation in the extent of direct democracy is also due to diverging definitions of the domains submitted to the mandatory referendum, different quotas or different time periods required to collect citizen signatures for an optional referendum or a popular initiative. Overall, there is a west–east divide with respect to the extent given to direct democracy, direct democracy being more extensive in German-speaking cantons (in the east), than in French-speaking cantons (in the west) (Trechsel and Serdült 1999). In any case, Swiss direct democracy leads to numerous occasions to vote. On average, citizens are called to vote on up to thirty objects of local, cantonal or national relevance every year, and Switzerland is the undisputed world record holder in popular votes (Papadopoulos 1998: 42).

Long considered as a source of inefficiency, the overall effect of direct democracy in Switzerland is seen more positively today. Extensive empirical analysis based on comparisons between cantons with high and low degrees of direct democracy has found a high degree of direct democracy to be associated with high government performance (see Eichenberger 1999; Freitag and Vatter 2000), low tax evasion (see Pommerehne and Weck-Heckmann 1996; Frey 1997) as well as with high individual happiness (Frey and Stutzer 2000). However, the Swiss case also illustrates the 'broken promises' (Papadopoulos 2001) of direct democracy. Direct democracy reinforces corporatist schemes of decision making, since political parties and organised interests cooperate in order to minimise the risk of negative votes (Neidhart 1970). Moreover, referenda tend to be used by groups who defend the status quo and thereby have a structurally conservative effect (Papadopoulos 1994). Analyses of political participation also inspire sobering thoughts. Turnout in popular votes is low, averaging roughly 40 per cent, and participation is socially stratified. Middle- and upper-class citizens participate far more than those from the lower class: 'the choir of Swiss direct democracy sings in upper and middle class tones' (Linder 1994: 95). In addition, 20 per cent of the population do not have Swiss citizenship and are therefore not entitled to vote.

Direct democratic procedures are part of normal politics in Switzerland and hence citizen voting on matters of area-wide public policy is also very frequent. A very interesting case in point is the setting up of an area-wide public transport system (S-Bahn) in the Zurich metropolitan area (Kübler 2004a): no less than nineteen votes on this project took place between 1970 and 2001.[6] Similarly, referenda proved to be moments for politicising area-wide cooperation in the field of higher education and research[7] in the Geneva-Lausanne area, thereby generating a public debate on a policy field that used to be limited to a very restricted circle of interested persons (Schwab 2004). In general, two effects of frequent citizen voting at the local level should be emphasised. On the one hand, direct democracy has proven to be a 'Damocles sword' (Papadopoulos 1998: 146) in urban and metropolitan policy-making. Repeatedly, promising projects were rejected by way of referendum, mostly at a very advanced stage of planning. Examples can be found in area-wide transport (Kübler 2004a), but also in urban development more generally (Cattacin 1994; Bassand *et al.* 2001). Very often, negative popular votes on single projects resulted in frustration and political stalemate, leading to paralysis of the wider policy field. On the other hand, direct democratic decision making can constitute a considerable political resource. If governmental projects are approved by a popular vote, the resulting legitimacy boost can translate into a dynamisation of the planning process. The Zurich area-wide transport system undoubtedly is a case in point: after clear approval in the early 1980s, it could be developed into a highly performing metropolitan transport network during the 1990s.

Thus, direct democracy has always been an important factor for sectoral urban and metropolitan policy-making in Switzerland, and will continue to be so in the future. In addition, there currently seems to be something of a direct democratic agenda in the debate on area-wide governance of metropolitan areas, where direct democracy is increasingly seen as a possible corrective for insufficient accountability of intergovernmental networks. In the Lucerne metropolitan area, for instance, rights for referenda and initiative were built into the new inter-communal coordination scheme for public transport set up in 1998. Similarly, direct democratic instruments (initiative and referendum) on an area-wide, that is, supra-communal, scale were some of the first institutional elements to be agreed upon in the currently ongoing pilot projects in the metropolitan areas of Bern, Fribourg and Lausanne. This is quite remarkable, since in these very same projects, the communes ferociously opposed direct election of the governing body. If these projects ever end up with effectively producing strengthened bodies of area-wide coordination – which is far from being evident at the time of writing – they are very likely to be headed by a government and a parliament whose members are elected by the communal authorities (indirect account-ability), but include extensive possibilities of direct citizen participation at the same time. It may therefore well be that direct democratic procedures will constitute the main (if not the only) vector for the emergence of an area-wide political sphere in Swiss metropolitan areas.

In any case, legitimacy of the local political system in Switzerland is high: trust in local government is higher than trust in governmental authorities at any other state level (Kübler *et al.* 2002: 99). Hence, there is no evidence that metropolitan policy-making through supra-local coordination schemes has led citizens to perceive local authorities to be more and more irrelevant, as this has been suggested by some authors (Lowery *et al.* 1992). Nevertheless, recent research has shown that the legitimacy of local authorities (measured by satisfaction with the functioning of democracy in one's commune) resides far less in the quality of public service which these authorities produce, and far more in the possibilities of citizen participation which they provide. Perception of involvement, participation and politics determines satisfaction with local democracy much more than the perception of service quality (Kübler *et al.* 2002: 121). In other words, legitimacy is primarily composed of input legitimacy, whereas output legitimacy comes far behind – this is still consistent with the image of the strong input orientation of the Swiss local government system (Hesse 1991).

Participation and metropolitan governance capacity

Hence, it seems that because of the strong emphasis on input-related democratic procedures in the Swiss local government system, as well as because of extensive direct democracy, metropolitan governance by way of intergovernmental cooperation does not seem to pose a significant threat to democratic structures and processes. In other words, there is no evidence that 'output is in and input is out' (Linder 1998: 101) in Swiss metropolitan areas. If this is the case, we should however focus also on the other side of this relationship: how does citizen participation affect the ability to achieve area-wide governance?

Studies so far conducted on this subject mainly address planning issues. Joye *et al.* (1995) have shown in a comparison of six Swiss cities that the extent to which direct citizen participation is granted, that is, the existence of opportunity structures, has a strong effect on the state's capacity to act. In this respect, the NIMBY ('not in my backyard') phenomenon, describing the behaviour of citizens affected by a certain policy who negate both the state's right to define public objectives and the right of policy experts to define public problems, has to be mentioned. While in the city of Bern citizen participation on the neighbourhood level is developed to an extent that it prevents any actual city planning, there are no channels for neighbourhood interests in the city of Geneva, a situation that favours city-wide planning. Citizen participation does not take place unless the respective interests can be organised on the city level. This in turn partially leads to NIMBY effects in neighbourhoods negatively affected by planning decisions regarding transport and living conditions. This city-wide scope of participation procedures helped establish the successful positioning of Geneva in the international city competition, assisted strong city development, attracted high-tech firms, and resulted in the effective protection of rural zones. The authors conclude that strong citizen participation at the local level helps improve living conditions with rather domestic and neighbourhood orientations as well as with specific focus on transportation issues, while a rather representative democratic culture helps promote the city as a whole and emphasises an exterior orientation.

Sager *et al.* (1999) come to a somewhat similar conclusion regarding the coordination performance of transport and land use policies in urban areas. Their comparison of four agglomerations shows a much better consideration of transport-inflicted problems in the two cities of Basle and Bern, with elaborate participation, than in the two cities of Geneva and Lausanne, with primarily representative opportunity structures. Focusing on processes of policy coordination, Kaufmann *et al.* (2003) find furthermore that in the two cities where participatory democracy is very much in practice, namely Bern and Basle, this contributes to the abandonment of the rationality of power among public actors in favour of approaches aiming at common policy solutions. The presence of multiple actors stimulates the habitual play of coalitions; for specific problems, the two cities build *ad hoc* commissions outside the institutional structure of departments, which to a certain extent separates them from the sphere of power games inherent in the public service sectors, thereby inducing a shift from interest-oriented to common problem-solving approaches. Conversely, permanent commissions with a strong political presence, such as those in Geneva and Lausanne, may constitute an obstacle to coordination, since they represent typical forums for the expression of approaches based on power. This acquires particular relevance in contexts where democracy tends to be representative, as is the case in Geneva and in Lausanne, where permanent commissions are sectoral and headed by elected representatives.

As for the question in how far representative, that is, political bodies, should be integrated in the actual policy coordination, Sager (2002, 2005), in a comparison of nine urban infrastructure projects in Basle, Bern, Geneva and Lausanne, finds that strict separation of the technical and political spheres is an important condition for the achievement of common and broadly accepted solutions. His case studies show that negotiations with different communities tend to be interest driven rather than aiming at problem solving. Accordingly, projects comprising 'open' networks lead to misunderstandings due to different problem perceptions. This again can encourage power struggles that will prevail over action-oriented attitudes. This effect, however, can be compensated for by the organisational structure of the processes: first, centralisation facilitates both positive coordination and an orientation towards common policy solutions since there is a central transmission belt for all interactions that, on the one hand, enhance the liability of the contacts because there are no parallel information flows, and, on the other, enable multilateral negotiations by abridging the distance between the actors involved. Second, the separation of negotiating from the political sphere turns out to be crucial for preventing advantage-maximising strategies. Since experts tend to favour evidence-based policy solutions rather than the maximisation of relative gains for their respective community, their negotiations basically tend to be less marked by politics. The more policy decisions are left to experts, that is, the higher the room for manoeuvring by the administration, the less competitive is the coordination process even in fragmented territorial settings. Sager (2002) argues here that, due to their technical nature, certain policy issues demand expertise more that they demand participation. However, the importance of bureaucratic autonomy understood as discretion within strict borders set by the political sphere might be due to Switzerland's tradition of a weak state and subsidiarity, while in the other European countries, traditions of strong states imply stronger participation and democratic control of the bureaucracy in policy processes (Sager 2004).

Conclusion

Building metropolitan governance in Switzerland

Institutional fragmentation in Swiss metropolitan areas is high, and, as a corollary, the achievement of area-wide governance is a continuous topic of concern. Due to widespread reluctance, local autonomy and high institutional hurdles, signifi-cant reform of territorial institutions has not taken place in Swiss metropolitan areas since the early twentieth century. Intergovernmental, purpose-oriented cooperation has proven to be the only practicable way to achieve area-wide governance. Consequently, there are countless structures, mechanisms and governing bodies producing such area-wide cooperation. In this sense, *new regionalism* appears to have been the major thrust of Swiss metropolitan gover-nance since World War II. On the one hand, weakly institutionalised regionalist arrangements have proven to be flexible enough to adapt to the local features of the institutional framework, the various types of actors as well as the political cleavages found in any given metropolitan area. The great variety of such arrangements across metropolitan areas and across policy sectors indicates that there is probably no *one best approach* to handle the challenge of area-wide governance. On the other hand, arrangements of area-wide governance in Swiss metropolitan areas were quite successful. The performance of metropolitan public services can be quite high (e.g. public transport), and the outcomes of metropolitan policy-making mostly meet the expectations of the citizenry. Until recently, the success of such intergovernmental arrangements mainly depended on the participating actors' adoption of conflict-avoiding strategies. This may also explain why core cities usually turn out to be in a rather weak position compared to smaller communes: in order to foster trust, core cities tended to accept arrangements that put them into disadvantage, rather than having no area-wide governance at all. However, with the new *agglomeration policy* of the federal government implemented from 1999, there is reason to argue that incen-tives set by higher state levels – and especially by the Confederation – will become a second important element in building metropolitan governance capacity. At the same time, this will probably result in a strengthening of the core cities with respect to other metropolitan players, since core city humility will no longer be the sole crucial element for achieving area-wide governance. Nevertheless, current trends in Switzerland indicate that more of the already known is to be expected. The strengthening of area-wide governance in metropolitan areas will see more intergovernmental forums, more purpose-oriented cooperation, more policy networks. The coming about of genuine regional institutions will be exceptional – if they materialise at all. To date, the creation of a new regional layer of multi-purpose government between the cantons and the communes is projected in only one metropolitan area – the rather small Fribourg agglomeration. After nearly ten years, the institution-building process is still far from completion, and observers are sceptical whether there really is enough political will to achieve an institution whose scope will be more than the sum of its parts (Dafflon and Rüegg 2001).

Democracy in Swiss-style metropolitan governance

In the theoretical chapter to this volume, Kübler and Heinelt suggested three dimensions along which the democratic question within metropolitan governance in any given metropolitan area should be assessed: (1) how area-wide governance arrangements affect the tension between openness and closeness of policy-networks; (2) how they affect the current relationship between input- and output-legitimacy; and (3) how they affect the relationship between civil society and the state. How does the Swiss case present in the light of these three dimensions?

First, balancing the tension between the required openness and necessary closeness of policy networks indeed constitutes the core issue of Swiss metropolitan governance. Due to federalism and high territorial fragmentation, a high number of institutional players are found in almost every field relevant to metropolitan policy-making. As has been argued elsewhere (Sager 2002, 2004), this multi-actor context did not foreclose coordination and instead has led to substantially rational policies thanks to the openness of the decision-making process. But the real problem resides in the implementation of the policies that have been decided upon, where insufficient closeness of the process has often resulted in politically motivated vetoes during the implementation process. Achieving area-wide governance in Swiss metropolitan areas essentially seems a constant struggle for a level of closeness that is sufficient for a minimal capacity to act within the regional scope. In this sense, it is not network openness that is under threat in Swiss metropolitan governance, but rather a minimum of network closeness that still needs to be attained.

Second, with respect to the relationship between input and output legitimacy in metropolitan areas, Switzerland's long tradition of citizen involvement in public affairs via direct democratic procedures needs to be emphasised. Especially in comparison to other countries, institutionalised opportunities for direct citizen participation are very extensive in Swiss metropolitan governance. Significant policy decisions are almost always submitted to a (facultative) referendum. If anything, there is more of a democracy overload than a legitimacy deficit. Due to widespread resistance against attempts of curtailing citizens' rights (Linder 1994: 137), extensive direct democracy will continue to be a central feature of metropolitan policy-making in Switzerland. As we have argued above concerning area-wide, supra-communal referenda and popular initiatives in pilot projects in Bern, Fribourg and Lausanne, there is even reason to believe that direct democracy rather than representative institutions will be the major vector for the emergence of an area-wide political sphere. Hence, in spite of the absence of area-wide democratic institutions in Swiss metropolitan areas, there is no evidence that current arrangements of area-wide governance would tend towards a withering away of the input-dimension in metropolitan politics.

Third, with respect to the relationship between civil society and the state, there is a traditional weakness of state institutions in Switzerland (see Kriesi *et al.* 1995) and, as a corollary, widespread involvement of non-governmental agencies in public policy-making (see Bütschi and Cattacin 1993). This tradition has left its mark on governance arrangements in metropolitan areas ever since. Not only are private actors, non-governmental organisations and voluntary sector associations thoroughly consulted during formulation of metropolitan policies. They are also charged with carrying out public tasks, and therefore play a central role in the implementation of these policies. And, as we have argued above, non-governmental agencies sometimes even constitute the main vector for a truly regional scope. However, the strong position of non-governmental agencies in area-wide governance arrangements raises the question of the extent to which (territorially fragmented) governmental institutions are still capable of controlling the activities of their non-governmental partners. With the wave of new public management that swept across Swiss local government during the 1990s, a set of new legal instruments has been introduced (especially performance agreements and controlling) in order to increase the capacity of governmental institutions to steer and control their non-governmental partners (see Ladner *et al.* 2000). The use of such performance agreements to regulate relationships between state agencies and non-governmental organisations has become very common in the implementation of area-wide policies in Swiss metropolitan areas, and there is evidence that pluralism and innovation potential are reduced by such attempts at extending state control over non-governmental agencies (Wälti and Kübler 2003). Hence, current trends in metropolitan governance building in Switzerland suggest that while involvement of non-governmental organisations is getting more and more substantial, the parallel extension of state control may simultaneously reduce the contribution of these non-governmental institutions to political pluralism.

As a conclusion, we would argue that metropolitan governance in Switzerland basically consists of area-wide steering of sectoral public policies responding to sectoral metropolitan problems. So far, the multitude of policy relevant actors, the strength of the existing democratic institutions – especially direct democracy – as well as the traditional weakness of the state in the Swiss context helped to keep openness of policy networks high, maintain the strong input orientation of the local government system, and associate the forces of civil society with area-wide public policies. In this sense, the Swiss answer to the democratic question within metropolitan governance is certainly not alarming, in spite of the absence of regional institutions. However, if Swiss metropolitan areas clearly have emerged as spaces of policies which are reasonably sound in democratic terms, they are far from featuring an autonomous public sphere. Most often, public political debate is concerned with issues and problems *within* metropolitan areas, and there is little emphasis on the challenges that metropolitan areas face as a whole and that may request them to act and react as such. The public debate on Swiss metropolitan governance actually consists of a multitude of sectoral debates on how to resolve problems of area-wide governance in various policy fields. If metropolitan areas are to be considered communities of destiny – and there is evidence that we should do so (Kübler *et al.* 2001) – democratic metropolitan governance should not stop at delivering area-wide public services. It should also provide arenas for the metropolitan community to express itself and to debate collectively on the ways in which it wants to act upon its fate. In this realm, Switzerland's performance leaves a great deal to be desired.

Notes

1 Daniel Kübler and Brigitte Schwab's contribution to this chapter is based on the research *Gouvernance métropolitaine et légitimité*, financed by the Swiss National Science Foundation's Priority Programme 'Switzerland towards the future' (grant #5004–58522), conducted at the Laboratoire de sociologie urbaine of the Federal Institute of Technology in Lausanne between 2000 and 2003. Fritz Sager draws on his PhD thesis *Vom Verwalten des urbanen Raums*, accepted by the University of Bern in 2002 (Sager 2002).

2 The Swiss Statistical Office speaks of 'agglomerations' (*Agglomerationen/ agglomérations/agglomerati*) to describe these functionally integrated urban spaces (Schuler 1994). For the purpose of this chapter, we however use the term *metropolitan areas* as a synonym.

3 The approval of amalgamation by the concerned communes is required in most cantons. Only in the cantons of Thurgau and Ticino can communes be compelled to disappear without their consent. But even in those two cantons, it is current practice to hold a referendum in the communes concerned by amalgamation. So far, forced amalgamation has happened only once.

4 Communes in Switzerland are fiscally autonomous. They raise communal taxes on income and property and they are competent to fix the communal tax rate. This has led to important fiscal competition between communes. On average, 70 per cent of communal income stems from taxes and fees. Only 18 per cent of communal income stems from transfer payments made by higher state levels – the lowest proportion found among all Western European countries (Steiner 2002).

5 Source: Swiss Statistical Office, population census data 2000.

6 Seven of them related to the financial involvement of the canton in the construction of the system; twelve took place in the city of Zurich and adjacent communes and concerned planning decisions and credits related to new stations.

7 In this case, cooperation concerned the joint implementation of capital-intensive research infrastructure, such as CERN (European Organisation for Nuclear Research), and the establishment of a pole of competence in life-sciences at the Swiss Federal Institute in Lausanne.

Bibliography

Arn, D. and Friederich, U. (1994) *Gemeindeverbindungen in der Agglomeration*, Zurich: NFP 'Stadt und Verkehr'.

Bassand, M., Compagnon, A., Joye, D., Stein, V. and Güller, P. (2001) *Vivre et créer l'espace public*, Lausanne: Presses polytechniques et universitaires romandes.

Bütschi, D. and Cattacin, S. (1993) 'The Third Sector in Switzerland: The Transformation of the Subsidarity Principle', *European Journal of Political Research*, 16: 362–379.

Cattacin, S. (1994) *Stadtentwicklungspolitik zwischen Demokratie und Komplexität*, Frankfurt: Campus.

Cohen, J. and Roger, J. (eds) (1995) *Associations and Democracy*, London: Verso.

Dafflon, B. and Rüegg, J. (2001) 'The Case of Fribourg: A Model for Switzerland? Some Notes on a Recent Institutional Innovation', *Swiss Political Science Review*, 7: 134–141.

Eichenberger, R. (1999) 'Mit direkter Demokratie zu besserer Wirtschafts- und Finanzpolitik: Theorie und Empirie', in H.H. Arnim (ed.), *Adäquate Institutionen: Voraussetzungen für 'gute' und bürgernahe Politik?*, Berlin: Duncker und Humboldt.

Freitag, M. and Vatter, A. (2000) 'Direkte Demokratie, Konkordanz und wirtschaftliche Leistungskraft. Ein Vergleich der Schweizer Kantone', *Schweizerische Zeitschrift für Volkswirtschaft und Statistik*, 136: 579–606.

Frey, B.S. (1997) 'A Constitution for Knaves Crowds out Civic Virtues', *Economic Journal*, 107: 1043–1053.

Frey, B.S. and Stutzer, A. (2000) 'Happiness, Economy and Institutions', *Economic Journal*, 110: 918–938.

Germann, R.E. (1999) 'Die Kantone: Gleichheit und Disparität', in U. Klöti, P. Knoepfel, H. Kriesi, W. Linder and Y. Papadopoulos (eds), *Handbuch der Schweizer Politik/Manuel de la politique suisse*, Zurich: Verlag NZZ.

Geser, H. (1999) 'Die Gemeinden in der Schweiz', in U. Klöti, P. Knoepfel, H. Kriesi, W. Linder and Y. Papadopoulos (eds), *Handbuch der Schweizer Politik/Manuel de la politique suisse*, Zurich: NZZ Verlag.

Hesse, J.J. (ed.) (1991) *Local Government and Urban Affairs in International Perspective*, Baden-Baden: Nomos Verlag.

Hirst, P. (1994) *Associative Democracy*, Cambridge: Polity Press.

Joye, D., Huissoud, T. and Schuler, M. (1995) *Habitants des quartiers, citoyens de la ville?*, Zurich: Seismo.

Kaufmann, V., Sager, F., Ferrari, Y. and Joye, D. (2003) *Coordonner transports et urbanisme*, Lausanne: Presses polytechniques et universitaires romandes.

Kriesi, H., Koopmans, R., Duyvendak, J.W. and Giugni, M.G. (1995) *New Social Movements in Western Europe. A Comparative Analysis*, London: UCL Press.

Kübler, D. (2004a) 'Métropolisation à la zurichoise: tertiarisation, fragmentation et démocratie directe', in B. Jouve and C. Lefèvre (eds), *Horizons métropolitains*, Lausanne: Presses polytechniques et universitaires romandes.

——(2004b) 'Städte und Agglomerationen in der Schweiz: eine Herausforderung für Politik und Institutionen', in C. Suter, D. Joye and I. Renschler, (eds), *Sozialbericht 2004*, Zurich: Seismo.

Kübler, D. and Schwab, B. (2006) 'New Regionalism in Five Swiss Metropolitan Areas. An Assessment of Inclusiveness, Deliberation and Democratic Accountability', *European Journal of Political Research*, forthcoming.

Kübler, D. and Wälti, S. (2001) 'Gouvernance métropolitaine et démocratie: l'exemple des politiques de lutte contre la drogue', *Revue suisse de science politique*, 7: 1–25.

Kübler, D., Joye, D. and Schwab, B. (2001) 'Identity, Community and Institutional Reform in Swiss Agglomerations', *Swiss Political Science Review*, 7: 126–134.

Kübler, D., Schwab, B., Joye, D. and Bassand, M. (2002) *La métropole et le politique. Identité, services urbains et citoyenné dans quatre agglomérations en Suisse*, Lausanne: LaSUR/EPFL.

Ladner, A., Arn, D., Friederich, U., Steiner, R. and Wichtermann, J. (2000) *Gemeindereform zwischen Handlungsfähigkeit und Legitimation*, Bern: Institut für Politikwissenschaft/Institut für Organisation und Personal.

Linder, W. (1994) *Swiss Democracy: Possible Solutions to Conflict in Multi-Cultural Societies*, New York: St Martin's Press.

——(1998) 'Deregulierung – ein politisches Instrument für viele Ziele', *LeGes*: 95–109.

Lowery, D., DeHoog, H. and Lyons, W.E. (1992) 'Citizenship in the Empowered Locality: An Elaboration, a Critique and a Partial Test', *Urban Affairs Quarterly*, 28: 69–103.

Neidhart, L. (1970) *Plebiszit und pluralitäre Demokratie*, Bern: Francke.

Papadopoulos, Y. (ed.) (1994) *Elites politiques et peuples en Suisse. Analyse des votations fédérales: 1970–1987*, Lausanne: Réalités sociales.

——(1998) *Démocratie directe*, Paris: Economica.

——(2001) 'Citizenship through Direct Democracy? The "Broken Promises" of Empowerment', in C. Crouch, K. Eder and D. Tambini (eds), *Citizenship, Markets, and the State*, Oxford: Oxford University Press.

Pommerehne, W.W. and Weck-Heckmann, H. (1996) 'Tax Rates, Tax Administration and Income and Tax Evasion in Switzerland', *Public Choice*, 88: 161–170.

Sager, F. (2002) *Vom Verwalten des urbanen Raumes*, Bern: P. Haupt.

——(2004) 'Institutions métropolitaines et coordination des politiques publiques: une AQOC des arrangements politico-administratifs d'articulation entre urbanisme et transports en Europe', *Revue internationale de politique comparée*, 11: 67–84.

——(2005) 'Mertropolitan Institutions and Policy Coordination. The Case of Land Use and Transport Policies in Swiss Urban Areas', *Governance*, 18, in press.

Sager, F., Kaufmann, V. and Joye, D. (1999) 'Die Koordination von Raumplanung und Verkehrspolitik in urbanen Räumen der Schweiz: Determinanten der politischen Geographie, der politischen Kultur oder der institutionellen Struktur?', *Schweizerische Zeitschrift für Politikwissenschaft*, 5: 25–56.

Savitch, H. and Vogel, R.K. (2000) 'Paths to New Regionalism', *State and Local Government Review*, 32: 158–168.

Schenkel, W. and Güller, M. (2000) *Zusammenarbeit und Koordination zwischen Bund, Kantonen und Städten im Rahmen der Agglomerationspolitik: Vorstudie im Rahmen des Agglomerationsberichtes 2001*, Zurich: ARE/seco.

Schuler, M. (1994) *Die Raumgliederungen der Schweiz/Les niveaux géographiques de la Suisse*, Bern: Bundesamt für Statistik.

Schwab, B. (2004) 'La métropolisation politique du bassin lémanique en question', in B. Jouve and C. Lefèvre (eds), *Horizons métropolitains*, Lausanne: Presses polytechniques et universitaires romandes.

Schweizerischer Bundesrat (1999) *Bericht über die Kernstädte, Bern*, Bundesamt für Raumentwicklung und Staatssekretariat für Wirtschaft.

——(2001) *Agglomerationspolitik des Bundes*, Bern: Bundesamt für Raumentwicklung.

Steiner, R. (2002) *Interkommunale Zusammenarbeit und Gemeindezusammenschlüsse in der Schweiz*, Bern: Haupt.

Tobler, G. (2002) 'Agglomerationspolitik des Bundes: Ziele, Strategien, Massnahmen', *Forum Raumentwicklung*: 5–7.

Trechsel, A. and Serdült, U. (1999) *Kaleidoskop Volksrechte. Die Institutionen der direkten Demokratie in den schweizerischen Kantonen, 1970–1996*, Basle: Helbing & Lichtenhahn.

Wälti, S. and Kübler, D. (2003) ' "New governance" and Associative Pluralism: The Case of Drug Policy in Swiss Cities', *Policy Studies Journal*, 31: 499–525.

12 Conclusion

Hubert Heinelt and Daniel Kübler

Setting out for a cross-national assessment of metropolitan governance, the authors of this volume basically had two issues in mind. On the one hand, there was the aim to work out the ways in which area-wide governance capacity has been or can be strengthened in order to make metropolitan areas fit for dealing with current and future challenges. On the other hand, there was the question of the consequences that various ways of achieving area-wide governance in metropolitan areas bear with respect to democratic legitimacy. In this concluding chapter we try to sum up and discuss the main findings presented in the previous chapters.

Concentrating on the two basic issues around on the reflection in this volume are centred, we first highlight aspects identified in our cases which support the development of metropolitan governance. This is important because the strengthening of area-wide governance capacity in metropolitan areas usually means to overcome a multitude of resistance. Additionally, we point out some 'dangers' of which one should be aware when trying to build new governance capacity at a metropolitan level.

Second, we come back to the 'democratic question' within metropolitan governance by positioning cases presented in this book within the 'cube of democratic metropolitan governance' developed in Chapter 2. The aim of this endeavour is not to asses the democratic character or quality of particular metropolitan governance arrangements – which would have been a too normative perspective. Rather, we would like to answer the question as to what modes of democratic policy-making in metropolitan areas fit specific conditions, and – as far as the information given in the individual cases allows such considerations – we try to draw some conclusions about their limits and potentials.

Different routes towards metropolitan governance – and how to open and follow them

Nowadays the classical controversy between proponents of the *metropolitan reform tradition* and those adopting a *public choice perspective* on metropolitan governance may still play a role by marking general arguments relevant to the debate – by advocating annexation and the creation of area-wide metropolitan governments on the one hand, or by defending fragmentation of metropolitan areas into a multitude of autonomous local jurisdictions as beneficial for effective and efficient metropolitan service delivery as well as for local identity and therefore for local democracy, on the other. However, as we have argued in Chapter 2, in current debates on how to govern metropolitan areas, the emphasis – according to so-called *new regionalism* – is much less on territorial boundaries of the traditional local government structure, but rather on arrangements between various public agencies and private actors at different territorial levels for the purpose of defining and delivering urban services with an area-wide scope. Although new regionalism emphasises the importance of such network arrangements for governing metropolitan regions, by moving the focus away from local or metropolitan government to metropolitan governance the trust in a one-fits-all model for metropolitan reform also got lost. Instead, interest is placed on case-related networks by which governability is (intended to be) reached. In this respect, *new regionalism* reflects a move from normative concepts or concepts from which clear guidelines for 'good governance' can be drawn – inherent in the *metropolitan reform tradition* as well as in the *public choice perspective* – to an empirical analytical one.

An empirical analytical point of view is helpful to concentrate on the question why and how metropolitan governance capacity has been achieved at all – be it in line with the 'classical' perspectives or in accordance with new regionalism. And to discover and clarify conditions for metropolitan governance the danger of being intellectually blocked by a specific normative pre-decision has to be avoided. This seems to be important because the responses to the challenges of governing metropolitan areas (and issues) are quite different – as has been demonstrated in the previous chapters: There are cases where 'old regionalism' (according to the model of the metropolitan reform tradition) has survived (Madrid, where area-wide governance draws heavily on the Autonomous Community) or has been newly applied (London, Montreal, Toronto, Hanover, Stuttgart and the Rotterdam city-province as it was planned). There are cases of new regionalism where area-wide governance is clearly centred around network arrangements involving a broad range of public and private actors (Barcelona, Helsinki, Los Angeles, the English cases outside London, the Swiss cases; Rotterdam after the failure of the city-province). There are hybrid cases as well, that is, networks mainly built on municipalities but also open to others (such as planned in Athens), and there are – most interestingly – cases such as Hanover (and similarly Stuttgart) where we can observe, on the one hand, a 'traditional' metropolitan reform (with the creation of a metropolitan government with a directly elected president and a metropolitan/regional council), and, on the other hand, the emergence of new forms of network governance involving the newly established metropolitan/regional government and private actors.[1] Finally, we find 'weak' inter-municipal cooperation, that is, arrangements where the autonomy of the cooperating municipalities is not questioned (the French cases presented in this volume and most of the German cases except for Hanover and Stuttgart, as casually mentioned by Fürst in Chapter 10). Furthermore and interestingly, one can observe different routes towards metropolitan governance within the very same country (as shown by the chapters on Spain, England and Germany in this book).

Against this background the question arises: how can we explain these different pathways towards metropolitan governance? As has been argued in Chapter 2, a single model of metropolitan governance is not likely to emerge, since increasing governance capacity in metropolitan areas is strongly determined by given spatial economic, social and political conditions, and depends on *cooperative actor behavior*, *adequate incentive structures* and *territorial political leadership* being developed and 'exploited' under certain local conditions. These reflections (hypothesis) seem to be confirmed in general, and they can be specified and developed further.

Cooperative actor behaviour

Actor behaviour is crucial for metropolitan governance in the sense that cooperative orientations are vital rather than confrontation or imposed reform (on the part of whosoever). This applies clearly for network formation according to the approach of new regionalism because it relies on voluntary entries and the compliance of involved actors. But it applies for the institutional consolidation of metropolitan government as well because in cases where consolidation (and annexation) is achieved by octroi in upper-level government (or by parts of metropolitan elites) it is not only in danger of being undermined by disobedience and subversive destruction by subordinated actors, but can also give reason for an uprising by local people – leading to opposition to an imposed reform (as the Rotterdam case demonstrates). Coordinating activities and cooperating with the aim of solving common metropolitan problems or even increasing individual interests by joint actions is usually based on mutual respect of the other actors. This respect has to become manifest already before an explicit ('positive') coordination of activities is taking place by what has been called (by Scharpf 1991: 102) 'negative coordination', that is, by taking the interests (and power resources) of others into account for our own actions without talking/interacting with them directly. Among the cases analysed in this book such cooperative behaviour seems to have been important everywhere, but it was absolutely crucial in the achievement of area-wide governance capacity in Barcelona, the Swiss and most of the English cases. And as these examples show, a policy style based on such cooperative behavioural patterns can more easily be developed and sustained on the basis of a particular political culture, that is, a common understanding of what is appropriate or not, and a social network system which is able to sanction (mis)behaviour.

Adequate incentive structures

A next factor that has proven to be important in building metropolitan governance capacity are incentives set by upper-level governments. These can be positive incentives, such as grants, financial subsidies, more competencies, etc., in the case of strengthened area-wide governance. There can also be negative incentives, such as the 'shadow of hierarchy' (Scharpf 1992), that is, the threat of a solution for metropolitan challenges/problems imposed by upper-level government.

More particularly, such positive or negative incentives set by upper-level governments have been important in Germany and Switzerland (state incentives granted for area-wide cooperation in metropolitan areas), in Greece (ministerial support for initiating projects for area-wide governance in the Attica region), in Finland (the central government's restructuring of the welfare state, leading to a reuniting of local governments in the Helsinki area), but especially so in France (new framework law for the creation of the *Communautés d'agglomération*). However, as especially the French examples clearly demonstrate, it depends on local actors, their abilities and their willingness to perceive incentives as such and how (if at all) to make use of them.

Moreover, big events taking place in a particular metropolitan area may open 'windows of opportunity' (Kingdon 1984), in the sense that they can put area-wide governance on the political agenda and thereby frame actor behaviour in a certain sense. For instance, the organisation of the Olympic Games strongly pushed forward area-wide governance in Barcelona (Olympic Games of 1992) and Athens (Olympic Games of 2004), where the need for regional planning in general and the construction of public metropolitan infrastructure in particular, related to the games but also to the question of what should happen after the games, have fostered the emergence of public–private networks of area-wide cooperation. In this respect, such big events can also be seen as components of an incentive structure for metropolitan governance capacity.

Territorial political leadership

Political leadership, as a means to foster area-wide governance, has been pursued most easily under conditions where the local government system formally provides specific individuals (mayors) with a leading role. This is especially the case in countries such as France, Greece, Spain (i.e. countries of the Franco group) and Germany (i.e. a country of the North and Middle European type of local government systems, where the role of mayors has been strengthened by direct election), or in a metropolitan area where a special status for a mayor has been created (as in London). However, as the differences between cases in these countries demonstrate, it is not just the formal authority dedicated to an office holder that is decisive. Rather, it is the performance of a specific role, and this role has not only to be fulfilled by one person (the leader), it can also be exercised by a group. What is needed (by leadership of a single person or a group) is to open up area-wide coalitions and a new path to metropolitan governance by stimulating cooperation (networking) and facilitating consensus between actors about the understanding of 'the' problem at hand, the need to solve it and how to solve it best. A basic component of these tasks is trust: a leader has to be trusted as a broker and this means as an actor without a selfish interest or as the 'agent' of her/his 'principles', that is, her/his organisation of origin. In this respect a particular leadership style is needed to achieve and to increase metropolitan governance capacities differently from those dominant in the past, that is, party leaders or clever representatives of local communities but also 'pure' administrative and/or technical experts (as Goldsmith made perfectly clear in Chapter 6).

Trust in political leaders is also crucial when it comes to network arrangements in which public as well as private actors are involved and outcomes have to be reached by bargaining (and not by the imposition of majority decisions). In this case, political leaders have to be trusted as agents of representative bodies and the common interests of the citizenry, and accountability is a precondition for the evaluation of political actors' performance in this respect – not least in respect to the legitimacy of decisions reached by such bargaining systems (Haus and Heinelt 2005). The case of the '*Hannover Impuls*' mentioned by Fürst in Chapter 10 is a good example of this: the mayor of Hanover and the president of the newly created metropolitan regions represent the city, respectively the region, on the supervisory board of this public–private partnership – together with two representatives from the business sector.

Beside this horizontal scale of network and consensus-building, leadership can be essential on a vertical scale as well, that is, by attracting support from upper-level government or by trying to prevent or defend interventions from upper-level government. In this respect one has to be aware that such 'multi-level games' are not only 'nested games' (Tsebelis 1990) but first of all strategic games, and as such 'multi-level games' cannot be played by a noisy network community itself, they have to be played by a clever agent – or better, a team captain.

Leaders are not only important as brokers and agents in fostering metropolitan governance capacity. They can also play a decisive role in initiating the process towards this goal. This is not just a task of agenda setting by declaring that a reform is needed. More importantly, critical junctures can be created by leaders to break the frozen landscape of the status quo. In this sense, 'big events' such as the Olympic Games, World Expeditions (EXPO), etc. not only appear as incentive structures that modify actors' behaviour (as mentioned above), but also as *created challenges* with new opportunities for political leadership in metropolitan governance, which can then last beyond the point of time when such an event takes place.

Of course, initiation of metropolitan governance building and moving this process forward by political leaders (and political elites) is not restricted to 'big events' as critical junctures. Rather, it is the articulation and the communicative expression – or social construction – of challenges which call for particular responses. In this respect the 'framing' of a metropolitan governance agenda and a respective pathway is crucial as a general topic. This refers not least to the observation (made in most of the presented cases) that a specific notion of globalisation is expressed in political debates. As far as a specific understanding of the global context and related challenges as well as of dangers becomes hegemonic in the political debate and public sphere, this impacts significantly on the question of how to (re)scale governing activities. This can lead to an unexpected paradigm shift (as exemplified by Fürst for Germany) and a related alternation of the 'mental maps' or beliefs of actors about what is possible and (normatively) right – or not.

Can there be a best practice?

As the North American cases described in this book demonstrate, answers to the question of how to (re)scale governing activities can be quite different because they depend on the concrete content of political and public debates and on how these debates impact not only on the mobilisation of specific interests but also on area-wide social movements. This can be related to the 'central problem of local governance' to stabilise temporarily 'everyday actions and transactions of individuals, collectives and institutions' under conditions of complexity (Keil 2000: 760 with further references), and as Keil and Boudreau clearly pointed out (in Chapter 7), a remapping of political and administrative boundaries is a crucial strategy to alter or defend such particular stability. And as the Rotterdam case clearly shows, the realisation of a well-meaning (although technocratic) metropolitan reform can be blocked by a social movement stimulated by public debate about this reform. Furthermore, the Rotterdam case is a warning that a debate about a metropolitan reform can easily be used for political polarisation and mobilisation by populist leaders. Therefore, emphasis should be given to place because the identity of people is not least place-based and the identification of people with a particular community (feeling of belonging) plays a crucial role in interest mediation and subordination under a political order. However, collective action and democratic participation (in any form whatever) can also be central means for the construction of 'place' (Pratchett and Wilson 1996).

Additionally, inter-regional lesson drawing (Rose 1991) – if not policy transfer – plays a crucial role in altering governance capacities in metropolitan areas. As made clear by nearly most of the presented cases referring to national as well as international experiences, impacts on the cognitive level, that is, on problem perceptions and beliefs as to how to respond best to challenges for governing metropolitan areas. Although there might be no 'best practice' from a scholarly point of view and a direct replication of a particular case is not likely either, the 'competition' between different models (e.g. the Hanover or Stuttgart model especially in Germany, or the London and Barcelona version of metropolitan governance in more general terms) influences the debates and the actual institutional design of metropolitan governance. This become obvious in Chapter 5, where the process of designing an institutional structure for Athens/Attica is described.

Features of democratic metropolitan governance

Chapter 2 emphasised that an analysis of metropolitan governance in the era of new regionalism should not be focused on governmental organisations (and their reform) but broaden the perspective to cooperative arrangements which allow private interest groups as well as collective actors from civil society to participate. Furthermore, we argued that an assessment of the democratic character in metropolitan governance should not be limited to the involvement of citizens through equal voting rights and representation, or the accountability of decision-making authorities. Instead, also relations between governmental bodies and non-governmental actors and the forms which allow the participation of the latter should be reflected. By taking into account the whole range of participatory practices (or options) for the purpose of achieving area-wide governance (from voting via negotiation to deliberation), considerations on democratic metropolitan governance would not only refer to the model of 'liberal democracy' but also to that of 'deliberative democracy'.[2] In this sense, the analytical framework outlined in Chapter 2 was synthesised into a 'cube of democratic metropolitan governance' (see Figure 2.2 in Chapter 2) featuring on (1) input-respectively output-orientation of the national local government system (according to the typology developed by Hesse and Sharpe 1991), that is, the allocation of tasks and competencies regarding service provision and local interest mediation and self-government within particular (vertical) power relations between different territorial levels of government; (2) closedness and openness of policy networks between public and private actors; and (3) the strength or weakness of civil society.

How can the cases portrayed in the various chapters be placed within this cube? The chapters presented in this volume suggest that there are patterns relevant to the position of the described cases which depend to a high degree on the different local government traditions found across the countries under scrutiny.

The North and Middle European pattern

Let us first consider the cases falling into the *North and Middle European type*, that is, those in Finland, the Netherlands, Switzerland and Germany. Here, local governments not only have a broad range of competencies in terms of service provision (from public transport and nursing to planning as well as to social assistance and local economic development) combined with a relatively high degree of fiscal autonomy and financial discretion. And one has to emphasise that all this is constitutionally guaranteed. Local government in these countries also rests on a strong sense of local self-government *by the people*, that is, input legitimation.[3] Not surprisingly, governing local affairs is perceived as a task of local government and, consequently, metropolitan governance is seen (and actually is) either an affair of horizontal intergovernmental (municipal) cooperation – as in the cases of Helsinki, Rotterdam after the city-province failure, and in Switzerland – or as an issue of local government reform in the sense of establishing a new authority with new competencies at the metropolitan level – as in the cases of Stuttgart, Hanover or the projected Rotterdam city-province. Nevertheless, issue-based networks between municipalities and private actors (mostly from the business sector) do exist, but they are perceived more or less as 'necessary exemptions' from the 'right order', and within them local (or metropolitan) political leaders (accountable to 'their' council and citizenry) usually get a strong position.

If these observations are true – and there is a lot of evidence for it – a first general conclusion would be that local government systems characterised by a strong output-orientation as well as by focussing on input legitimation based on equal voting rights and representation tend towards metropolitan governance arrangements that are dominated by municipalities. Although attempts in increasing area-wide governance concentrated either on strengthening horizontal intergovernmental cooperation or on establishing area-wide metropolitan governments, emphasis is also placed on the involvement of societal actors, but this depends on local conditions and reform capacities mentioned in the previous section.

In terms of democratic legitimacy, the general focus on local (or metropolitan) government in these countries seems not a problem at all because such arrangements rely not only on traditional forms of democratic participation (by vote) and relatively clear structures of accountability (which is crucial from the perspective of 'liberal democracy'). Furthermore, based on a specific common understanding (or widespread meaning system and behaviour patterns; Scott 1994: 57ff.), these ways of governing metropolitan affairs are perceived as appropriate in the respective counties. Regarding effectiveness the answer is not so clear. One can argue that countries subsumed under the North and Middle European type of local government – and metropolitan government as well (at least after an 'appropriate' reform) – have the competencies and (financial) resources at their disposal to govern metropolitan areas effectively. This may be true in relative terms, that is, in comparison to countries with other local government systems. However, it is hard to believe that metropolitan governments under such 'favourable' conditions are without any need to mobilise the resources of others as well. And if this is true, self-confident and self-containing metropolitan government can become a weakness in governing metropolitan affairs because it can lead to denying the importance of networking with private actors and of involving civil society. And the stronger metropolitan government seems to be (or perceives itself to be) the greater this danger becomes (as Fürst argues in Chapter 10).

The Anglo pattern

The situation is quite different in the countries belonging to the *Anglo group*. Here, the low legal status of local government makes metropolitan governance building tributary to higher government interventions. In England, for instance, local governments have suffered from the effects of constantly changing roles in service provision, imposed by the 'reforms' of Margaret Thatcher and her successors among the Tories, and their reversal by 'New Labour' in a second phase. Quite similarly, Canadian local government structures are at the mercy of the higher level, though this is the province and not the central state, as in

England. In Toronto and Montreal, metropolitan reforms have significantly altered existing structures. Such frequent rescaling of local government results in weakening local government with respect to the broad spectrum of other (newly created) government organisations, quasi-governmental bodies and private actors engaged in delivering services or, more generally, policy outputs formerly provided by the 'local state'.

Such a constellation requires cooperation between these different public and private actors to secure a comprehensive local service package. Against this background, governing local affairs implies networking and the involvement of actors relevant to achieving effectively particular policy objectives (outputs). In such a way, legitimacy can be reached by governance *for the people* (output legitimation). At the same time, legitimacy through governance *by the people* (input legitimation) can be reached as well. But this does not mean participating politically in urban affairs just by elections for local government and through council decisions. Options to express opinions and concerns and to make them decisive by being (collectively) involved in those arenas where decisions are taken, outside city halls as well, can be of more importance for input legitimation in a context such as the English one. Consequently, governing a metropolitan area is, on the one hand, not bound per se to the city halls in that area and can, on the other hand, rely on already existing horizontal relation not centred on local government but on a broader spectrum of different societal actors relevant to solving concrete problems and resolving conflicts at any stage.

Therefore, one is tempted to conclude, the *Anglo type of local government favours societally opened governing arrangements in metropolitan areas.* To achieve effective policy outputs network-based governance is needed to pool resources and competencies, and to bring legitimacy in such arrangements, a participatory governance approach is essential. However, as we know from reflections on bargaining systems (based on game theory; see Ostrom 1990; Ostrom *et al* 1994; Scharpf 1997), there are a lot of obstacles to overcome to realise the potentials of such constellations, and it depends on the structures or the institutional design of arenas and on actor behaviour to achieve actually effective and legitimate policy outputs (see the section on 'Different routes towards metropolitan governance' above). In England, the establishment of a directly elected mayor for London, as well as the introduction of a local government scheme with a directly elected mayor as an option for the whole country points to a strengthening of local government – or at least of the mayor. But this has not been done to substitute or to roll back governance arrangements. On the contrary, this has been done to increase the effectiveness and the legitimacy of network-based governing activities by bringing in accountable political leadership (see Hambleton and Bullock 1996; Hambleton 1998, 2002).

The Franco pattern

If the local government system plays a crucial role for creating particular metropolitan governance arrangements, what about the third type, that is, the

Franco type of local government? In this case, the picture seems not so clear at first sight, if we look at our examples. The two Spanish cases, that is, Madrid and Barcelona, have followed different tracks. And the proposed perspective for Athens looks extraordinary but the actual development is still uncertain. Finally, the chapter on France flashes on several interesting cases. However, one common feature is remarkable: metropolitan governance is strongly influenced by vertical (inter)governmental power relations or interventions from upper-level government mediated by local political leaders. This feature applies also to other cases not subsumable under the Franco type (for instance, the English cases, and most obviously London; see the chapter by Goldsmith), but there it appears more or less in the context of one-sided central government intervention to 'improve' or weaken local or especially metropolitan government, which can be related to the unitary structures of political systems cross-cutting the distinction between the three local government types mentioned above (see Page and Goldsmith 1987; Page 1991).

In the Franco-type cases under consideration it is obvious that local political leaders try to play a 'multi-level game' according to their individual interests, sometimes in favour of metropolitan governance or a specific form of it – sometimes not. This fits nicely in the general characterisation of the Franco type because it is argued (see Chapter 2) that the essence of local government in the respective countries is political rather than substantial in respect of the provision and implementation of public policies. Consequently, 'political localism' (Page 1991) characterising these countries is focused on the representation of local interests against higher levels of government where the powerhouses are situated. And this is carried out by local political leaders. How differently this can be performed in respect to metropolitan governance is demonstrated by the cases of Madrid and Barcelona. In both cases, local leaders have played a crucial role but in one case (Madrid), the local and regional government structures have been stabilised with no or only the traditional (corporatist) forms for involving organised interest. The other case (Barcelona) highlights the importance of the mayor of the core city in facilitating and stabilising societally wide open governance structures. The same is demonstrated by the different responses to the French programme, where leadership by local actors (mayors and/or prefects) was crucial for the creation of new *Communautés d'agglomération*. To sum up, we could conclude: *the Franco type of local government, per se, favours neither the involvement of societal actors in policy making (and the model of deliberative democracy) nor local/metropolitan government (and the liberal model of democracy). Which development metropolitan governance building takes here (if any) is strongly related to strategic choices of local political leaders and, of course, their locally determined political options to pursue their plans.*

A further special feature seems to be obvious in some of the Southern European countries. Looking at the Spanish cases and at Athens, the involvement of social partners in a formalised way is astonishing. For Greece and Spain, this involvement of social partners has to be seen in the context of a general attempt to achieve governability by 'social dialogue', etc. (see, for Greece,

Heinelt *et al.* 1996).[4] This means that in a time in which in Northern and Middle European countries – formerly characterised by neo-corporatism – the trust in these forms of interest mediation has been lost, elsewhere the 'corporatist Sisyphus is headed back up the hill' (Schmitter and Grote 1997: 37). But here the typically closed network structure of neo-corporatist governance arrangements is opened and the involvement is not restricted per se to particular actors 'licensed' (by the state) to represent specific interests (Schmitter 1979).

General conclusion

As shown by the concluding considerations on building a capacity for metropolitan governance (in the section 'Different routes towards metropolitan governance') as well as on features of democratic policy-making in metropolitan governance arrangements (in the section 'Features of democratic metropolitan governance'), there is no 'best practice'. Some general lessons can be drawn on how to build and increase the capacity to govern metropolitan areas in relation to *actor behavior, incentive structures* and *territorial political leadership*, and some general patterns of the democratic character of metropolitan governance arrangements can be detected which reflect particular institutional context structures for achieving democratically legitimised governing activities. However, with respect to the development and maintenance of area-wide governance capacity as well as with respect to answers to the democratic question, it becomes clear that place matters. But this is not meant in a static way – pointing to place-related 'objective' driving forces. On the contrary, 'dynamics of place' matter insofar as they result out of local processes of defining metropolitan challenges/problems, of mediating conflicts on how to solve them and of defining and pursuing common objects about how to govern a metropolitan area effectively and in a way that is perceived as legitimate.

However, what is the relevance of such 'dynamics of place' with respect to the broader structural or institutional context? This question is important because the emphasis given to place-related dynamics does (or should) not imply that everything can happen at a certain place – providing local heroes behave properly. To reject an 'anything goes' approach without ending up with determinism, the relation between structure and process (or actors) has to be considered in a dialectical way. A lot of work has been done by the social science community on this issue, and, to mention just the more recent approaches, the actor-oriented institutionalism (Mayntz and Scharpf 1995; Scharpf 1997) and the (different directions) of neo-institutionalism (Hall and Taylor 1996) should be quoted.

For the concrete topic at stake here, that is, the creation of governing capacity and democracy in metropolitan areas, an 'older' contribution to this debate can be helpful: the two-filter model developed by Elster (1979: 113; see for it and its application, for example, Windhoff-Héritier 1991: 38–39; Heinelt and Mayer 1992: 14–16). In this model, the societal context in general (e.g. globalisation) and the institutional structure in particular (e.g. the local government systems with their specific distribution of resources/power as well as the normative ideas and values embedded in them) are considered a first filter. This filter can be altered by the creation of special 'incentive structures'. This can be done from 'above', that is, by upper government levels, as in the case of the new French framework law for the creation of the *Communautés d'agglomération*, or locally, for example by featuring big events. However, the first filtering process still offers actors a more or less broad 'feasible set' from which they have to choose, in a second filtering process, one of the possible or available options. The basic components of this second filtering process consist of what has been called above the 'dynamics of place', that is, the political definition of metropolitan challenges/problems, the mediation of conflicts as to how to respond to these challenges/problems, as well as the definition and pursuit of common objectives about how to govern a metropolitan area effectively and in a way that is perceived as legitimate. To do this in a way that capacities for metropolitan governance are increased (or even stabilised), the aspects mentioned above are decisive: cooperative orientations of actors and respective behaviour are essential, as well as a visionary and consensus-facilitating leadership style and locally established incentive structures. The latter refer not only (as just mentioned) to big events, but also and more importantly to spatially embedded informal and locally designed formal rules for interaction (e.g. for the exchange of information and consultation before decisions are taken) as well as for defining a space-related 'logic of appropriateness' (March and Olsen 1989).

In this way, actors are not only able to choose a particular pathway to governing metropolitan areas, they are also in a position to reshape the constrains and to exploit the enabling potentials of the given contextual conditions. However, as has been shown by the presented cases, the ability of actors to reshape and to exploit contextual conditions are related back to institutional structures: On the one hand, the North Middle European type of local government induces limited reshaping and exploiting activities of local actors due to the strong autonomy and relative high degree of resources of local government, as well as to a particular meaning of the 'appropriateness' (i.e. a government-oriented image) of governing metropolitan affairs in a democratic way. On the other hand, under the two other types of local government – that is, the Anglo and the Franco type – activities of actors to achieve metropolitan governance are suffering under a lack of autonomy and resources. This calls for and can be compensated by the vibrancy of the local (civil) society, the involvement of resourceful (economic) actors and the communicative performance of political leaders in creating visions and facilitating consensus. This does not mean that the vibrancy of civil society, the involvement of economic actors and/or the communicative performance of political leaders do not play any role in achieving metropolitan governance under the North Middle European type of local government, but their potentials are harder to mobilise due to choices actors have to make under their respective institutional conditions. However, taking and pursuing a certain choice depend under any circumstances on a locally settled reshaping and exploitation of contextual conditions (see Haus and Heinelt 2005: 33–34).

Notes

1 This refers to the *Hannover Impuls* mentioned by Fürst in Chapter 10, a public–private partnership in which the metropolitan region and the city of Hanover, as well as major local enterprises or big enterprises with local branches are involved to foster the economic competitiveness of the region.
2 See for this distinction also the considerations by Schaap (in Chapter 9) related to the attempts to increase governance capacity in the metropolitan region of Rotterdam.
3 This applies especially to the Swiss cases where local referenda are a crucial means of governing by the people and for input legitimation.
4 For Spain, it may be explained as a legacy of the corporatist political system of the Franco era. But this explanation is not plausible because a lot of other legacy of this time has been questioned fundamentally in Spain.

Bibliography

Elster, J. (1979) *Ulysses and the Sirens*, Cambridge: Cambridge University Press.
Hall, P.A. and Taylor, R.C.R. (1996) 'Political Science and the Three New Institutionalisms', *Political Studies*, 44(5): 936–957.
Hambleton, R. (1998) 'Strengthening Political Leadership in UK Local Government', *Public Money and Management*, January–March: 41–48.
——— (2002) 'The New City Management', in R. Hambleton, H.V. Savitch and M. Stewart (eds), *Globalism and Local Democracy: Challenge and Change in Europe and North America,* Basingstoke: Palgrave.
Hambleton, R. and Bullock, S. (1996) *Revitalising Local Democracy – the Leadership Options*, London: Association of District Councils/Local Government Management Board (now Local Government Association/Improvement and Development Agency).
Haus, M. and Heinelt, H. (2005) 'How to Achieve Governability at the Local Level? Theoretical and Conceptual Considerations on a Complementarity of Urban Leadership and Community Involvement', in M. Haus, H. Heinelt and M. Stewart (eds), *Urban Governance and Democracy: Leadership and Community Involvement*, London: Routledge: 12–39.
Heinelt, H. and Mayer, M. (1992) 'Europäische Städte im Umbruch – zur Bedeutung lokaler Politik', in H. Heinelt and M. Mayer (eds), *Politik in europäischen Städten. Fallstudien zur Bedeutung lokaler Politik,* Basle/Boston/Berlin: Birkhäuser: 7–28.
Heinelt, H., Getimis, P., Bekridaki, G., Dedousolpoulos, A. and Gravaris, D. (1996) *Probleme politischer Steuerung in Griechenland*, Opladen: Leske & Budrich.
Hesse, J.J. (ed.) (1991) *Local Government and Urban Affairs in International Perspective*, Baden-Baden: Nomos Verlag.
Keil, R. (2000) 'Governance Restructuring in Los Angeles and Toronto: Amalgamation or Secession?', *International Journal of Urban and Regional Research*, 24(4), December: 758–781.
Kingdon, J.W. (1984) *Agendas, Alternatives and Public Policies*, Boston: Little, Brown and Co.
March, J.G. and Olsen, J.P. (1989) *Rediscovering Institution: The Organizational Basis of Politics*, New York: Free Press.
Mayntz, R. and Scharpf, F.W. (1995) 'Der Ansatz des akteurszentrierten Institutionalismus', in R. Mayntz and F.W. Scharpf (eds), *Gesellschaftliche Selbstregulierung und politische Steuerung*, Frankfurt/New York: Campus: 39–72.

Ostrom, E. (1990) *Governing the Commons: The Evolution of Institutions for Collective Action*, Cambridge: Cambridge University Press.

Ostrom, E., Gardner, R. and Walker, J. (1994) *Rules, Games and Common-Pool Resources*, Ann Arbor: The University of Michigan Press.

Page, E. (1991) *Localism and Centralism in Europe*, Oxford: Oxford University Press.

Page, E. and Goldsmith, M. (1987) *Central and Local Government Relation*, Beverly Hills: Sage.

Pratchett, L. and Wilson, D. (eds) (1996) *Local Democracy and Local Government*, Basingstoke: Macmillan.

Rose, R. (1991) 'What is Lesson-Drawing?', *Journal of Public Policy*, 2(1): 3–30.

Scharpf, F.W. (1991) 'Games Real Actors could Play: The Problem of Complexity', *Journal of Theoretical Politics*, 6: 27–53.

—— (1992) 'Die Handlungsfähigkeit des States am Ende des zwanzigsten Jahrhunderts', in B. Kohler-Koch (ed.), *Staat und Demokratie in Europa*, Opladen: Leske & Budrich: 93–115.

—— (1997) *Games Real Actors Play: Actor-Centered Institutionalism in Policy Research*, Boulder: Westview Press.

Schmitter, P.C. (1979) 'Still the Century of Corporatism?', *Review of Politics*, 36: 85–131.

Schmitter, P.C. and Grote, J.R. (1997) *The Corporatist Sisyphus: Past, Present and Future*, Florence: EUI Working Paper SPS No. 97/4.

Scott, W.R. (1994) 'Institutions and Organizations. Towards a Theoretical Synthesis', in W.R. Scott and J.W. Meyer (eds), *Institutional Environment and Organizations: Structural Complexity and Individualism*, London: Sage: 55–80.

Tesbelis, G. (1990) *Nested Games: Rational Choice in Comparative Politics*, London: Pinter.

Windoff-Héritier, A. (1991) 'Institutions, Interests and Political Choice', in R.M. Czada and A. Windoff-Héritier (eds), *Political Choice. Institutions, Rules and the Limit of Rationality*, Frankfurt/Boulder: Campus/Westview Press, 27–52.

Index

accountability 14, 15, 23, 24 n.4, 175–7, 192, 195
actor behaviour 10–11, 22–3, 52–3, 190, 198
actor-oriented institutionalism 198
administrative interest intermediation 16, 18
agency level of governance 152
agenda 21 processes 154, 165 n.5
agglomeration policy, Switzerland 169, 175, 181
Akerman, T. 17
Alapuro, R. 117
Almond, G. 141
amalgamation *see* consolidation
Amsterdam 137
Anglo group countries 2, 4–5, 20, 195–6, 199
anti-globalisation movement 103
Antikainen, J. 127
Arn, D. 173, 176
Arpaillange, C. 34
Artal, F. 51
Association of Greater Manchester Authorities (AGMA) 92
associative democracy 15, 21, 177
Athens 3–4, 63–80, 189, 193, 197; administrative structure 65–6; civil society 76–7, 78; economic competitiveness 64; economic and social committee 70, 72, 74, 77, 78; employment 64; metropolitan association of local authorities 69, 73–4, 77, 78; metropolitan government 69, 71–3, 77, 78; metropolitan regional authority ('mixed form' of governance) 69–71, 75–6, 77, 78; Olympic Games (2004) 3, 67, 191; planning procedures 72; policy networks 77, 78; political elite 70, 71, 76–7; population 64;

prefectoral system 66, 71, 72; strategic planning 74–5
Australia 20
Austria 20
authenticity of state action 14

Baden-Württemberg 160
Badie, B. 21
Bahamonde, O. 49
Bang, H.P. 15
Baraize, F. 11, 35, 36
Barcelona 3, 47–62 *passim*, 189, 190, 193, 197; Association of Municipalities 52; civil society 58–9, 60; General Metropolitan Plan 51, 53; metropolitan bodies 51–2, 53; Municipal Metropolitan Entity of 50; Olympic Games (1992) 3, 47, 54, 58, 191; policy networks 55–7; strategic planning 54, 55–6, 58–9, 60; territorial plans 49; Urban Development and Common Services Commission 49
Barcelona Metropolitan Corporation (CMB) 50–1
bargaining/political exchange 16, 17, 18
bargaining power 17
Basel-Stadt 173
Basle 170, 171, 180
Bassand, M. 178
Baumheier, R. 158
Bavaria 160
Belgium 20
benchmarking 58
Benz, A. 10, 14, 16, 162, 164
van den Berg, L. 10, 162
Berlin 151
Bern 170, 175, 178, 179, 180
Béziers 35, 36, 38
Bilbao 50, 53

Birmingham 84, 92, 93
Birnbaum, P. 21
Blair, T. 88, 97 n.6
Blanc, A.-C. 34
Blotevogel, H.H. 151
Bordeaux 36, 38
Bossong, H. 155, 165
Boudreau, J.-A. 4–5, 100–16
Bourque, P. 104
Braun, E. 162
Bremen 151
Brenner, N. 9, 14, 101, 108, 158
Brugué, Q. 57
Brunila, B. 120
Buck, N. 91
Bullock, S. 196
bureaucracy 16
Burns, J. Mc G. 36
Bush, G.W. 106
business sector: Germany 154, 155, 159,
    160, 163, 164, 165; *see also* corporate
    actors
Bütschi, D. 183

Cachet, A. 138
Caillosse, J. 37
Canada 4–5, 20, 100–16, 195–6; legal-
    institutional framework 101–2; political
    culture 102; *see also* Montreal, Toronto
cantons, Swiss 170–1, 173, 174
Carens, J.H. 102
Casado, C. 50
Castells, M. 103
Castilla-La Mancha 50
Castillo, F. 50
Catalan Autonomous Community 3, 51–2
Cattacin, S. 178, 183
central government 4
centralisation 21, 140, 180
centrality charges, Switzerland 172–3, 174
chambers of commerce 18, 55, 154
Chambéry 37
charter movement, North America 109,
    111–12, 113
Chevènement Law 30, 31–3, 35, 37, 39, 42
citizen participation 14, 196; Finland 129;
    France 43; Greece 76, 77; Netherlands
    140, 141–2; public choice theory and
    12–13; Spain 58–9, 60; Switzerland 6,
    169, 177–80, 182–3; *see also*
    participatory (direct) democracy,
    representative democracy
citizenship 12, 13–15, 18
City of Culture Foundation 124

City of London 82, 91, 96
city marketing 54
City Pride initiative 88, 93
city-provinces, Netherlands 5, 134, 138–9,
    144, 189, 194
civic virtues 13
civil society 18, 142, 194, 195, 199; Athens
    76–7, 78; Barcelona 58–9, 60; England
    95; France 43; infrastructure of 16;
    Madrid 55, 58, 60; Rotterdam 148;
    strength/weakness of 21, 22, 23, 78, 95,
    194; Switzerland 176–7, 183, 184
civil society-state relations 15, 17, 18–19,
    20–2, 58–9, 60, 148
clientelism, Greece 72–3, 74, 75
Clinton, B. 106
Clogg, R. 63
Clos, J. 53, 54
co-governance, Netherlands 136
Cohen, J. 15, 177
Cole, A. 22, 43, 93–4
Coleman, J.S. 22
Colomé, G. 53, 56
Comisiones Obreras (CCOO) 55
Communautés d'agglomération (CUA) 3,
    29–46, 191, 197, 199
Communautés de communes 30
Communautés urbaines 30, 31
communes: France 3, 29–46, 191, 197,
    199; Switzerland 170, 171
communitarianism 12, 103, 104
community attachment 12, 193
Community Safety Units 90
Community Solidarity Grant 40
Como-Chiasso 171
competitiveness: international 1, 103,
    104, 110–11, 113, 126, 130; regional
    159–60, 165
compromise 15
Condé, Y. 36
Confederation of Enterprises of Madrid
    (Ceim) 55
conflict-avoiding behaviour 6, 181
consensus 15, 199
consolidation, institutional 4, 9–10,
    11–12, 127, 140, 190; North America
    100, 106–8, 109, 110, 111, 112
cooperation 140–2, 189, 190, 194, 199;
    culture of 33–4; German regions 153–5,
    156–7, 158, 159, 164; Helsinki
    metropolitan area 123–5, 127, 128, 129,
    131, 194; inter-communal (France) 3,
    29–46, 191, 197, 199; issue-based 6,
    153–4, 194–5; Netherlands

municipalities 134, 135, 137, 144–5;
  Swiss metropolitan areas 169, 173–5,
  176, 181, 194; voluntary versus forced 13
corporate actors 18, 55, 56, 154, 155
corporate citizenship 159, 163
corporate taxes 30, 118, 128
cosmopolitan localism 1
crime, London 90
Croucher, S.L. 102
Culminatum 124
cultural diversity 104

Daemen, H.H.F.M. 141, 143
Dafflon, B. 182
Dahl, R.A. 14
Davis, H. 92
Davis, M. 103, 106
Deas, I. 92, 93
decentralisation 21, 136, 140, 141, 142
decision modes 15, 16–18, 19, 23
Delémont 175
deliberation/debate 14–15, 16, 17, 18, 19,
  23, 194
deliberative democracy 194, 197
democracy 2, 8, 11–23, 43, 75–6, 130,
  193–8; associative 15, 21, 177;
  deliberative 194, 197; liberal 194, 195,
  197; overhead model of 14, 176;
  participatory (direct) 43, 134, 140–6
  passim, 169, 177–80, 182–3, 194;
  representative 14, 43, 134, 140–7
  passim, 175–7, 180, 194, 195; *see also*
  input legitimisation
democratic deficit 39–41, 112–13
demographic diversity 104
Derksen, W. 136, 138
Desfor, G. 109, 113
Development Councils (France) 43
DiGaetano, A. 152, 154, 157
Dobson, F. 89
Dolwitz, D. 159
Dotation Globale de Fonctionnement
  (DGF) 32
Downs, A. 10

ecological modernisation 104
economic development 40, 41; Helsinki
  123–5, 126; London 90–1
economic restructuring, Germany 152, 165
Economou, D. 66, 76
Edelenbos, J. 142
education policy, London 86, 87
effectiveness of state action 14; *see also*
  output legitimisation

efficiency 20, 75–6
Eichenberger, R. 9, 13, 177
Elcock, H. 11
electoral systems, proportional 21
Elster, J. 198
enabling state 158
England 81–99, 190, 195, 196; *see also*
  London
environmental policy 40, 41
Escaffit, C. 35
Espoo 119, 120, 121, 122, 128, 130, 131
*Établissement public de cooperation
  intercommunale* (EPCI) 39
Eurocities 119
European Union (EU) 135, 152; Finnish
  membership 117, 118, 119; funding
  policy 92, 94, 158
evaluation instruments 58
events, place-related 22, 47, 54, 58, 191,
  192, 199
EVLN (*Exit, Voice, Loyalty and Neglect*)
  model 12

Fair of Madrid (Ifema) 55
federalism 21
federation of local governments 163, 164–5
Finland 5, 117–32, 191, 194; *see also*
  Helsinki
Flynn, N. 85, 86
Font, J. 57
Foods, R. 106
Fortuyn, P. 134
fragmentation, institutional 6, 8, 9, 12–13,
  107–8, 169, 171, 189
France 3, 20, 29–46, 189; citizen
  participation 43; civil society 43;
  housing policy 40, 41; incentive
  structures 31–3, 42; inter-communal
  cooperation 3, 29–46, 191, 197, 199;
  political leadership 36–9
Franco group countries 2, 3–4, 20,
  196–8, 199
Frankfurt 153, 155, 156, 159, 160, 164
Frêche, G. 35
Freitag, M. 13, 177
Frenzel, A. 160
Frey, B.S. 9, 13, 177
Fribourg 170, 175, 178, 182
Friederich, U. 173, 176
Frisken, F. 9, 10
Fuchs, S. 164
functional interest intermediation 10, 17, 18
*Functional Overlapping Competing
  Jurisdictions* (FOCJ) 13

functional urban regions (FURs) 127
Fürst, D. 5–6, 151–68

Gainsborough, J.F. 11, 103
Garber, J.A. 102
García de Enterría, E. 50
Garrard, J.A. 81
Garside, P. 82, 83
Gateshead 94
Geneva 170, 171, 173, 179–80
gentrification 104, 170
Germann, R.E. 171
Germany 5–6, 20, 151–68, 189, 191, 193,
    194; business sector 154, 155, 159, 160,
    163, 164, 165; cooperation 153–5,
    156–7, 158, 159, 164; economic
    restructuring 152, 165; incentive
    structures 159, 165 n.4; planning
    associations and districts 152, 155;
    policy networks 154, 158; public-
    private arrangements 154, 155, 157,
    165, 192, 200 n.1
Geser, H. 170
Getimis, P. 3–4, 63–80
Gilbert, L. 104
Giuliani, R. 104
globalisation 1, 14, 103, 106–10, 158,
    192–3
Goldberg, M.A. 101
Goldsmith, M. 4, 20, 76, 81–99, 101, 197
Gomà, R. 57
Gore, A. 106
Greater London Authority (GLA) 4, 96
Greater London Council (GLC) 84, 86
Greece 3–4, 20, 29, 191, 197; *see also*
    Athens
Green Belt 83
Grote, J.R. 198
growth-machine theory 103
Guéranger, D. 33
Güller, M. 174

Habermas, J. 15
The Hague 137
Hahan, J. 104–5
Haila, A. 5, 117–32
Hall, P.A. 33, 198
Hambleton, R. 196
Hamburg 151, 159, 160
Hannover Implus 165, 192, 200 n.1
Hanover 6, 152, 153, 155, 159, 160–3,
    165, 189, 193, 194
happiness 13
Harding, A. 92, 93

Harvey, D. 101
Haus, M. 199
Hebbert, M. 92, 93
Heinelt, H. 1–7, 8–28, 188–202
Heinz, W. 14, 157
Helsinki 5, 117–32, 189, 191, 296;
    economic development 123–5, 126;
    housing policy 122, 129, 131;
    inter-municipal cooperation 123–5,
    127, 128, 129, 131, 194; policy
    networks 117, 125–6; utilities 122–3
Helsinki Club 124–5, 126, 130
Helsinki Development Corporation 124
Herbert Commission Report 84
Hesse, J.J. 2, 19–20, 48, 179
hierarchical administrative interventions
    15, 16, 18
Hirst, P. 15, 177
Hlepas, N. 3–4, 29, 63–80
Hoffmann-Martinot, V. 52, 58
Hogen-Esch, T. 109
housing policy: France 40, 41; Helsinki
    122, 129, 131

Imbroscio, D.L. 102
incentive structures 11, 23, 190–1, 198,
    199; France 31–3, 42; Germany 159,
    165 n.4; Spain 53; Switzerland
    175, 181
inclusiveness 14–15
income tax 118, 122, 184 n.4
infrastructure, public 1
Inner London Education Authority (ILEA)
    86, 87
Innopoli 124
input legitimisation 14, 19–20, 23, 95,
    194, 195, 196; Greece 78; Rotterdam
    148; Spain 57–8, 59–60; Switzerland
    179, 182–3; *see also* democracy
institutional consolidation *see*
    consolidation
institutional culture 33
institutional fragmentation 6, 8, 9, 12–13,
    107–8, 169, 171, 189
institutional learning 31, 33–6
institution building 33–6
interest intermediation 16–19, 194;
    administrative 16, 18; civil society
    related 17, 18; functional 10, 17, 18;
    territorial 10, 16, 18, 164
International Olympic Committee 67
Ireland 20
issue-based cooperation 6, 153–4, 194–5
Italy 20

'jacobinism' 29
Jarvis, H. 102
John, P. 22, 36, 43, 93–4, 96, 137, 140
joint decision trap 10
Jonas, A.E.G. 103
Jouve, B. 11, 53

Kafkalas, G. 67, 75
Kaufmann, V. 180
Kauniainen 120, 121, 122
Kautto, M. 117
Keating, M. 48, 100, 108
Keil, R. 4–5, 100–16, 193
Kickert, W.J.M. 133, 140, 141
Kingdon, J.W. 22, 191
Kipfer, S. 102, 104
Kohler, B. 109
Kolbe, L. 121
Koliopoulos, J. 63
Kooiman, J. 10
Koppenjan, J.F.M. 137, 138
Kramer, J. 84
Kriesi, H. 21, 183
Kübler, D. 1–7, 8–28, 169–87, 188–202
Kujath, H.J. 152, 158, 160
Kymlicka, W. 102

Ladner, A. 173, 183
land scarcity 153
land use, regional 152
Lankinen, M. 118
Lastman, M. 104
Latendresse, A. 43
Lausanne 170, 171, 175, 178, 180
Le Galès, P. 5, 10, 11, 14, 54, 96,
    117–32, 157
Le Havre 36
Le Saout, R. 42
Leach, S. 91
Leeds 84, 93–4
Lefebvre, H. 113
Lefèvre, C. 9, 11, 75, 157, 158
legitimisation, input and output *see* input
    legitimisation, output legitimisation
Leguina, J. 53
Lehmbruch, G.L. 10
Lehning, P.B. 102
Lehto, J. 117
lesson drawing, inter-regional 153,
    159, 193
Levine, J.N. 154
liberal democracy 194, 197
liberalism: notion of citizenship 12, 195;
    see also neo-liberalism

Linder, W. 173, 175, 178, 179, 183
Liverpool 84, 94
Livingstone, K. 86, 88–90, 91
local autonomy 9, 10, 108, 109, 111, 136,
    140, 155, 189, 199
localism: cosmopolitan 1; political
    20, 197
London 81–4, 86–91, 95, 96, 189, 191, 193
London Assembly 88, 89, 91, 96
London Boroughs Grants Committee
    (LBGC) 87
London Coordinating Committee 87
London County Council (LCC) 81,
    82–3, 84
London Development Agency (LDA) 90
London First campaign 87–8, 96
London Planning Advisory Committee
    (LPAC) 87
London Pride Partnership 88
London Residual Body (LRB) 87
López, M. 49
Los Angeles 4, 100, 104–13 *passim*, 189
Loughlin, J. 48, 135
Lowery, D. 11, 12, 179
Lowndes, V. 142
Lucerne 171, 175, 178
Lugarno 170, 171
Luhmann, N. 141
Lyons, W.E. 12

Madrid 3, 47–62 *passim*, 189, 197;
    Autonomous Community of 3, 47, 50,
    53, 55, 58, 59; Chamber of Commerce
    and Industry (CCIM) 55; civil society
    55, 58, 60; General Plan of the
    Metropolitan Area of 48–9; General
    Urban Plan for (1946) 48;
    neo-corporatism 55, 58; policy
    networks 55
Magnusson, W. 107
Major, J. 87
majority decisions 15, 16, 18, 23
Makrydimitris, A. 65, 75
Malaga 53
Maloutas, T. 66, 76
Manchester 84, 92–3
Mantes-La Jolie 34, 38
Maragall, P. 51, 52
March, J.G. 199
Marin, B. 10
Marseilles 36, 39
Marsh, D. 159
Martin, P. 105
Mavrogordatos, G. 78

Mayer, M. 198
Mayntz, R. 10, 198
mayors, elected 4, 88–9, 95, 104–5, 159,
    191, 196
Mercer, J. 101
mergers, municipal *see* consolidation
Messner, D. 158
'Metropolitana' 159, 166 n.10
metropolitan areas 8
Metropolitan Police Authority (MPA),
    London 90
metropolitan reform tradition 8, 9–10, 11,
    12, 13–14, 15, 188–9
Michel, H. 36
Miller, D. 104, 110, 112
Miller, G.J. 102
mobility of persons and goods 1
Molotch, H.L. 103
Monnikof, R. 142
Montpellier 35, 36, 38
Montreal 4, 100, 102, 104, 105,
    107–13 *passim*, 189, 196
Montreal Citizens Movement 102
Morrison, H. 83
Mossberger, K. 76
motivation, intrinsic (of individuals) 13
Munich 152, 153, 155, 156, 160

Nantes 44
negotiation 15, 23
Négrier, E. 3, 11, 29–46, 54
Neidhart, L. 177
Nel lo, O. 53
neo-communitarianism 103, 104
neo-corporatism 10, 55, 160, 198
neo-institutionalism 33, 198
neo-liberalism 4, 100, 101, 103, 108,
    113, 158
Netherlands 5, 20, 133–50, 194; *see also*
    Rotterdam
Neuchâtel 175
Newcastle 84, 94
New Labour 4, 195
new public management 58, 140, 158,
    162, 183
new regionalism 8, 9, 10–11, 13–15,
    18–23, 133, 140, 174, 181, 189, 190
New Towns policy 83
New Zealand 20
Nicholls, W.J. 109
NIMBYism 104, 179
Nokia 119, 120
Norris, D.F. 9, 10, 151, 152, 156, 157
North America 4–5, 20, 100–16

North and Middle European countries 2,
    5–6, 20, 194–5, 199
North Rhine-Westfalia 160

Oakersond, R.J. 13
Offe, C. 164
O'Leary, B. 86
Olive, M. 35
Olsen, J.P. 199
Olympic Games (1992 Barcelona) 3, 47,
    54, 58, 191
Olympic Games (2004 Athens) 3, 67, 191
Oppenheim, J.P. 35
Ostrom, E. 9, 12, 196
Otero, L.E. 49
Oulu 128
output legitimisation 14, 19–20, 23, 95,
    194, 195, 196; Greece 78; Rotterdam
    148; Spain 57–8, 59–60; Switzerland
    179, 182–3
overhead democracy model 14, 176

Page, E. 20, 197
Papadopoulos, Y. 65, 177, 178
paradigm change 5, 158, 160, 161–2,
    163, 193
Parks, R.B. 13
parliamentary institutions 16
Parry, G. 142
participation, citizen *see* citizen
    participation, participatory (direct)
    democracy, representative democracy
participation rights 13
participatory (direct) democracy 43, 134,
    140–6 *passim*, 169, 177–80, 182–3, 194
Pastor, M. 113
Peck, J. 93
Peters, B.G. 135
Phillips, C. 104
Pimlott, B. 86, 87, 88, 90
place 22, 193; dynamics of 198, 199
place-related events 22, 47, 54, 58, 191,
    192, 199
planning associations, Germany 152, 155
planning districts, Germany 155
policing, London 90
policy networks 9–10, 15, 18–19, 189, 190,
    195, 196; accountability issues 14;
    Athens 77, 78; Barcelona/Madrid 55–7,
    59; closedness/openness of 19, 23, 55–7,
    59, 77, 78, 95–6, 147–8, 182, 194;
    England 95–6; Germany 154, 158;
    Helsinki metropolitan area 117, 125–6;
    Rotterdam 147–8; Switzerland 174, 182

political behaviour, individual 12–13
political culture 152; Canada-US
  variations 102; local 35–6;
  territorial 33–6
political identity 41, 66, 71, 76
political leadership 11, 23, 31, 96, 191–3,
  196, 197, 198, 199; France 36–9;
  prefectoral 37–9; Spain 53–4;
  Switzerland 175; transactional 36;
  transformational 36–7; trust in 191–2
Pommerehne, W.W. 13, 177
Pontier, J. 35
popular initiative 177, 178
populism 108
Portugal 20
Poupeau, F.M. 34, 35
power, rescaling of exercise of 108, 110
Pratchett, L. 193
prefectoral systems: Athens 66, 71, 72;
  France 37–9
Priebs, A. 161
property rights 102, 113–14 n.3
public choice approach 8, 9–10, 12–13,
  13–14, 15, 188–9
public-private arrangements 10, 189, 191;
  Athens 64; England 89, 93, 94;
  Germany 154, 155, 157, 165, 192,
  200 n.1; Switzerland 174
Pujol, J. 51
Purcell, M. 112
Putnam, R.D. 21, 22

Quebec 101, 105–6
Quilley, S. 92

Radaelli, C. 42
Rantala, E. 128
Rao, N. 86, 87, 88, 90
rational choice theory 13
Reagan, R. 106
Redcliffe-Maud Report 84–5
Redford, E. 14
referenda, Switzerland 177–8, 200 n.3
regional assemblies 94, 155
regional associations, Germany 155–6
regional conferences, Germany 156, 158,
  165 n.5
regional development agencies: Germany
  155, 156, 163, 164; UK 4
regional planning associations, Germany
  152, 155, 161
regional policy/government: Finland
  127–8; Germany 151–65; Netherlands
  137–50; North America 103

Rennes 37, 44
representative democracy 14, 43, 134,
  140–7 *passim*, 175–7, 180, 194, 195
Rhodes, G. 83
Rhodes, R.A.W. 10, 140, 141
Riordan, R. 104–5
Ritter, E.-H. 152
Rodríguez Alvarez, J.M. 48, 50, 52, 53,
  55, 58
Rogers, J. 15, 177
Rose, R. 153, 159, 193
Rotterdam 5, 133, 134, 137–9, 143–8,
  190, 193; as city-province 5, 134,
  138–9, 144, 189, 194; City-Region
  144–5, 146–8; civil society 148; policy
  networks 147–8
round tables 158
Rudolph, A. 160, 161
Rüegg, J. 182
Ruiz-Gallardón, A. 53
Rusk, D. 10

Sager, F. 6, 169–87, 180, 181, 182
St Gallen 170, 171, 175
Sandberg, S. 119
Saukkonen, J. 121
Savitch, H. 10, 19, 176
Scandinavia 20; *see also* Finland
Schaap, L. 5, 133–50
Scharpf, F. 10, 14, 47, 54, 159, 190, 191,
  196, 198
Schenkel, W. 174
Schmitter, P.C. 10, 198
Schubert, H. 154, 163
Schwab, B. 6, 19, 169–87
Schwarzenegger, Arnold 105
Scott, W.R. 195
secessionism 102; Los Angeles 4, 100,
  106, 107, 108, 109, 110, 111, 112
segregation, social 1, 76, 171–2
separation of powers 21
Serdült, U. 177
Seville 53
Sewell, J. 107
Sharpe, L.J. 2, 19–20, 48, 86, 91
Sheffield 84
Siitonen, E.-R. 119, 128
Smallwood, F. 83
smart growth 104
Smith, A. 36
social capital 22, 152, 164
social movements 4, 101, 108–9, 110,
  111, 193
social renewal 133, 148 n.1

social segregation 1, 76, 171–2
social services, Finland 118, 121–2, 131;
    see also welfare state
Soja 103
Sørensen, E. 12, 15
space, functional specialisation of 1
Spain 3, 20, 47–62, 191, 197; Autonomous
    Communities 48, 49; Local Government
    Law (1985) 48; Social Councils 58; *see
    also* Barcelona, Madrid
spatial development strategies (SDSs) 90–1
spatial mobility 1
special joint authorities, Germany 154
state, weak and strong 21
state-civil society relations 15, 17, 18–19,
    20–2, 58–9, 60, 148
Steinacher, B. 162
Steinbock, D. 119
Stoker, G. 10, 42, 76, 95
Stone, C. 11, 82, 93
strategic planning: Athens 74–5;
    Barcelona 54, 55–6, 58–9, 60; English
    metropolitan counties 85–6
Strom, E. 152, 154, 157
structural level of governance 152
Stuttgart 6, 152, 153, 155, 156, 160, 162,
    163–4, 165, 189, 193, 194
Stutzer, A. 13, 177
subsidies, state, Finland 118
suburbanisation 1, 103, 153, 170, 172
Swanstrom, T. 11, 158
Switzerland 6, 20, 169–87, 189, 190, 191,
    194, 200 n.3; agglomeration policy 169,
    175, 181; centrality charges 172–3, 174;
    citizen participation 6, 169, 177–80,
    182–3; civil society 176–7, 183, 184;
    incentive structures 175, 181;
    intergovernmental cooperation 169,
    173–5, 176, 181, 194; policy networks
    174, 182; political leadership 175;
    public-private arrangements 174;
    transport policy 178, 180; urbanisation
    169, 170, 173
Swyngedouw, E. 22
Syndicat d'Agglomération Nouvelle
    (SAN) 39
*Syndicat intercommunal à vocation
    multiple* (SIVOM) 39
Syndicat intercommunal à vocation unique
    (SIVU) 39

Tampere 128
taxes 184 n.4; corporate 30, 118, 128;
    income 118, 122, 184 n.4

Taylor, I. 93
Taylor, M. 33
Taylor, R.C.R. 198
territorial interest intermediation 10, 16,
    18, 164
Teuvo Aura 121
Thatcher, M. 86, 195
Theodore, N. 108
Thorbecke 135
Ticino 170, 173
Tickell, A. 93
Tiebout, C.M. 9
Tobler, G. 175
Tomàs, M. 3, 47–62
Toonen, Th.A.J. 133, 135, 136
Toronto 4, 100, 102, 104–13 *passim*,
    189, 196
trade unions 18, 55, 56
transport policy: London 89–90;
    Switzerland 178, 180
Travers, T. 91
Trechsel, A. 177
Trom, D. 104
trust 191–2
Tsebelis, G. 192
Tsoukalas, K. 66
Tully, J. 102
Turku 128
van Twist, M.J.W. 141, 147
two-filter model 198–9
typology of local government 2–3, 19–20

Union of Baltic cities 119
Unión General de Trabajadores
    (UGT) 55
United Kingdom 4, 20; *see also* England
United States 4–5, 20, 105, 106;
    legal-institutional framework 101–2;
    political culture 102; *see also*
    Los Angeles
Urban Network Study (Finland) 127
urban sprawl 1, 8, 126–7, 170
urbanisation, Switzerland 169, 170, 173
Usannaz-Joris, M. 37
utilities, Helsinki 122–3

Valencia 50, 53
Vancouver 104
Vantaa 120, 121, 122, 124, 128
Vartiainen, P. 127
Vatter, A. 13, 177
Verba, S. 141
Veremis, T. 63
Viikki 124

Voelzkow, H. 157, 160
Vogel, R.K. 10, 19, 176
Voiron 34, 38
Vuosaari 121

van Waarden, F. 19
Wälti, S. 14, 174, 176, 183
Weck-Heckmann, H. 13, 177
welfare state: Finland 5, 117, 118, 119,
    121–2, 130, 191; Netherlands 136
Wiechmann, Th. 152, 154, 155
Wilson, D. 103, 193
Windhoff-Héritier, A. 198

Winnipeg 104
Winterthur 170, 171
Wisler, D. 21
Wissen, M. 109
Wolch, J. 113
world social forum 103

Young, K. 82, 83, 84, 86, 111
YTV 122–3

Zaragoza 53
Zug 173
Zurich 170, 171, 173, 174, 175, 178